Approaching
World
Religions

Edited by
Robert Jackson

John Murray

World Religions in Education
Series Editor: Robert Jackson

Approaching World Religions
Robert Jackson (editor)

Approaches to Islam
Richard Tames

In preparation
Approaches to Christianity
Approaches to Judaism
Approaches to Hinduism

Also edited by Robert Jackson

Perspectives on World Religions (School of Oriental
and African Studies, University of London)

To the memory of Everroy Robinson,
a Jamaican student of religious education
at the University of Warwick, who died in 1981

© John Murray (Publishers) Ltd 1982

First published 1982
by John Murray (Publishers) Ltd
50 Albemarle Street, London W1X 4BD

Photoset in Great Britain by
Photobooks (Bristol) Limited

Printed in Great Britain by
Richard Clay (The Chaucer Press) Ltd,
Bungay, Suffolk

British Library Cataloguing in Publication Data

Jackson, Robert
Approaching world religions.—(World
religions in education; 1)
1. Religious
200   BL80.2

ISBN 0-7195-3913-7

Foreword
by Professor Ninian Smart

This volume is a sign of the great advance which the study of world religions has made both in schools and beyond. There can be little doubt that for both social and personal reasons young people need to become acquainted with something of the range of human beliefs and practices. This is so for personal reasons, because for good or ill our world is now a plural one, in which the different religious traditions are meeting in our cities and through the media. It is no longer possible for the Christian or the Hindu to isolate himself or herself from other faiths. It is better for people to face this pluralism and benefit from its riches rather than to retreat into too closed a commitment. Socially, the exploration of religion is obviously important, since it is necessary for people of different persuasions and customs to live together in their immediate environment and in the world at large. There is increased recognition of this in our schools, and this book is a notable contribution to this process of exploration.

Unfortunately, despite the fact that religious education shows very considerable liveliness and is one of the most interesting areas of the curriculum, the image of the subject is often inadequate. Because of a past in which the study of religion has been seen largely within the context of commitment, our educational system is neglectful of what I sometimes now call 'worldview analysis'. When I say 'our' I am really referring to the educational systems of the western world as well as to the British scene. The neglect can be put in the following way. Whereas it is common for students in schools to study economics, and whereas universities usually have departments of political science, there is a tendency to ignore traditional belief systems and to neglect political education. Thus we often turn out people who have a technocratic view of the world which ignores some of the deep spiritual, ideological and cultural forces which help to shape human history and contemporary society. Consider: the tendency in theology is to undervalue the non-Christian religions; the slant in political science is towards the study of secular ideologies; the tendency in philosophy is to look at a selective set of western beliefs and values; the trend in sociology is to deal with our own society; the scope of anthropology covers small-scale societies in the main; often history is western-centred. All these areas can make an excellent contribution to the exploration of worldviews, but it is in the field of religious studies and religious education perhaps that we come nearest to a systematic study of human belief systems.

There was a time when I would typically have the following conversation in a train or a plane. Someone would ask me what I did and I would tell them that I taught religious studies in a university. The interlocutor would then say, 'What do you think of Seventh Day Adventism?' And I would say, 'I really don't know anything about it.' The interlocutor would be outraged: 'You teach religion in a university and you don't know anything about Seventh Day Adventists?' Nowadays I claim to be involved in worldview analysis, and a person on a train or a plane replies, 'How interesting. And how do you go about that?' I reply, 'Suppose you want to explore the meaning of a worldview – let us suppose for the sake of argument it is Seventh Day Adventism – then what you need first of all is some structured empathy. . .' Thereafter we can pursue a creative conversation.

The present volume is the beginning of a series which will continue the work which has gone on so fruitfully since the 1960s in extending the scope and expertise of religious education. It will help us to see what methods and approaches will be appropriate in our educational system. There is no denying that teachers in the field need help, partly because the demands of multi-faith education are great, and partly because it is necessary to avoid the impression that this somehow subtracts from teaching in the field of Christianity. Indeed I believe firmly that Christian studies in schools (for instance as described here by Dr Owen Cole) benefit greatly from crosscultural fertilisation. Moreover I think that the worries which people have about possible threats to existing commitments can themselves be used fruitfully, although they raise some of those vital questions which are dealt with in the section of this book on commitment.

The fact that our society is increasingly pluralist is also, for all its tensions, a creative thing. I believe that the life of Britain and of other western countries is greatly enriched by the presence of Asian, African and other populations in our midst. However, the problem of pluralism is not just a matter of the classroom. It is clearly important that professional people, such as the police, need a deeper background in pluralist values than our traditional education provided. Thus the section in this book on pluralism, though aimed in the direction of the school system, has a far-reaching significance for society at large. It is incidentally therefore difficult to separate our proposals for religious education from political issues, since there are those who are hostile to pluralism, partly because of a perceived threat to themselves.

The storm which blew up a few years ago about the Birmingham syllabus as a result of the proposal to incorporate a section on Marxism is a symptom of the fact that very few people can distinguish between teaching which is concerned with exploring and understanding a belief system, and teaching which is designed to hand on or inculcate a belief system. Very few people still can stand back enough to understand values with which they disagree. The fruits of such a failure have been seen in so many places. They have been seen sometimes in the work of missionaries swift to categorise other people's beliefs as idolatrous; in Henry Kissinger's failures in Iran; in the way Chamberlain failed to appreciate the plain significance of *Mein Kampf*; and even in the writing of partly sympathetic scholars on Buddhism, such as the late R. C. Zaehner. So it is important that religious educators should demonstrate how without losing their integrity they can successfully bring out the human meaning and living force of ideas and practices often very different from their own.

This itself relates to issues about personal development too, which are treated here in an important section. For young people are not only searching for commitment perchance; they are also struggling with strong feelings which can both get in the way of and be harnessed to that voyage into other people's feelings and ideas which we all continually need to make. In this respect the exploration of world religions and the more general task of worldview analysis is a noble and creative exercise of the imagination.

As I have indicated, though the main emphasis in religious education is on the traditional systems of beliefs and the symbols implicit in our everyday life, we cannot escape the modern age. In Cambodia, for instance, what we saw was not just religion in dialogue with religion. What we saw was religion in often bloody encounter with the bombs of liberal democracy, the guns of rural Marxism in the style of the Khmer Rouge, and the tanks of orthodox Vietnamese Marxism. In our own society the options include humanism and other nontraditional ways of looking at the world. Nor is this all. The world has always produced new religious movements, and our own day is no exception. These new movements themselves represent items on the agenda of the human soul. I like to think of every system of belief and practice, whether it be good or evil, whether it be Buddhism or Nazism, whether it be ancient or modern, as representing an answer to questions lodged deep in human souls and societies. For this reason it is necessary that religious education should deal seriously with the moral and political questions and the concluding section of this work explores this relationship.

But writings in this field must, as I have indicated, be practical. It is therefore a useful feature of this book that it begins with a firm rooting in the educational situation.

Religious education and the study of world religions have, as I have indicated, greatly flourished in this country in the last two decades. We live in an exciting time. Nevertheless, it is important that we see the problem of religious education in the wider educational perspective of the world. There is no reason why similar styles of exploration of world religions in education should not occur in many other countries. The principles of personal and social understanding are the same wherever we may be. But in many countries the sort of approach so admirably promoted in this book would be ruled out. There are many countries where education is closed. These countries promote in modern form that old post-Reformation principle *cuius regio eius religio*. Only now it tends to be *eius ideologia*. This shows that a presupposition of world religions in education is a new pluralistic humanism. But it is also one which takes seriously the human spiritual search, whether that ends with orthodoxy or a radical stance. It is thus a kind of spiritual and pluralistic humanism, which is surely what the educational system needs to be suffused with. We should therefore be grateful for the visions and practicalities contained in the following pages.

University of Lancaster and University
of California, Santa Barbara
St Andrew's Day

Preface

There has been an enormous growth of public interest in the study of world religions in recent years, reflected in broadcasting (particularly in such a lavish television series as *The Long Search*), in a proliferation of books aimed at the general reader, and in the growth of full-time and extramural courses in colleges and universities, including the Open University. Though the reasons for this growing awareness are many, the presence in our own society of significant numbers of followers of religions other than Christianity is an important factor in stimulating people to explore particular religions for the first time and to look at Christianity afresh as a world religion in its own right.

Parallel developments have been taking place in our schools where many courses in religious education have been reorientated to embrace the study of a variety of the world's religions. There are some excellent examples of world religions approaches to RE currently to be found in British schools, provided by imaginative and skilful teachers. These are not confined to multicultural schools, although there are special opportunities there for developing courses in world faiths.

In spite of the trend towards multi-faith RE, there are many RE staff who trained before teacher-education courses included the study of world religions, and there are many non-specialist teachers in primary and secondary schools who would like to adopt a multi-faith approach, and need help in introducing world religions into their syllabuses. There are also many others – teachers, students and parents – who have serious reservations about the inclusion in RE of religions other than Christianity. This book is addressed primarily to these groups of people, although we hope that its contents will encourage teachers already engaged in multi-faith RE to reflect further upon their approaches and methods.

The first section of the book – The Classroom – is full of practical advice about how to teach world religions courses in different kinds of primary and secondary schools. The contributors write from their own direct experience of multi-faith RE, and the positive response of young people, together with the useful advice and information they offer, should inspire many teachers to try out new ideas in RE lessons.

The rest of the book aims to remove the reservations and doubts about the teaching of world religions expressed in recent years by many parents and teachers. The contributors consider the implications for RE of the pluralistic nature of our society (Chapters 5–7), the personal commitment of teachers and pupils in relation to a multi-faith religious education (Chapters 8–10), the relevance of a multi-faith RE to the developing personal views and feelings of the children and young people in our schools (Chapters 11–13), and the relationship between religious education and other areas of the curriculum fundamentally concerned with values (Chapters 14–16).

To make the book as flexible as possible, there is a separate introduction to each section. These are intended to set the issues under discussion in the wider context of religious education in schools, and to relate the chapters in each section to one another. Where it may be helpful to the reader, summaries of the main arguments of the chapters that follow are included; and when material pertinent to issues discussed in one section occurs in other sections reference is made to it.

Suggestions for further reading are placed, as appropriate, at the end of sections or chapters. The reading lists include comments by contributors on recommended books and articles.

All the contributors are professionally engaged in religious education or religious studies in schools, colleges or universities and many are involved in the development of RE through such bodies as the Schools Council, the Shap Working Party on World Religions in Education, the National RE Council and the International Seminar on Religious Education and Values. It will soon become apparent to readers – and this is deliberate – that the contributors do not have completely unanimous views about religious education. What we do have in common, however, is the knowledge, based on teaching experience, that a multi-faith approach to RE develops children's interest in the subject of religion, and the conviction that an exploratory, non-dogmatic study of religions is educationally desirable in today's world. Our collective hope is that by sharing our experiences and deliberations with other teachers we can help and encourage them to join their students in approaching world religions.

Robert Jackson
University of Warwick
January 1982

Acknowledgements

I am grateful to all the contributors for their support and patience while this book was being compiled, to my colleagues Dennis Starkings and Peter Gardner at the University of Warwick for their wise counsel, to Ann Cochrane at John Murray for her expertise and encouragement, and to my wife Rosemary for her understanding, tolerance and secretarial skills.

RJ

Contents

Notes on the Contributors

OWEN COLE is Senior Lecturer in Religious Studies at West Sussex Institute of Higher Education, Bishop Otter College, Chichester, and a founder member and former chairman of the Shap Working Party on World Religions in Education. He edited *World Faiths in Education* (Allen & Unwin, 1978) and with Piara Singh Sambhi wrote *The Sikhs: Their Beliefs and Practices* (Routledge and Kegan Paul, 1978). His recent publications include *Thinking About Sikhism* (Lutterworth, 1980), and *Five Religions in the Twentieth Century* (Hulton, 1981).

BRIAN GATES, previously Principal Lecturer in Religion at Goldsmiths College, University of London, is Head of Religious Studies and Social Ethics at St Martin's College, Lancaster. He is Deputy Chairman of the RE Council of England and Wales and of the Shap Working Party on World Religions in Education. He is editor of *Afro-Caribbean Religions* (Ward Lock, 1980). A book based on his doctoral thesis, *Religion in the Developing World of Children and Young People* (University of Lancaster, 1976), is to be published shortly.

MICHAEL GRIMMITT was the first Director of the RE Resources and In-Service Training Centre and Principal Lecturer in Religious Education at Westhill College, Birmingham before taking up his current post as Lecturer in Religious Education at the University of Birmingham. His publications include *What Can I Do In RE?* (Mayhew-McCrimmon, 1973 and 1978), and, with Garth Read, *Christians Today* and *Teaching Christianity in RE* (both Kevin Mayhew Ltd, 1978). He is Reviews Editor of the *British Journal of Religious Education*.

RAYMOND HAMMER has taught at St Paul's University, Tokyo, at the Universities of Durham and Birmingham and at the Queen's College, Birmingham. He is currently Director of the Bible Reading Fellowship, London, and is a consultant to the Archbishop of Canterbury on Interfaith Relations. His publications include *Japan's Religious Ferment* (SCM Press, 1961), *Commentary on Daniel* (CUP, 1976), and 'The theological perspective in the encounter of religions', in R. Jackson (ed.), *Perspectives on World Religions* (School of Oriental and African Studies, 1978).

ALLAN HAWKE taught religious education in secondary schools and at Coventry College of Education before becoming Principal Lecturer and Head of Religious Studies at Bretton Hall College of Higher Education, Yorkshire. He taught for a year in Afghanistan and has travelled in India and Nepal. He is a tutor for the Open University course 'Man's Religious Quest'.

JEAN HOLM is Principal Lecturer in Religious Studies at Homerton College, Cambridge. Her publications include *Teaching Religion in School* (OUP, 1975), and *The Study of Religions* (Sheldon Press, 1977), in the series *Issues in Religious Studies* of which, with Peter Baelz, she is General Editor. She is chairman of the Schools Council Religious Education Committee.

JOHN HULL taught in schools and colleges in Australia and England before taking up his present post as Senior Lecturer in Religious Education in the Faculty of Education of the University of Birmingham. His publications include *Hellenistic Magic and the Synoptic Tradition* (SCM Press, 1974) and *School Worship: An Obituary* (SCM Press, 1975). Since 1971 he has been Vice-Chairman of the Christian Education Movement and editor of the *British Journal of Religious Education* (formerly *Learning For Living*). He is co-founder and co-chairman of the International Seminar on Religious Education and Values, and a member of the Shap Working Party on World Religions in Education.

ROBERT JACKSON, General Editor of the present series, is Senior Lecturer in Arts Education at the University of Warwick. He edited *Perspectives on World Religions* (London: School of Oriental and African Studies, 1978), and is a regular contributor to BBC radio programmes for schools on world religions. He is a member of the Shap Working Party.

ERIC PAIN, a former Advisory Teacher in Religious Education, is Deputy Head of France Hill School, Camberley, Surrey. He is co-author with John Elliott of *Sex, Marriage and Family Life* and *Education, Work and Death* (Lutterworth, 1975, *Life Cycle* series), and he contributed to the unit on *Pilgrimages* in the Schools Council series *Journeys into Religion* (Hart-Davis, 1977).

ROBIN RICHARDSON, now Adviser for Multicultural Education with Berkshire Education Authority, is a former Director of the World Studies Project, and also of the Bloxham Project. Until 1979 he was editor of the educational journal *The New Era*. His publications include *Images of Life* (SCM Press, 1973), *Learning for Change in World Society* (One World Trust, 1976), and various curriculum materials including *Frontiers of Enquiry* (Hart-Davis, 1971) and *World Studies* (Nelson, 1977).

DENNIS STARKINGS is Lecturer in Arts Education at the University of Warwick. He is the author of *British Democracy in the Twentieth Century* (Faber, 1969), and co-author with Marion Would of *Reconciling the World* (Faber, 1970). With Robert Jackson he is editor of *Resource*, a journal for teachers of religious and moral education.

RICHARD TAMES is Deputy Organiser of Extramural Studies, School of Oriental and African Studies, University of London. He held a number of teaching posts before becoming secretary to the Council of the Hansard

Society for Parliamentary Government. His publications include *People, Power and Politics* (Nelson, 1978), *The Arab World Today* (Kaye and Ward, 1980), and *Approaches to Islam* in the present series.

MARILYN THOMAS is Head of Religious Education at Hornsey Girls' School. She is a former teacher-fellow in World Religions and Education at the School of Oriental and African Studies, University of London, and she is author of 'World religions in a comprehensive school', in R. Jackson (ed.), *Perspectives on World Religions* (London: SOAS, 1978).

SIMON WEIGHTMAN is Lecturer in Hindi at the School of Oriental and African Studies, University of London. His publications include *Hinduism in the Village Setting* (Open University, 1978), and 'Hinduism and religious education', in R. Jackson (ed.), *Perspectives on World Religions* (London: SOAS, 1978).

PETER WOODWARD is General Inspector of Schools for the City of Birmingham Education Department. He edited *World Religions: Aids for Teachers* (CRC, 1971). His other publications include 'World religions: practical considerations', in Ninian Smart and Donald Horder (eds), *New Movements in Religious Education* (Temple Smith, 1975), and he is scriptwriter and adviser for the schools television series *Believe It or Not*, and a member of the Shap Working Party.

Part One

The Classroom

Introduction

This section deals with the practicalities of introducing world religions into the curriculum of different types of schools in a variety of social settings. Jean Holm deals with primary schools, while Eric Pain and Marilyn Thomas discuss religious education in two comprehensive schools, one multi-cultural and the other not. Drawing on his experience as an adviser, Peter Woodward offers practical guidance to teachers in both primary and secondary sectors on multi-faith religious education.

Teaching about world religions should be considered in relation to the general picture of religious education in schools, and the following remarks are intended to set the opening chapters of this book in a wider context.

Primary Schools

The impression given by reports from HMIs, by lecturers engaged in teacher education and by many teachers is that primary school RE generally is in a poor state. Of the various contributory factors the following are particularly significant. The first is pressure on the curriculum. Primary school teachers are expected, in theory, to be familiar with all aspects of the curriculum, but at the same time they are under pressure from parents and others to give particular attention to the basic skills of numeracy and literacy. It is significant that the presence of coherent, well-constructed reading and mathematics schemes in infant, junior and middle schools is all but universal while the conduct of religious education – as distinct from assembly – is left all too frequently to the discretion of the individual teacher. Recent agreed syllabuses produced by some local authorities offer guidance to primary teachers, but experience has shown that these are of limited practical value unless used by teachers as a basis for designing RE programmes to meet the needs of particular schools.

A second, more fundamental, factor is the confusion felt by teachers concerning the subject's aims. In primary schools teachers still commonly assume that the role of RE is to establish and foster religious faith, an assumption which prompts many of them to oppose the place of RE in the curriculum or at least to decline to teach it. Some primary teachers on in-service courses have been pleasantly surprised to find that most RE literature published in the last decade has emphasised the *understanding* of religion as the key aim of RE, and has regarded nurture in a life of faith to be the responsibility of the home and of any religious community to which the child's family may be affiliated.

A third factor, associated with confusion over aims, is concern about the relationship between religious commitment and religious education. 'Should I teach RE if I'm not a regular churchgoer?' is still a common question. The commitment issue is so important that a whole section of this book has been devoted to it. For the moment, suffice it to say that it has been found that once teachers have a clear idea of the subject's aims and have resolved any tensions they may feel about commitment, their interest and involvement in RE often develops quickly.

A fourth reason for RE's decline in primary schools, particularly in infant schools, is the view that young children are incapable of understanding religious ideas. Ronald Goldman's research, published in the early 1960s, emphasised that while young children are capable of feeling emotions associated with religion, their understanding of religious ideas is limited but may develop through a series of stages, from the intuitive (up to a mental age of 7–8 years) to the abstract (from mental age 12–13+). Curriculum material for younger children based on Goldman's work avoided the introduction of religious language, and usually made no explicit reference to religion. Instead children were introduced to 'religious' emotions by reference to situations familiar to them in their own experience. Thus 'love' would be explored through such a theme or topic as 'people who help us', and 'awe' or 'wonder' would be experienced directly, for example in response to the birth of animals or the growing of seeds.

It should be noted that Goldman was not primarily concerned with the discussion of aims, and the traditional 'nurturing' aim was regarded as axiomatic. Goldman's particular theological view – a Christian theology of human experience – is implicit in his own work and in much of the curriculum material modelled on his ideas; teachers having theological opinions different from Goldman's, and those with no theological position, have found difficulty in identifying such material as *religious* education, although its general educational value is usually affirmed. It is possible, however, to use insights from Goldman's work which help in the preparation of RE materials for younger children. As Jean Holm points out in Chapter 1, young children can be introduced at a very early age to certain aspects of religion as it is lived by people. The teacher does not introduce abstract ideas, but in discussing simple factual material capitalises on children's questions, experiences and interest. World religions are not *taught* in any formal sense, but they *are* learnt about. Jean Holm also makes it clear that provided that difficult and abstract ideas are avoided, young children can enjoy absorbing a great deal of information about religions as well as discovering something of religious feeling. Recent research in religious education – particularly the work of Brian Gates – offers evidence that many young children can understand a good deal more about religion than they are able to express in language, and there is considerable scope for investigating the use of such media as art, music and drama, as well as writing, in the exploration of religion. (See Brian Gates's contribution, Chapter 11, and the publications of the Schools Council Project on Religious Education in Primary Schools for further details.)

Finally, as both Jean Holm and Peter Woodward observe, some of the best primary RE currently being taught is in multi-faith schools. Many teachers in such schools have worked out the question of RE's aims for *themselves* because of the immediate needs of the children in their classes. When a range of religions is represented in a class it is evident that a 'nurturing' aim is inappropriate. RE is seen to be concerned with the sharing of experience – with the understanding and appreciation of one another's faiths. Furthermore the data of religion – its festivals and fasts, its prayer and devotion, its rites of passage – are immediately available (albeit piecemeal) in the presence and contributions of pupils. Teachers who in earlier days may have spurned RE as evangelism or even as indoctrination find themselves *interested* in RE because they are interested in and concerned for their pupils.

Secondary Schools

Since there are more RE specialists in secondary than in primary schools, the results of research and curriculum development in the subject tend to be known and acted upon in the former relatively quickly. Nevertheless, there is still a shortage of secondary specialists, and the subject is too often left in the hands of staff who have no formal qualifications in RE. This state of affairs is an important factor in accounting for the wide variety of aims and subject matter to be found in the RE syllabuses of secondary schools.

Chapters 2 and 3, by Eric Pain and Marilyn Thomas respectively, illustrate how experienced specialist RE teachers have set about re-examining the aims and content of their subject. Both take account of recent thinking on RE in devising syllabuses and teaching methods to meet the particular needs of their own pupils. Like Peter Woodward (Chapter 4) they are concerned to work out clear educational aims, and to tackle the problem of selecting material from the enormous resources of the world's religions in achieving them. While Eric Pain and his colleagues adopt a basic course in religious language and terminology followed up by a study of two or three religions for their fourth- and fifth-year examination students, Marilyn Thomas favours a thematic approach for her first- to third-year pupils. In his overview, Peter Woodward emphasises that although a multi-faith approach is suitable in *any* school, the precise contents of courses should vary according to the geographical setting and social composition of schools.

Other matters raised in Chapters 2–4 include the role of the teacher in exploring world religions with children; the rethinking of examination procedures; the use of visits and audio visual aids to increase pupils' interest in and sensitivity to religion; and the crucial issues of satisfactory provision on the timetable for RE, and the appointment by schools of adequate numbers of professionally trained RE teachers.

Further issues raised in the opening chapters, relating to religious commitment, to the implications for religious education of the pluralistic nature of our society and to the relevance of RE to the personal lives of pupils, receive detailed discussion in later sections of the book.

R.J.

1
World Religions in Primary Schools

Jean Holm

'When should you start teaching world religions?' Many primary school teachers, remembering their own experience of the comparative study of religion in the sixth form, feel that world religions are too difficult for young children.

In one sense they are right. It is quite impossible for children of primary or even middle school age to understand even their own religion properly, let alone other religions.

But the expression 'teaching world religions' is a misleading one, suggesting as it does schemes of work on Islam, Hinduism, etc. What happens if we put the question with which we began in a different form? If, instead of asking, 'When should you start teaching world religions?', we ask, 'When can children start learning about world religions?' The answer will now be, 'In the reception class'. It will, of course, be incidental learning, and it will arise from the children's own background and experience. It may be sparked off by a child's response to a story, or it may perhaps come from a contribution to the morning 'news time'. We must not forget that Christianity is a world religion. Among the great variety of experiences which small children regard as important and therefore want to share with their teacher, there are bound to be such things as Easter eggs and Christmas presents and activities; and there is always someone who wants to talk about a family christening or wedding. These are all part of what are called the phenomena of religion, that is, the ways in which a religion is expressed in the life of an individual or of a religious community.

In the multi-faith class the things the children want to talk to their teacher about will come from more than one religion. But even where there are no pupils of other faiths the class will still be learning about the phenomena of religion.

The teacher will deal with the child's contribution in the field of religion in exactly the same way that she deals with contributions about the new hamster or auntie coming to stay or the family holiday. By her interest and her questions she will encourage the child to talk about it, and she will help the rest of the class to understand and appreciate what he says.

Talking about the phenomena of religions in the context of the children's experience is a reminder of three important characteristics of religions.

Firstly, they are not just sets of beliefs and practices written down in books. They are *lived by people*. So we shall not just tell the class about the life of Muhammad and the Five Pillars of Islam. Instead, we shall help them to enter imaginatively into the life of a Muslim family, to try to understand what Islam is like in practice, especially as it affects the children of the family.

Secondly, when we talk about a religion we are talking about *someone's faith*, so we must treat it as we would like our own faith to be treated. We must help the children to see it from the point of view of the person concerned, to try to stand in his shoes, and to realise that it is profoundly important to him.

Thirdly, religion is always intertwined with the *culture* of the person who practises it, so in the classroom we shall not try to isolate what we consider to be 'religious' – beliefs, worship, etc. – but we shall include all those aspects of the culture through which the religion is expressed: food, dress, customs, dance, music, etc.

It is much easier to follow these guidelines in a multi-faith class. The children are a constant reminder that religions do not exist in a vacuum, but are made up of particular people and expressed through particular cultures. We know that to make a negative statement about a child's religion is to hurt that child and to depreciate his sense of identity. When there are no children of other faiths in the school we have to make a conscious effort to develop that sensitivity which is necessary for talking about other people's religions.

Schemes of work

Children's incidental learning about religions, through discussion of something brought into the classroom, or seen on television, or encountered in a story, will remain important right through the primary school, but how do we set about organising more systematic learning?

In a multi-faith class this can start quite early, even in the infant school, because the emphasis will be on sharing. Festivals are excellent for sharing because, although they are significant for the community as a whole, they are times of particular delight for children and they almost always involve parties, presents, special food and new clothes.

The teachers of one junior school, where children from minority ethnic groups make up 85 per cent of the school population, decided one year to celebrate the major festivals of all the religions represented in the school. As Eid, Divali, Christmas came round they were 'celebrated' by all the classes, and each class made a contribution to the assemblies. The children were able, with pride, to share their particular cultural background, through dress, dance, food, hairstyles, art, jewellery, worship and information about the practices of their religious community. However, as one of the teachers said, 'We soon discovered that although the Italians and West Indians were Christians, they did not have the same opportunities to share their culture within their religion. So we decided to have a Carnival Celebration or Caribbean week for the West Indians and an Italian week for the Italians, where they could illustrate their forms of worship, bring artefacts and generally share their culture.' The festival experiment was a great success. All the pupils participated and knowledge of the various religions spread throughout the school. But most of all the 'host culture' for each festival took pride in identifying with its own culture.

Teachers may well protest that one cannot just do festivals year after year. Obviously there is more to the study of religion than festivals, but we have to remember that children do not regard the annual celebration of festivals as boring repetition. They look forward to them with keen anticipation. And after all, schools have a long tradition of 'doing' Christmas every year! To recognise the festivals of the children in the class is one very important way of acknowledging the children's significance and valuing their identity.

Festivals can be handled in different ways. One year it may be enough, particularly at the junior school stage, to wish the Jewish children a 'Happy New Year' at Rosh Hashanah or the Hindu children a 'Happy New Year' at Divali and to allow them to talk to the rest of the class about how their family is celebrating the festival. Another year the festivals may be part of a wider scheme, such as a study of the local community, which, in addition to all the usual ingredients – buildings, occupations, public services, etc. – would include customs and ceremonies in the homes and places of worship of the different religious groups.

A different angle on festivals can be given by including them in a topic on *Time*. The cycle of the religious year is one way of measuring time, and the festivals linked with seasons – spring festivals, such as Passover, Holi, Easter, and autumn festivals, such as Sukkot (Tabernacles), Divali, Harvest – are appropriately dealt with in this context. One school included annual festivals in its study of seasonal patterns, within a topic on *Patterns*.

In the multi-faith school *Families* and *Growing up* are examples of topics which make it possible for younger children to share their own cultural background with the rest of the class and to learn about the cultural background of other children.

But what about schools where there are no children of other faiths? They are of course deprived of the opportunities we have been describing of discovering through first hand experience the different ways of doing things in different cultures; but there are variations even within the same culture. Children can be helped to accept and respect differences through finding out about such things as likes and dislikes within the class, family customs, and so on, or through good children's literature, which makes possible an exploration in some detail of characteristics and situations which distinguish people from each other. This is a most important foundation on which can be built an acceptance of the value of other cultures and religions.

'We don't do anything on world religions because we have no immigrants in our area', said the headmaster of a lively rural primary school, well known for its imaginative teaching. 'These religions are outside the children's experience.' 'But didn't you do Tutankhamun?' 'Yes, but that was different. We took the children to London to see the exhibition.' The school is only 60 miles from London, but it is less than 20 miles from a large town with a high proportion of so-called 'immigrants'. Moreover, it could be argued that the religions practised in Britain in the twentieth century are much closer to the children's experience than the culture of ancient Egypt, or for that matter the culture of the ancient Greeks or the Vikings which junior school children study with such enthusiasm.

The argument about starting from the children's experience is an important one in the infant school, but by the time children are about eight or nine they are capable of being interested in a whole range of topics. They have a natural curiosity, and they enjoy acquiring knowledge. However, in addition to the characteristics of religions already mentioned, there are other points to remember if the children are to find learning about contemporary religions as absorbing as they find learning about ancient cultures.

1 We must *start with the concrete*, that is, with what can be seen, either literally or in pictorial form. Children in the junior school are at the concrete stage of thinking. They are capable of quite extensive questioning and discussion, but they need as a basis a solid foundation of factual information.

2 Children need *lots of detail*. Juniors love collecting things, including facts. They soon lose interest in something if it is being treated superficially. And the more removed a topic is from their immediate experience the more important it is that they should be given plenty of accurate information. Confusion and misunderstandings about world religions are an almost inevitable consequence of topics being dealt with too quickly and too superficially.

3 We need to develop a *positive attitude* towards religions. This does not mean pretending that every aspect of every religion is perfect. What it does mean is that we should introduce children first to those aspects which they are likely to admire. For example, it is better for children to meet Muslim art and architecture or Arabic script before they learn about the Muslim prayer positions. This is especially important if they do not know any Muslim children, or if there are tensions between ethnic groups in the local community. The last thing we want is for children to laugh at other

people's ways of doing things, particularly when they involve something as central to a religion as its worship. If they find Muslim geometric patterns and Arabic script fascinating they are much more likely to take a positive interest in aspects of the religion which might otherwise seem odd.

4 The pupils should be learning about *living religions*. The emphasis should therefore be on what it is like to be a Jew or a Hindu or a Christian today. We have to resist the temptation to deal first with the origins of a religion. This is far too complex a subject for children of primary school age to understand without distortion, and if we present it to them in 'simple' terms which they can 'understand', then we shall without doubt have given them a misleading and inaccurate 'understanding'. It is only when pupils have developed the ability to handle historical concepts, that is, not before about 13 or 14, that they can take a real interest in movements in history. (See page 10 for the problem of teaching about the founders of religions.)

5 The children need access to a *variety of resources*. Ideally they should be able to make visits to the places of worship and the homes of adherents of the religions they are learning about, they should be able to see and if possible handle religious objects, for instance a joss stick holder or an image of Ganesha used by Hindus, a Seder dish used by Jews at Passover or a nine-branched candlestick used by them at the festival of Chanukah. If the children cannot have firsthand experience of these things they must have clear and accurate pictures and descriptions. Again, ideally they should have access to some of the literature which the religious community uses. Books, pamphlets, posters, and so on, which are produced for the community's own children are excellent, but even adult literature, such as a book used in worship, can be useful. Sometimes older juniors will be able to use it for reference purposes; but even if the content is too difficult for children, simply handling a book which is important to the adherents of the religion being studied helps to bring that religion to life and to make the study authentic. (See page 14 for further discussion of resources.)

6 Children need to undertake *practical activities* related to the religions they are learning about. Merely copying facts out of books is a completely inadequate way even of mastering those facts, let alone learning what it must be like to be an adherent of a religion. Just as children need a variety of resources to help them to understand something as complex as a religion, so they need a variety of ways of expressing what they are discovering about the practice of a religion. For instance, in addition to such familiar activities as drawing, painting, making models and wall charts, they could prepare food, learn a traditional song (and tape it), write out prayers or short passages from the scriptures and decorate them with the characteristic symbols and art forms of the religion, reproduce key texts in the appropriate script – Arabic, Hebrew, Punjabi, Gujarati, and so on. The activities must be imaginative and varied and they must give an accurate picture of the religion.

In a school which is not multi-faith an excellent scheme to introduce nine or ten year olds to a systematic study of world religions is *sacred places* – learning about the places of worship of two or more religions. It illustrates how we can put into practice the principles outlined in the last six paragraphs. Top juniors enjoy finding out about different kinds of buildings – their characteristic architecture, furnishings, forms of decoration and symbols, the placing and use of the scriptures – and the ways in which the adherents of the religions use the buildings, for worship and for other activities.

Children of this age cannot comprehend a religion's beliefs about God or salvation or the nature of man. These belong to the adult reflective activity which we call theology, and even the adherents of a religion themselves seldom study their beliefs in any systematic way. Rather, the beliefs are expressed through the different aspects of the religion such as worship, prayer, meditation, sacred buildings, places of pilgrimage, festivals, scriptures and other sacred writings, and the way in which the children are brought up. As our pupils learn about these aspects of a religion, focusing particularly on what can be seen and what people do, they are gradually building up an understanding of the things which are important in the religion, and laying a foundation for a much later study of a people's beliefs, the nature of their faith, the significance of their worship, and so on. It is also at this later stage that it becomes relevant to look back to the origins and the historical development of a religion.

Founders

Religious education books frequently recommend that founders of religions should be studied in the primary school. How sound is this advice? Of course children should become familiar with the names of the founders of the religions practised in Britain (where there are known founders), and by the end of the junior school stage they should know something of the significance of the founder within a particular religion. For example, they should know that Muslims object to being called Muhammadans because that seems to suggest that they worship Muhammad, whereas they believe that Muhammad was a wonderful human being but not in any sense divine.

However, a study of the life and work of the founder of a religion is inappropriate in the primary school, for two main reasons. First, founders are concerned with belief systems and, as we have seen, any adequate understanding of beliefs and their relationship to one another is impossible for children at this age. It is true that most lives of founders written for children focus on ethical teaching more than on beliefs, but we are giving a misleading impression of what founding a religion involves if we suggest that the founder's main achievement was to teach that people should be honest and sincere and that they should love and care for others. At this rather simple level such teaching can be found in all religions.

What caused a man to become a founder of a new religion lies at a much deeper level.

It may perhaps be argued that no serious harm can come from showing children that the ethical teachings of the founders of different religions are similar. However, there is a more serious objection to teaching about founders.

This objection relates to the fact that a new religion always arises from an existing one, keeping some features of the original religion and rejecting or modifying others. The process is highly complex and it requires considerable maturity to understand not only the inevitable tensions it creates, but also the genuine anxieties of sincere people who believe that truth is at stake, and feel threatened by the new teaching. This is reduced to such a simplistic level in the stories of founders written for children that the impression is often given that all those who supported the founder were 'good' and all those who opposed him were 'bad'. If our aim is to help pupils to develop a positive understanding of religions, we shall be making the achievement of that aim virtually impossible if, for example, in learning about the founder of Sikhism or Christianity the children come to regard Muslims or Jews as villains.

Of course it is appropriate that children in school should learn more about the founder of the religion which has had a major influence on the culture of the country than about the founders of other religions. Children in Britain will therefore learn about Jesus. This does not mean that our approach will be the same as it was when the aim of religious education was confessional. Instead of assuming that Jesus is the Son of God, or even just the greatest teacher of ethical values, we have to help the pupils to see him as the founder of a world religion and to understand something of his importance for Christians. The problems this raises, particularly at primary school level, are so complex that they cannot be dealt with here; they require a separate and detailed discussion.

The same or different?

In the days when the study of religions was confined to a short course in the sixth form, the emphasis was put on the differences between religions. Now we are possibly in danger of going to the other extreme, especially in the primary school, partly because of the tendency to oversimplify for young children and partly because we are no longer trying to demonstrate the superiority of one religion over its 'rivals'. We have to tread a very narrow path if we are to help children to see both what religions have in common and what distinguishes them from one another.

Topics such as *sacred places* and *festivals* and *signs and symbols* are useful for keeping this balance, but we get into deep water if we try to do cross-cultural schemes on subjects like the heroes or the stories of world religions. One cannot find comparable examples, even in the five main religions represented in Britain. Must the heroes, for example, be historical characters? If so, that would probably exclude one of the main Hindu heroes, Rama, whose significance in Hinduism is completely independent of any historical situations or events. It would be confusing to children to have historical characters from some religions and mythical characters from others, all called 'heroes'. It would also be confusing if we were to select figures from very different periods in history, with different sets of values. Children might be tempted to think that the religion represented in the later period was superior to one whose 'hero' lived in much earlier times; but it is not possible to find heroes from each religion, contemporary with one another and suitable for primary school children.

What about stories? Surely we are on safer ground here? Children love stories, and it is often through stories that we can gain an entry into the 'feel' of another culture. This is certainly true. There are many stories drawn from different religious traditions which are suitable for children.

The problem arises when we try to set stories alongside one another as illustrations of different religions. For example, if we wanted to have a scheme on myths in the religions represented in Britain, what would we choose? The Hindu myth would be easy. The story of Rama and Sita is central in popular Hinduism, and is suitable for primary school children. What would we choose as a Christian myth? Would the stories of King Arthur be appropriate? But they are legends rather than myths, and in the junior school we help children to distinguish legends from myths proper. Genesis I is sophisticated theology, expressed through a borrowed Mesopotamian myth, but even if it was regarded as a myth, should it illustrate Christianity or Judaism in our scheme? Muslims would strenuously deny that there were any myths at all in Islam. And before we have even started to ask about myths in Sikhism we have discovered that a scheme on myths in world religions could be only an artificial construction, which would not be true to some of the religions and which would inevitably fail in its original purpose of illustrating one theme from different religions.

As we have already seen, however, the fact that such schemes are impossible does not mean that stories from the different religious traditions cannot be told to children. Sometimes a story may stand on its own, and be told just because it is a good story. If the children are learning about a religion's festival we may tell a story which is associated with that festival. Or if they are learning about boys and girls growing up in a particular religious tradition it would be appropriate for them to hear one or more of the stories which those boys and girls enjoy. Our main criteria in selecting the stories will be that they are stories which the religious community itself would be happy to have told, and that they should be suitable for the age and background of the children in the class.

Judaism – a world religion

Teachers who say that they do not approve of world religions in the primary school, and that they are sticking to good old-fashioned Bible stories, seem to be quite unaware that they are actually teaching two world religions – Christianity and Judaism – albeit in a way which does justice to neither. The children may be learning stories from the Christian (and the Jewish) scriptures, but they are certainly not learning about Christianity or Judaism as living religions. However, the distortion of Christianity is as nothing compared with the distortion of Judaism which results from this kind of approach.

In the first place, 'the Jews' are presented as opponents of Jesus. The fact that he himself was a Jew, as were his disciples and all the earliest Christians, is ignored. The stories in the gospels of Jesus' confrontations with the Pharisees are treated as straightforward historical accounts, and children are given the impression that all the Pharisees were legalistic hypocrites. Most primary school teachers are not RE specialists, and they cannot therefore be blamed for not knowing that the Pharisees were the most devout group within Judaism and that their teaching had a great deal in common with the teaching of Jesus; or for not knowing that the gospels took their present form at a time when the Christian Church was emerging as a separate religion from Judaism, with all the tensions that involved. The responsibility lies primarily with those who write books for teachers and pupils to use, but if we are aware of the problem we can at least be alert to the dangers of stereotyping.

Secondly, the impression is given that Judaism came to an end when Christianity began. This is not confined to Bible-based religious education. It is astonishing how many teachers who are happy to teach world religions use only biblical material to teach about Judaism, ignoring all the developments of the past 2,000 years. When they teach about Passover, they focus not on the Jewish family's celebration in the late twentieth century, but on either the slaughter of the Passover lambs in the Temple in Jerusalem in the first century or the story of the origins of the festival at the time of Moses. Similarly, a description of Jewish worship is more likely to contain details of the Tabernacle and the Temple than of the synagogue today.

One of the problems is that while many people are aware of their lack of knowledge of Islam, Hinduism and Sikhism, they feel more confident about handling Judaism because of their familiarity with the Bible. But because Judaism is a religion with 2,000 years of history since biblical times, and because Jewish interpretations of its Bible (the Christian Old Testament) are in any case not identical with Christian interpretations, we have to be particularly careful about how we present Judaism to children.

Resources

It is unfortunate that few books about world religions take the approach that is required if children are to understand what it is like to be an adherent of a religion. Almost all the available books, even those written for children, start with the origins of the religion and include something about its history and its main beliefs before describing its practices. A notable exception is the *Understanding your Neighbour* series published by Lutterworth. The books in this series deal mainly with the practice of the religions in Britain where they are minority faiths, and where therefore the expression of the religion is different from what it is in its own cultural setting.

Another problem is that many authors attempt to summarise a religion in one small book. How can children possibly do detailed work on a festival that is described in a few sentences, or undertake a study of sacred places if the books they are using give only the briefest information about the mosque or synagogue or gurdwara?

Generally speaking, the best literature is that produced by the religious community itself, especially when it is in the form of books or leaflets on individual aspects of the religion. There is a wealth of this kind of material available from Jewish sources, and an increasing amount available from Muslim sources, though as yet there is not the same kind or quality of literature available for Hinduism and Sikhism.

As we have already seen, children need more than books if they are to get the feel of a religion. Multi-faith schools have a tremendous advantage here, as families are often prepared to lend objects or to bring them into the school for the children to see. Other schools in towns or cities where there are religious communities will find that the communities are usually very willing to help when there is a genuine desire to learn about their religion.

With a little ingenuity a school can build up an inexpensive collection of useful resources which illustrate religions and cultures: festival greetings cards, calendars, prayer leaflets, examples of the script of languages (e.g. in newspapers circulating among the different ethnic groups in Britain or brought back from a holiday abroad), postcards, travel brochures, photos from colour supplements and so on.

In some localities primary and secondary schools have combined to create a joint bank of resources. This is a great help to the primary schools, with their limited funds for individual subjects, and a very useful collection can be built up when a number of teachers pool their knowledge and experience of different religions and make available copies of slides or prints.

We end this chapter as we began it, with the pupils. They are one of our most important resources. Whether the class is multi-faith or not, there will be some pupils who come from families where religion is practised. By sharing their experience of the different aspects of their religion, such children can make an invaluable contribution to the class's understanding of the nature of religion. There is, of course, much more to be learnt about religions at secondary school, but the realisation that they are *lived by people* is an excellent foundation for later study.

See page 47 for further reading for Chapters 1-4.

2

Developing a
World Religions Course

Eric Pain

This chapter is an account of the development of a world religions orientated course at France Hill School, Camberley, a mixed comprehensive of 1,450 pupils aged 12 to 18. It is written in the hope that others may learn something of benefit from our experiences. Any success we have had has been due to a number of factors, among which are a clear idea of the subject's aims accepted by colleagues in the school and by parents on educational grounds, an adequate number of qualified members of staff and the collective will to make the subject as demanding and as popular as any other subject in the school. I am convinced that given similar staffing and resources any school could make a success of religious education. The 'Cinderella' status of the subject in many schools is caused by inadequate and (all too often) unqualified staffing, insufficient lesson time and poor resources. It has nothing to do with the subject itself, which – in our experience – generates a great deal of enthusiasm and interest among pupils.

Aims and principles

It might be useful at this point to summarise the department's ideas about the aims and principles which underpin our RE courses. Our view is that the basic aim of religious education is to give pupils some understanding of religion. But the pupil should also be encouraged to develop a critical appreciation of religion in formulating a – perhaps provisional – philosophy or theology of life. Religious education should be 'open'; it should neither aim to foster nor to undermine beliefs held by pupils; it should develop knowledge, understanding and the ability to evaluate ideas.

Such an approach demands an adjustment of the traditional view of the RE teacher's role and in this connection it is useful to draw a clear distinction between the role of the family and the role of the school in the advancement of religious education. If RE is to be open and exploratory the teacher cannot expect to be an evangelist, an oracle or in any way prescriptive. Rather he should be a guide, more experienced than his students may be, but none the less a co-explorer and a catalyst. Through careful questioning or the presentation of new evidence, he can help pupils to consider fresh angles or alternative viewpoints. The teacher should expect to experience new insights himself and in a sense his pupils will have to educate him. Sometimes it will be necessary for a teacher to withhold his own experience and understanding *for a while* in order to allow his pupils to develop their own. This is not always easy in practice, but it is essential as a general principle. In this way pupils can be encouraged to see themselves as students of religion. This is important because it helps to focus attention on the nature of religion itself and shift the emphasis away from 'What sir believes'. As long as pupils feel that RE is about teachers trying to get them to believe what *they* believe it is likely to be a negative and unsatisfactory business. It is much more worthwhile to bring pupils into a dialogue with religious experience itself. This can be liberating for both pupil and teacher. There is much more likelihood that the teacher will be able to act as catalyst and guide when he is not constantly defending his own beliefs; the pupil is also more likely to be able to become a co-investigator, an active participant in the learning process.

If such an admittedly idealised state of affairs is to approach reality it is essential that one's studies should have a historical and world perspective. This is partly because religion has universal significance, and partly because without a world view our pupils would be offered a parochial, partial, inward-looking and therefore distorted picture.

Even more important than this, the inclusion of material from religions other than Christianity is an indication to pupils that a diversity of views is permissible. Thanks to the mass media all of us are made aware daily of the existence of beliefs and philosophies different from our own. Any intelligent and thoughtful person will be challenged by them, our pupils no less than others. Unless we recognise this, pupils will feel that we are deliberately keeping information from them. In this situation we should approach the beliefs of others with a concern for accuracy, a sensitivity to the feelings of others and a desire to understand.

Adopting a world perspective emphasises our determination to present a broad picture but, for obvious reasons, some selection from the richness of religious experience at our disposal must be made. We should not try to study every major belief system, for this would lead to the superficiality of the 'Cook's tour' syllabus. Nor should we try to devise a 'Consumers Association Survey' perhaps unintentionally leading to a best buy. Our way of solving the problem of selecting material is through the identification of central concepts and issues which have application and importance across the range of religious experience. A syllabus does not have to be thematic in structure but it must involve continual reference to, and re-examination of, these core concepts and issues.

Of course it is naive to assume that the right aims will carry us through. There are other necessary conditions for successful RE teaching including proper staffing, adequate resources and a measure of educational and political know-how. None of these can be achieved overnight and the account that follows covers a period of eight years or so at France Hill.

Preparing the ground

In 1974 the RE department consisted of the departmental Head (Geoffrey Taylor) and myself (a former Head of RE and advisory teacher for RE). RE was allowed one double lesson (70 minutes) or two single lessons per week in the first two years. In the fourth and fifth years RE was an option; about ten students were preparing for O level. There was one sixth-form A level student who was taught by the Head of Department in 'free periods' and after school.

Our lower school work was designed as a two-year course which, borrowing a title from Ninian Smart, we called 'the religious experience of mankind'. The first year covered the historical development of religions from earliest times. This was followed by a year devoted to living world religions including Hinduism, Judaism, Islam, Buddhism and Christianity. Within the various topic headings we always looked for key concepts and selected lesson material accordingly.

A primary aim at that time was to increase the interest of lower school pupils in the study of religions. Many of them came to us plainly not expecting to enjoy RE. We believed that if we could build up their confidence through developing their skill in using religious concepts, they would discover the interest of the subject for themselves and begin to enjoy it. It was necessary to explain to them that we were adopting a different approach. From time to time discussions about the philosophy behind our teaching arose in class and we considered these to be an important part of our RE programme.

In order to give the reader an insight into the balance we hoped to achieve between getting pupils to understand religious concepts and encouraging them to formulate their own ideas on religious matters there follows an extract from a transcript of a tape-recorded third-year lesson about the soul taught by Geoffrey Taylor:

Pupil 1   I think it's something inside you, a microscopic dot almost like a small universe. Something really small but also really big, that you can explore. Maybe the revelations of God come out from that and, like the Universe, it has a soul itself.

Pupil 2   I think it's a place where all your worship is built up. All your previous religious ideas are stored there.

Teacher   What important quality does the soul have that people, almost from the beginning of time, have felt was its most important aspect?

Pupil 3   It's um . . . immortal. It never ages, never dies like the body does.

Pupil 1   Another idea of the soul, I think, is the belief that the soul is a kind of spirit, but sort of softened . . . a mild sort of spirit. I think of a spirit as being sharp, almost like the points of a star, but the soul being round, smooth. It doesn't do any good or harm. It is just immortal and goes on and never ages.

Such discussions demonstrate that young secondary pupils are capable of deeper levels of thinking than they are sometimes given credit for. They also show that the open approach can lead to genuine involvement and the possibility of a real dialogue between teacher and pupils. This happens, I believe, because pupils have a greater freedom to react to the lesson material and to express their emerging ideas without the inhibition imposed by the feeling that there is a right answer, which the teacher knows.

In three years we saw enough evidence of growing interest to warrant the appointment of a further two specialist RE teachers. The fourth-year O level group had increased to just over twenty pupils who were studying 'The Life and Teaching of Christ' and Islam. Yet, although we were encouraged by this enthusiasm and also by the high standards of discussion and written work achieved, the fact remained that only twenty-five pupils out of over three hundred opted for RE. One reason why the O level group remained relatively small was the lack of continuity between our lower school work and the rather traditional O level syllabus that followed. Those students who took the O level course worked quite well and we had a good pass rate. Nevertheless the enthusiasm and involvement we had seen in earlier years were lacking. We found that the study of a Gospel was too narrow a discipline for any but a small number of students. We felt that too often there was an underlying assumption in conventional examination syllabuses of aims which were not open and exploratory but closed. Furthermore, students tended to see the course as 'wading through a set book'. Then there was the problem of those students who opted for the course but were not able to reach the standard required for O level entry.

Another factor which inhibited the growth of our O level group was a compulsory fifth-form social studies course which effectively limited the range of options open to prospective O level students. We had to advance arguments for replacing this with an optional sociology course in order to secure sufficient space on the timetable to mount our new courses. At the same time we instituted a major reform of the timetable which involved changing to a twenty-five period week with one hour units and no split lessons. RE, like all other options, is now allocated three hours a week during the fourth and fifth years. I emphasise this point because some RE teachers may not appreciate that it is sometimes necessary to become involved in 'school politics' in order to change possibly long-held negative attitudes towards RE and to get a fair share of the timetable for their subject.

Our own public examination syllabuses

By early 1976 we had submitted proposals to London University and to the South-East Regional Examinations Board for Mode 3 syllabuses leading to O level and CSE respectively. The syllabus content for the last two examinations was to be exactly the same, but the manner of assessment was to be different. In this way we hoped to avoid the need to divide into GCE sheep and CSE goats by producing in effect a 'common exam', based on a syllabus which would enable us to build on the success of earlier years. Within an unusually short time the Examination Boards accepted our syllabus and we were able to offer it to our pupils in 1977 for examination in 1979.

There are three main elements in the syllabus. The first is a compulsory section entitled 'The Language and Terminology of Religion'. This is designed to give students a broad understanding of religion which they could apply to any belief system they might meet. The list of topics includes: Religion, Worship, Prayer, Sacrifice, God, Good and Evil, The Sacred, Holy Men, Revelation, Religious Response (theism, monotheism, polytheism, dynamism, humanism, agnosticism, etc.), Ritual, The Afterlife, Salvation.

The second element is the study of one or more of the three major examples of Western monotheism – Christianity, Judaism and Islam. We believe that these have been, and still are, so influential in Western life and culture that they must command an important place in the secondary RE syllabus.

The third element is the study of one or more from a group of religions which includes primal religions (primitive and traditional tribal religions), Hinduism and Buddhism. Hinduism and Buddhism were selected because we felt that a major Eastern religion should be studied. Primal religions are included because they offer a direct link with earlier work, which has proved absorbing to our students; they also provide a very useful way of introducing concepts in a variety of contexts which illustrate their meaning.

We try to present religions in such a way that pupils can begin to appreciate each of them as a living whole, and we have found Ninian Smart's six-dimensional analysis of religion (ritual, myth, doctrine, experience, ethics and the social dimension) very helpful in drawing attention to the organic character of religions.

Coursework assessment is made throughout the two years of study. For O level this carries up to 30 per cent of the final marks and for CSE up to 50 per cent. The final examination, in both cases, consists of a short-answer paper based chiefly on concepts, and a paper of longer essays.

The subject choice booklet

Once the syllabus had been accepted, it was necessary to inform our students of the new possibilities in RE. This was mainly done by the production of a subject choice booklet prepared in time for the beginning of the new course. In it we included some reference to the general approach to RE within the department, we gave an outline of the course content and methods of assessment, and we referred to teaching methods and resources. We also offered some information about RE and its relevance as a qualification for future careers; in our experience many employers are, amongst other things, interested in the ability to empathise that is developed in RE. Subsequently we included short passages written by students who had completed the course, describing some of their work in the subject.

The booklet was carefully produced and was well received by pupils and by their parents. Many parents said that whether or not their sons or daughters eventually chose to study RE they welcomed the fact that they were being fully informed about what was involved. Many parents of course have their own memories of RI or Scripture lessons and these are not always happy ones. Several have told us that they were against the choice of RE until they read the booklet and saw how different the subject was from 'what we did when we were at school'.

One of the interesting consequences of the kind of world religions course we offer is the remarkable amount of parental involvement. We are often told by parents how they have been following the course with their children through reading their work and discussing it with them. Some have even asked us to consider running an evening course for interested adults.

The response

As a result of all this effort, we were very encouraged when the number opting for RE in 1978 more than doubled. A year later we felt quite stunned when the number doubled again. There was a further small increase the next year but we suspect that we may have reached a plateau now. In both the fourth and fifth years we have four groups of about thirty students and this makes something like a third of the total number of students on roll. As far as numbers opting for the course are concerned RE is as healthy as any other humanities subject.

We are also seeing increased interest at sixth form level. Our new A level group is likely to comprise over a dozen students. In addition we are able to offer a one year O/A course in world religions which is getting a similar response.

Putting flesh on the bare bones

As with any course, what really counts is the way it is worked out in the classroom. In practice we decide which areas of the syllabus to study as a result of a democratic vote. The diagram shows the various options available.

compulsory		at least one of this pair must be selected		
the language terminology and concepts of religion	Group A	Judaism	Christianity	Islam
	Group B	primal religions	Hinduism	Buddhism

All students vote in accordance with the rules of the syllabus, which were devised for the reasons stated earlier (see page 20). In each of the three years so far the result has always been in favour of Christianity and primal religions. Twice the vote for the third choice went to Hinduism and once to Buddhism. This voting at the outset of the course underlines our expectation of the students' full participation in the course.

Many of the lessons now resemble those taught in the lower school, but the materials are more complex and the approach takes account of the greater maturity of the pupils and their more developed intellectual capacity. As I have said, the groups are mixed-ability and we have never found this too much of a problem. Each group remains with the same teacher throughout the two years. Teachers and students alike can now see the continuity between work in the first two years and the CSE/O level course, and we are often able to draw upon the knowledge and experience gained by pupils in the second and third years.

Here is an example, drawn from the teaching of a former colleague, Shirley Evans. She was teaching about Pentecost and realised that the class was finding considerable difficulty in understanding what Christians mean by the Holy Spirit. Suddenly one of her students asked, 'Is it anything like what the Polynesians call Mana?' (a topic studied in the third year). There was a pause while they all thought about this surprising juxtaposition of ideas. 'I mean, do Christians believe that through the Holy Spirit God's spiritual power is made available to them?' It was an observation which everyone found illuminating and helpful. Of course there is always the danger that *any* teaching can become dry and boring, but examples like this should indicate that this need not be the case.

We try to make the lessons as practical and as visual as possible. Over the years we have built up a very good selection of visual aids. These are all carefully indexed and filed in a simple but effective retrieval system. We have two teaching rooms used mainly for RE. Both have blackout facilities and are equipped with slide and overhead projectors and tape recorders. We also have access to a portable video-replay machine. Having a proper base for the subject means that we can display work done by pupils and set up audio-visual equipment with the minimum of fuss.

It is possible to give an idea of the approach we use by describing what happens in the primal religions section of the course. We may begin by studying the beliefs and practices of early man. Building up confidence by referring to what they already know, we introduce students to new materials. This could be a set of slides on 'The Dawn of Religion', and as the students watch and take notes we talk about the importance of the shaman and his role in connection with hunting, fertility magic and rites of passage. These features are constantly referred to as we proceed to study the Eskimos, the Aborigines and the beliefs of Polynesia. Here we usually use film and video material to help the students enter into an imaginative encounter with the culture of the people concerned. We also try to arrange at least one visit to the Museum of Mankind or the Horniman Museum. After one of these visits we usually ask the students to produce a project of up to 4,000 words, which forms the basis of their first assessment.

The use of visits

It was always intended that visits and visitors would form a key part of the course. At the suggestion of the students themselves, this has now grown to include visits abroad. During our first term on the new course one of the pupils suggested that we ought to go to see some cave paintings for ourselves. Less than a year later we visited the cave of Pech-Merle in the Dordogne Valley. Other visits have included a trip to Italy (which included an open-air papal audience), study visits to Guildford, St Paul's and Westminster Cathedrals and a very successful visit to the thriving and lively Millmead Centre (Baptist) in Guildford.

Such trips often produce worthwhile experiences which cannot be anticipated. For example, in Assisi we were shown round the basilica by a genial Franciscan who clearly impressed many of our students with his faith and good humour. On the coach afterwards there was a deep discussion about the monastic calling and the importance of sincerity in religion which could not have happened in the same way in the classroom. This too I would suggest is the best way for students to encounter commitment: by meeting committed people in a spirit of inquiry.

We have undertaken a project on worship in the community with students and staff from the University of Warwick. Ten students and two lecturers visited the school for two days to observe and to take part in our O level teaching programme. The Warwick students then planned a study weekend in Coventry for sixteen of our O level students and the four RE staff from the school. The first day included introductions to some of the living religions to be found in Coventry, discussions and visits by everyone to Coventry Cathedral and to the Hindu festival of Navratri. On the second day separate groups visited a Sikh temple, a West Indian Pentecostal church and a Greek Orthodox church. In all cases worship was taking place during our visits and the discussions which followed the visits (whether in the seminar room or on the bus or at a party!) showed the insights to be gained by pupils from a well-planned study visit. The Warwick University students were able to practise different teaching techniques, to try out different resources (slides, tape and artefacts) and they gained the invaluable experience of planning visits as part of a school's RE programme. This particular account illustrates how pupils from a more or less mono religious area can benefit from visiting a city rich in a variety of religious traditions. It also illustrates the sort of symbiosis that can take place when a school develops a link with an establishment where RE teachers are trained.

Evaluation

I hope that by now I have made it clear that our approach to religious education through the study of world religions is not rigid and fixed; it is constantly changing and developing. We feel it necessary to ask how far we are achieving our aims and whether our teaching methods are consistent with those aims. For instance, we are currently experimenting in order to use visual aids more effectively so that they stimulate discussion and reflection that leads to greater understanding, rather than simply conveying factual information.

We have found that having external moderators for our examinations has been most helpful in reviewing and evaluating our work. Their main responsibility is to see that our academic standards are comparable with those of externally set and marked O level and CSE examinations. There is nothing like conversation with an interested but neutral outsider to sharpen up one's thinking. It is difficult to assess religious sensitivity and understanding but somehow there are unmistakable signs which emerge over a period of time even in written work. The use of correct terminology and the careful description of ideas and beliefs provide some measure of the student's capacity to empathise.

In addition to projects, we use essays and short-answer tests as assessment tasks. The setting and marking of these is challenging and demanding but we probably end up gauging our students' understanding of religion more accurately than we did in the days of setting questions about the history of Israel or the literary criticism of the New Testament. Furthermore, students have remarked upon the amount of 'pastoral care' and personal interest shown by the RE staff. This is partly the result of our open approach because by definition it includes listening as well as telling.

Working together

The RE department, which now includes four specialists, has fortunately enjoyed considerable stability during the past few years and this has been very helpful for both curriculum development and our own development as RE teachers. We have arrived at a general working agreement about our aims, partly as a result of regular staff meetings. It is vital not to underestimate these as a force in promoting group cohesion. Of course we do not always agree, but there is no doubt that we have learnt a lot from one another in terms of subject expertise. We are able to draw upon the particular skills and strengths of the team. This includes sharing the burden of lesson preparation, which is particularly important when even the course content may be unfamiliar to those teaching it. Sharing ideas and knowledge is of great value in maintaining the morale and effectiveness of teachers. All heads of department would do well to remember the importance of securing the participation of their colleagues through real involvement in all aspects of the work. It is not enough to hand out a syllabus and tell them to get on with it.

Some problems present and future

One difficulty we are trying to overcome at the moment concerns the curriculum. At the time of writing we are still learning to see Christianity as a world religion. Of all the areas of study we have found the resources for teaching about Christianity to be the least satisfactory. Many books, for instance, are visually very uninteresting and they often deal with topics which are more suitable for Church Sunday schools than for State schools. The situation is gradually changing as new materials become available but much remains to be done. A related problem is that for Christian RE teachers, which I suppose most of us are, it is difficult to see the wood for the trees. We need to be able to stand back and present Christian beliefs and practices as we do those of other religions.

A problem we anticipate for the future concerns staffing, and it is common to all secondary schools. As we experience the effects of falling rolls and consequent cuts, there is obviously the danger that RE could gradually lose its place in the curriculum. This makes it all the more important that RE departments should be adequately staffed with professionally trained specialists.

Despite such problems I feel more optimistic about the future of religious education, after twenty years of teaching, than at any time since I began. There seems to be a greater consensus, at least among teachers, about the aims of the subject. We also have more *good* teachers, though never enough. Because of their influence we see the development of better syllabuses which in turn demand better teaching resources.

A few years ago I met an ex-pupil who came up to me, shook hands and said, 'Hello, Sir. I used to enjoy your lessons. Can't say I've finally worked out my beliefs yet but you made me think . . . and I haven't stopped thinking.' I have no idea how often this is the response to our approach to the teaching of religious education. I am not sure that we can expect more but I am convinced that we should not aim for less.

See page 47 for further reading.

3

Religious Education in a Multi-ethnic Comprehensive School

Marilyn Thomas

This chapter recounts the evolution of RE in a multi-ethnic comprehensive school of about 1,300 girls. In particular it charts the development of RE in the first three years from a syllabus consisting of biblical texts and church history to a multi-faith syllabus taught through themes and topics. The impression should not be given, however, that the new syllabus is a permanent fixture. RE is a living subject; it deals with a body of knowledge and experience which is continually expanding. As there is always something new to learn, RE needs an atmosphere in which it is possible to develop, adapt or change ideas. The importance of sharing underlies our syllabus and relationships inside and outside the classroom. The making of the new syllabus was a shared experience and the dialogue still goes on.

The syllabus for the whole school has gone through many changes during the last ten years. The first important changes were made within the examination syllabuses in the senior school, A level, O level and CSE. Now the circle has fully turned and we are again looking at new books and courses for examination classes. We are adding the London University Alternative O level syllabus for sixth-form groups and offering the full range of options from the A level syllabus. All of this is an exciting and challenging prospect.

Preparing for change

The following paragraphs are meant to give an idea of the planning that went into the new syllabus for years 1–3. We are fortunate in having three specialist RE teachers plus help from two others, so we were able to stimulate and encourage one another. RE is also reasonably well represented on the timetable. All girls in the first three years have two RE lessons and a homework assignment a week, and there was no danger of losing any of this by making changes.

The old syllabus had consisted of Old Testament studies in the first year, the life of Jesus based on the Gospels in the second year, and a history of the Church in the third year, beginning with the *Acts of the*

Apostles and ending with a limited excursion into world religions. We had not become bored with this syllabus, and as all of us then had Bible-based theology degrees, we felt safe with it! Our reasons for change were educational.

Firstly, it seemed absurd not to take account of the multi-ethnic composition of the school and the local population. The presence of members of various world faiths in the school community was an important factor in inducing us to redesign the syllabus. Secondly, we felt that since religion is a universal phenomenon, reflecting a search for truth, we should not impose strict limits on our exploration. Thirdly, we held the view that RE should help our pupils to understand the world in which they live. Without some knowledge of religion, how are pupils to understand history, politics, social pressures, art . . .? Fourthly, we agreed that RE should aim to give an understanding of the relationships between people who are part of different cultures and societies. Finally, we all felt that RE should relate to the experience of our pupils. Our summary aims were stated as follows: to create a religious awareness; to relate to the experience of the pupils; to give pupils a body of knowledge.

We were careful to consider possible criticisms of our ideas, and indeed discussed our own reservations. For example, some people were worried that there might not be enough space in a new syllabus for the study of Christianity. Therefore we made sure that Christianity was properly represented, and we subsequently found that in the new course we covered much of what was included in the old syllabus. We also feel that our approach in the new syllabus helps to give pupils a better understanding of Christianity. For instance, away from the biblical, historical approach it is easier for pupils to perceive Christianity as a living religion.

More difficult to cope with were our own anxieties about designing and teaching a new and demanding course. We all felt short of information as each of us was better qualified on paper in New Testament Greek than in Hinduism or Islam. Happily, we have learned much these last few years from excellent courses (such as those put on by the School of Oriental and African Studies at London University and by the Shap Working Party), from the increasing number of good books on world religions and from our own discussions.

Lack of resources (coupled with lack of money) seemed to be another major problem. Initially we overcame this by re-assessing the textbooks we already had in stock. Abandoning them as textbooks, we were now free to use a chapter or perhaps just a page or diagram. We put together a card index to help new teachers find their way through the books quickly. On the whole, children are not given books to keep for the term, but they see and use many more books than they did before. Over the last five years we have been able to buy books with our new syllabus in mind, but they are still used selectively and not worked through. One of the best results is that children are beginning to evaluate books for themselves: 'I don't like this book, Miss, it's preachy.' 'Why does this man assume that we are all Christians?' 'There's a mistake in this book, Miss.' They are quick to spot the hypocrisy of the author who begins with questions but ends assuming we have all reached his answers. Some ask for particular titles for the library, where the RE section has expanded and is well used, or for more copies for class use.

One difficulty is transportation. Although we have two RE rooms we still have to carry perhaps two or three sets of books to a lesson. Another is book loss; it is difficult to keep complete sets of books although we try to catalogue them and put the most formidable children in charge.

Knowing that teachers would feel pressed for time, we organised a large filing cabinet, placing all new work sheets, postcards and small pictures in the relevant drop file. This simple system has been a great help in promoting the sharing of ideas and methods. We now have a good collection of film strips, slides, postcards and posters. This was built up gradually using school requisition money and adding items ourselves. We hope to add more artefacts – a picture in a book is no substitute for handling the real thing. We have, for example, many objects associated with Jewish worship including a Mezuzah, prayer shawl and skull cap. The Hinduism box contains a beautiful sari (given to us by a Hindu mother), and the make-up and jewellery to go with it. The shopkeeper and his usual customers were puzzled to find an English lady buying such items, but they were delighted to discover that they were to be used in a classroom.

The syllabus

In order to achieve our aims we decided to use themes or topics. Many history teachers are now moving away from a chronological approach and developing 'patch history'. In the same way we decided to concentrate on the ideas involved, using examples to develop our theme. We have found that children are not confused or puzzled if we cut across the centuries. Topic work also gives us freedom, and avoids the arrogance of thinking 'We have done Hinduism this term'. It also helps reinforce ideas, and avoids false comparisons. Theologically it is good, for example, to be able to see Judaism as a living religion and not as an introduction to Christianity.

Our first-year syllabus contains five main topics: Early Ideas of Gods; Founders of Religions; In Search of Freedom; Rules for Living and People of Courage.

We all begin with the topic *Early Ideas of Gods* and then teachers are free to develop their own work scheme for the year. The introduction provides us with a link with history and a basis for the first three years. We begin with 'What is religion?'. Many pupils are surprised to find RE on their timetables, having received little teaching in their junior schools. Some have had an integrated day and although they have studied some religious topics, perhaps the story of Muhammad or parables told by Jesus, they would not be able to label them as religious. This leads on to naming the main religions in the world today, recognising their symbols, and sharing information. The class begins to come together, as children discover the relevance of religious practices in their homes and television programmes they see. It surprises me how much eleven-year-old children notice and remember from quite complicated programmes or chance encounters whilst out shopping. At this stage children are very open – 'My Dad says . . .' 'My Gran . . .' 'This lady down the road, Miss, well . . .'. We go on to 'How did all this start? How did religion begin?' We try very hard to avoid giving the impression that we have progressed from the primitive to some superior position. New words are learnt, like animism, polytheism, monotheism. The less able find these fun as they are learning new terms with everyone else.

In this section we include the story of Abraham with an emphasis on search within religion. It allows us to use the worship at Ur and Haran as an example of polytheism. The Fertile Crescent and Egypt are covered in history but through the gods of Egypt and Canaan we are able to introduce the idea of fertility worship. This topic is always met with enthusiasm; some go further and are able to link the search for prosperity with the aims of our own materialistic society. We end the topic with ideas on the Hebrew God, including the names for God in the Old Testament.

Founders of Religions allows us to look at the major religions represented in Britain today. We now use Hinduism as a bridge between Early Ideas of Gods and Founders of Religions. We have written our own booklet as a simple introduction showing how Hinduism began. There are many illustrations so that children of all abilities can learn something. Judaism allows us to bring together the stories of Abraham and Moses. Films and children's books have introduced some of this information already.

The story of Siddhartha Gautama becoming the Buddha is always greatly enjoyed. We give a brief outline of the life of Jesus, often concentrating on the events of Easter. Finally we trace the life of Muhammad up to the *Hijra* and gather together some information on Guru Nanak. Much of this work is done through work booklets in which opportunity is always given to the pupil to add information. Many pupils bring in objects to show the class: icons, pictures of scenes from the Bible, paintings of Guru Nanak. Interesting discussion arises over why Muslims will not represent Muhammad in any way; Muslim students often criticise pictorial material in textbooks.

It is fascinating to pick out titles given to these founders – Prophet, Buddha, Christ, Al Amin, Guru – and comment on their significance.

Students do, of course, have their own loyalties, but it is very rare for any unpleasant conflict to emerge during the study of this section. Perhaps this is because relationships in the class and school generally are fairly happy. Discussions over very particular points in the leaders' teaching are more likely in the senior part of the school where the students, having had basic information earlier and being more mature, translate conflict into academic argument.

There is a genuine interest in the course and students do not take advantage of information to insult or criticise others. At first-year level there is a great quest for knowledge. There is little desire to convert anyone. What students do want is for each religion to be fairly represented. So, for example, a group of Muslim girls will wait eagerly for us to come to the study of the life of Muhammad. With their enthusiasm and ability to produce extra information they will make their loyalty to Islam clear. They will have already studied the life of Jesus quite happily with the class, however, and will go on to show interest in the work of Guru Nanak.

As teachers we concentrate on the person and the story, and try with the class to find out why religious leaders had such an impact. We avoid making particular comparisons or judgements.

In Search of Freedom begins with a general introduction on the meaning of freedom. 'Freedom from slavery' is illustrated by the story of Moses and the Exodus. 'Freedom from disease', beginning with what it feels like to be ill, looks at some of Jesus' healing miracles. Also included are stories of people who worked for freedom against disease, poverty, ignorance. These stories are always popular and enable us to use modern examples too. The children are more involved with the concept than chronology and do not seem to be confused by studying Moses, Jesus, Martin Luther King and Mother Teresa, in the same half-term.

Freedom and *Rules for Living* go together. Are rules necessary? Can we really be free without them? In the general introduction students make their own rules for home, school, friends, the country. They sometimes make up adventure stories in which the characters invent rules in order to survive. The subject is always treated seriously and the rules are very strict. Looking at the main religions we include: Hinduism – religious duties for a devout Hindu; Judaism – the Law, concentrating on the Ten Commandments; Buddhism – Buddhist commandments for lay people and monks; Christianity – the Golden Rule, two or three Beatitudes, the use of parables, with the Good Samaritan as an example; Islam – the Five Pillars of Faith; Sikhism – the Five Ks.

The children notice for themselves that, for example, the kind of codes given for Hinduism and Judaism are very different. They are also able to make connections and spot similarities.

The final section, *People of Courage*, often left to the end of the year, is sometimes dealt with very briefly. Some people will have been considered under different headings and need only be mentioned again. We think it important to include women and to show their contribution to religious thought and society. This topic lends itself to project work, and by the end of the first year all girls should have developed skill in using the library, class libraries, and available textbooks.

We try to use many different ways of working so that pupils are used to project work, individual work sheets or longer work booklets, group work and class discussion. All girls, by the end of the year, will have built up a loose-leaf work file, divided into the topics covered. The less able need help in keeping their files in order but most are able to number pages and index them. Files are collected in several times during the year and are given a grade and comment at the end of the summer term.

The second-year syllabus covers: Signs and Symbols; Religious Buildings; Religious Leaders; Gifts to Gods – Worship; and Festivals. These can be attempted in any order.

Signs and Symbols is fun at this stage and involves much practical work. We hope it will also be an introduction to the use of symbolism and imagery in literature studied in the third year. We begin generally with signs we see and use in everyday life. We then look at the major religions in turn.

For Hinduism we look at *Om*, the markings used for devotees of Shiva and Vishnu, and the use of Yantras. Judaism provides a very full study: the Star of David, the Menorah, Ark, use of Phylacteries and Mezuzah. Christianity too provides many signs which girls are often able to see for themselves during their visits out of school. We include signs of the early Church like the fish; signs of the Gospel writers; signs used in Christian teaching. There are a great many, and often pupils add their own from what they have noticed in a church (like the use of liturgical colours), or found in a reference book. Although Islam prohibits images, Islamic art is very beautiful. Indeed the whole topic is visually stimulating, and would be hard to cover without posters, postcards, slides and art books. Most children are good at drawing, but they are given some duplicated material such as outline drawings and diagrams so that we can cover as much ground as possible.

We look at *Religious Buildings* as places of worship, not just as architectural curiosities. To begin with, there are general questions – What made people build? Why was so much effort put into making buildings beautiful? The building for worship is then named for each of the main religions, avoiding statements like 'A Muslim church is called a mosque'! We cover some historical ground within Judaism, including details of Solomon's Temple and Herod's Temple, as well as worship in the synagogue today.

This is the obvious stage in the year to arrange visits. A popular trip is an exploration of Westminster Cathedral and Westminster Abbey. As we are a London school we have also been able to take some classes to the Regent's Park Mosque where our guides have always been most generous with their time in providing information. The school timetable does not allow for endless visits, so we do not try to visit all the buildings studied but pick a few which will give a good impression of size and beauty. Much that is valuable can also be learnt in the classroom from slides and films. By the end of the year girls should be able to label outline plans correctly, putting in important objects, for example the *qibla* wall, *minbar* and *mihrab* in the mosque. They are also encouraged to develop one part of the work into a project.

Information and invitations come from the students, often at festival time or to a special event. Amongst other things I attended a Hindu festival celebration in Acton Town Hall and a monthly meeting held in the home of a Hindu student.

Religious Leaders follows naturally from the need to name the leaders of worship. We try to give them the right titles. We look at any special clothes worn, and the function of leaders in the organisation of worship and day-to-day living. We begin in a general way, looking at qualities of leadership and personality. There are different expectations and different functions, so all leaders cannot be grouped together and called priests. Within the topic we would normally cover: Hinduism - brahmin and sadhu; Judaism - in historical context, priest, prophet, pharisees and sadducees, before looking at the work of a rabbi today; Buddhism - the monk, and his community; Christianity - the organisation within the major churches, and the role of priest, minister, monk and nun; Islam - imam and muezzin. Many related questions arise on celibacy and the role of women within organised worship and in leadership.

Gifts to Gods - Worship is a very wide topic, and at first glance its adequate treatment seems impossible. From observing what people do we try both to gather information and deepen understanding. We look, for example, at prayer and the techniques people use to aid concentration and to show their devotion. One class studied prayer in Islam; they had seen slides of prayer positions, pictures of mosques and had heard a recording of the call to prayer. A Muslim girl in the class was asked by a friend, 'Show us'. She hesitated, and then said 'No, I can't *show* you but I *can* pray'. She organised herself, spread a coat on a table and then, concentrating very hard, began her devotions. The atmosphere at the end was electric.

Within this section too comes discussions on holy days and the use of music in worship.

The witness to one's faith through the keeping of regulations for food and clothing always stimulates much interest. Knowledge of such rules lessens prejudice and awakens a new awareness of the importance of religion in ordinary living. Many students fast during the year and their friends need to know why; or why certain foods are forbidden; why they are not allowed to keep up with the fashion if it means cutting hair or wearing revealing clothes. Outside the classroom the information is needed by the school kitchen too, and by anyone concerned with the collection of dinner money. At a recent conference at which Hindus, Muslims, and Sikhs were represented the main meal served was steak and kidney pie! I hope by the end of the second year our students will be better informed and more imaginative.

The last topic, *Festivals*, is wide but exciting. We try to cover major festivals, for example: Hinduism - Holi and Divali; Judaism - Passover,

Pentecost, Channukah, sometimes Purim; Christianity – Christmas, Easter, Whitsun; Islam – Eid ul Fitr and Eid ul Adha. The idea of celebration is most important and we try to involve the students by using pictures, music and food. This remains, however, a gesture on our part, a symbol of the real festival rather than a re-enactment. Everyone can try to find out about a festival and its significance but this will never be the same as the whole-hearted celebration of devout people. This year, for example, for Passover we collected items for the Passover plate. When I held up *charoseth* paste and asked 'What does this remind you of?' the quick reply was 'Cement'! I was delighted. But I have never felt it possible to go through the *Haggadah* as if it were actually Passover: it somehow seems arrogant and insulting. Items of food are easy to produce and the resulting excitement far outweighs the expense of ingredients and the time and effort spent in preparation. Many students will contribute items too, and all will eat whatever is offered! Some classes have made their own collection of festival recipes.

The third-year course is where we have made most additions to our original topics. As we aim for continuity, class and teacher have usually been together since the first year so particular needs and preferences have become obvious. The teacher chooses topics from a wider range, knowing that not all the suggestions can be covered. We may begin with Sacred Writings; Proverb, Fable, Parable; The Use of Myth; Folk Stories. We include project work on *Religion in Britain*, sometimes adding *Life in First-Century Palestine* to provide a background for those going on to further study in the fourth year. We have added a very popular topic – *Birth, Marriage and Death*. We are planning a new topic on *The Place of Women in Religion*.

When we began *Sacred Writings* we included details of early writing and writing materials. We have now dropped most of this subject matter, as students have some knowledge from history lessons and we want to add more that is relevant to *religious* education. Instead we concentrate on naming the sacred texts of the major religions and discussing the ways in which scriptures are used and treated with respect. For class use we find it easier to look at selected writings, using a book like *A Book of World Religions* by Geoffrey Parrinder. Where possible we have translations for the use of teachers and interested individuals. Many Muslim girls will not handle a copy of the Qur'an without proper preparation and we soon learnt not to ask girls to bring in texts from home.

The study of symbol in the second year is used fully in the literary study of *Proverb, Fable, Parable* and *Myth*. The echo through the study is 'Is it true?' We try to look beyond the stories to the writers' intention and skill. Often students are good at writing their own fables and parables and then trying them out on one another.

We are often criticised for leaving this kind of study until the third year; many teachers claim that this topic is more suitably covered in the first year. I still feel, however, that the intellectual operation involved in going beyond the story and manipulating ideas requires maturity. The story can be told when the child is young, but its regular repetition can reinforce misunderstandings as well as make it lose its freshness.

From fable and parable it is easy to move on to myth, and to recognise how difficult it is to express deep feelings and emotions in language. We have used very early myths from Egypt and Greece, and the early chapters of Genesis. We are gradually adding creation stories from the major religions as we find them.

Initially *Folk Stories* was based on the Bible and was included to ensure that students would recognise biblical references in literature. We found that classes greatly enjoyed stories like the Death of Sisera – the bloodier the better! Experience in telling and listening comes with the use of tape recorders and dramatised readings. Gradually we have added traditional stories from other religions too.

By the third year, pupils' knowledge of world religions has grown, so information can be more detailed. In project work students are encouraged to write their own ideas and comments rather than copy from a book or be content with pretty pictures. Within a topic like *Religion in Britain Today* the class will often be working as individuals, covering the religion of their choice. Some may well be writing about the ceremonies of the Jewish home whilst others want more information on Buddhist monasteries. Such research puts a heavy strain on the teacher, whose personal book shelves are often laid bare in the effort to find suitable material; but the time when projects are reviewed is exciting and rewarding.

Classes often look at the growth of the Church, making a general historical survey before considering the different buildings and ceremonies that we find today.

At this stage students are able either to learn more about their own background or to explore some new interest. We are fortunate in being able to use recorded television programmes so that everybody can be reminded of the basic facts in an enjoyable way. We have found such programmes particularly helpful with *Birth, Marriage, Death*. This topic questions the whole purpose of life, and the exploration of religious beliefs concerning these 'crisis points' stimulates valuable discussion. The first part of the topic has obvious attractions: discussion about death sounds more off-putting. Preparation has to be done with care; it is only sensible to make enquiries about the class from pastoral heads to find out if anyone has recently suffered death in the family. The pupils' initial reluctance takes us right into why people are afraid to talk about death, use so many euphemisms, or keep away from those who grieve. As well as studying customs and beliefs, we look at the ways in which suffering and death are portrayed in the media, especially in films and plays shown on television. In the end the response is often far greater than for the seemingly more attractive topic of marriage.

We have been accused of superficiality. All we can do is to lay a foundation in these three years, strong enough to be built on later. We can offer information and teach skills. We hope that at the end of our three year course students will know where to go for more information. They should have learnt how to question, how to argue coherently and logically, and to be discriminating.

Many choose to continue with their study of religious education for public examinations. They have a chance to study in more detail. We hope, however, that those whose subject choices take them away from RE will appreciate the value of their course in the first three years.

In the classroom we hope to create an atmosphere in which students can develop without fear of ridicule or embarrassment. The importance of sharing is fundamental. The teacher is not the authority, but also needs to grow and develop as ideas are shared. Students are not shocked by a straight 'I don't know', or 'I think I know how, or where, I can find out.' As a result of this approach we hope that students will see their religious education as a life-long process, and that they can go on learning and developing their ideas. If later they forget many of the facts we offer them, I hope that they will be able, nevertheless, to understand those whose view of life is a religious one.

See page 47 for further reading.

4
Multi-faith Teaching in Creative Classrooms

Peter Woodward

Religious education today is more concerned with asking the right questions than with providing the correct answers. The Jewish *hasid* who replies to a question with a question, and the Zen Buddhist abbot who offers a seemingly pointless riddle for his novices to ponder are creative models for the RE teacher. Nearer to home the widely held view that the role of RE is concerned with education and not with nurture has encouraged many teachers to develop in their pupils a questioning attitude, so that they – the pupils – may discover or develop their own individual viewpoints; or it has led them to present a variety of answers from a range of faiths or stances so that *on those issues where pupils need to make a choice* they may come to an informed and balanced decision between a reasonable number of different alternatives. Either way the teacher avoids the situation where he has the final solution, neatly packaged, ready to pass on to the pupils as the 'revealed' answer.

So in our search for what is creative in RE, questions are everything; questions succeed in our quest where statements fail – as may be seen from the many stories of the Hodja, the Sufi mystic who is always extricating himself from droll situations by standing the opposition on its head. The pan which the Hodja borrowed from his neighbour is an example. After he had finished using it, the Hodja (Nasrudin) took it back to the neighbour with a small additional pan tucked inside it. When the neighbour expressed his surprise, the Hodja explained that when he borrowed the pan, it was pregnant, and had now brought a child into the world. The man smiled and accepted the gift. A few days later the Hodja again borrowed the pan, but this time he failed to return it. When his neighbour angrily demanded its return, the Hodja explained that it had died. 'Don't make jokes with me,' replied the man. 'How can a pan die?' 'Well, if you can believe that it brought a child into the world,' said the Hodja, 'why can't you believe that it died?'[1] The following five questions are more prosaic, but in each response there is a supply of material from which the reader will find much to fashion his own answers.

The questions I wish to raise are practical questions about multi-faith approaches to RE.

1 *What* is good practice in multi-faith RE (a) in terms of content, and (b) in respect of method?
2 *Why* should the modern RE teacher operate on a multi-faith basis?
3 *How* does one (a) start, (b) continue, and (c) finish teaching in the field of world religions?
4 *Where* is a multi-faith approach possible?
5 *When* (at what ages) is it appropriate?

It will become clear, as we look at these five questions, that (in my opinion) some of the best teaching of religious education today is based on a multi-faith approach in a multi-cultural situation. For a variety of reasons, a restricted diet of pluralism, which matches and responds to the composition of the classroom, tends to produce both liveliness and balance. Why is this? Is it the result of youthful enthusiasm, or of novelty, of the provision of adequate books and resources of an enquiring nature, or is there some element inherent in the approach that produces such a result? Is it the match between audience and material, or is that not enough in itself? Can anyone teach in this fashion? What are the implications for initial (or for in-service) training of teachers?

1 What is good practice in multi-faith RE?

In terms of content good practice will include a study in depth of a single faith. There will also be a study of at least one other faith in *sufficient* depth to provide a valid yardstick for evaluating the first faith – though it will also be a legitimate study in its own right. In addition there may be the study of a number of themes across a number of faiths, possibly in preparation for examination work.[2] But at no time will there be a full study of such a wide range of faiths that the end product becomes superficial.

In terms of method good practice involves three items: sound, sympathetic and accurate description; an evocative approach that elicits insights; and a reflective element that encourages the pupils to ponder on deeper issues at as serious a level as they can manage. Each of these elements is essential if the RE is to be fully effective.

A Birmingham primary school recently concentrated on Divali as a festival of light for the whole school. Every class, infant and junior, made some contribution, the staff entered into the spirit of the festival, even turning up in saris for the week of the celebrations, and the tailor's dummy they hired for the occasion and decked out in Indian costume became the centrepiece and focus for much of their work. Their religious education gained a new dimension, first in amassing a store of factual information, secondly in developing insights into the nature of festival and celebration in another tradition, but also, thirdly, in a reflective pondering by staff and older pupils alike of the features that are common to more than one tradition. And the more frequently they have 'celebrated' festivals since then, the more natural it becomes for them to develop a further range of insights and to pursue them in ever greater depth.

Is this good practice? Who says so? Who is to judge? What are the criteria? Is it good community education without being good religious education? Or are the two interchangeable and inseparable at the primary level? Consider by contrast a secondary school in an area outside the city centre where black and coloured faces are present but are still very much in the minority.

This school lacks the opportunity for extensive first hand contacts in the local community, but takes its RE most seriously and employs a multi-faith scheme of work at all ages. The head of RE developed a simple but effective method of compensating for the comparative lack of local resources. A group of fourth and fifth year pupils was preparing for multi-faith options at O level and CSE.[3] Expeditions were, of course, made to a local mosque, synagogue, church and temple, but in addition a week's visit was arranged to Tunisia on a cheap-rate, out-of-season excursion. The pupils had a marvellous time and came back laden with resources. One enterprising lad, who had mastered the art of barter, visited Woolworth's before the visit and traded cheap British goods for a range of Tunisian artefacts during his busy week abroad! The particular lesson the group learnt about Islam was that *some* Muslims prohibit *some* non-Muslims from entering their mosques. The youngsters awarded these sticklers for protocol a bonus mark for being members of a faith that cared enough about the sanctity of its sacred buildings to make access difficult for the non-committed.

The frequency of such visits for pupils, and with it the practice of visits abroad for teachers to learn about Judaism, Islam or Hinduism at first hand, has grown rapidly recently. As a result many teachers have had their horizons pushed back and others have found that their approach to teaching has been greatly invigorated.[4]

Nearer home, visits to local places of worship are growing more and more frequent. Sadly, schools derive less value than they might from these visits, either through inadequate preparation (preliminary visit, clear objectives, adequate briefing) or because the communities do not provide the type of educational material the pupils require. Christian clergy frequently seem so anxious to play down the 'religious' angle that they limit their contribution to a social studies approach, and students who are looking for a statement of what is distinctive about Christian marriage or a theology of infant baptism are fed instead with details of wedding ceremonial and who holds the baby at a christening! Muslims and Sikhs often seem better able to emphasise the central place of worship in their faiths, though different problems may then emerge, such as their inability to answer specific questions posed by pupils, and the tendency to provide a much used 'package' of answers about basic aspects that are already familiar. A question and short answer approach can often provide the answer here.

The growth of examination syllabuses such as those referred to above, where sacred buildings and places of pilgrimage, worship, festivals, sacred writings, and rites of passage such as birth, marriage, death, and ceremonies of initiation are studied across three faiths, has encouraged a particularly creative approach,and not only in multi-cultural areas. It is interesting, however, to discover from an exploration of the special studies included in the assessment how approaches vary from area to area and from teacher to teacher. Schools where there are many children of Asian origin find it simple to produce glossy, colourful studies, rich in decoration and authentic in detail – though often light in evaluation – in a way which is 'foreign' to a more staid, traditional Christian (or post-Christian) community. Pupils whose families have sprung from the West Indies often explore the vital aspects of their beliefs about funeral rites or believer's baptism with panache and vigour (though with limited attention to perspective). Those whose background is restricted to Britain either try to emulate the above, with a limited degree of success, or produce clinical essays with minimal illustration. A small proportion only is left, who use their imagination to produce magnificent examples of flair and insight – and ones that genuinely constitute religious studies. Two instances of this last class come to mind. A fourth-year girl wrote innumerable letters to a Tunisian pen-pal, and then cut up and annotated his replies about what life for him as a Muslim was like. Her description proved both evocative and reflective. Another student wrote a mini-novel about a family's reactions to her heroine's visits to a variety of places of worship to find out how celebrations of birth, marriage and death took place there. The research was incredibly thorough and the statistical results were conveyed through the mouths of the other members of the family, whose recognisable viewpoints were consistently expressed and discussed at all stages. Is this good practice in RE? If so, is it because content and method have fused to an appropriate alloy where they support each other and become virtually inseparable? And is this the direction in which we should all be aiming?

Finally, a word about one of the more evocative sources of information for examination syllabuses (or for use with younger secondary pupils). For some years ATV has produced a series of ten programmes for schools called 'Believe it or not'.[5] These attempt to portray a faith from the inside, in terms of what it means to be a Muslim, Jew, Hindu, Christian or Sikh, rather than in a purely descriptive or external manner. The thematic programmes focus on their material in such a way as to raise questions about worship and celebrations, in each case through the eyes of two or three different communities. Is this good practice? Or is the development of such material for RE akin to spoonfeeding the pupil and usurping the role of the teacher? What is good practice here? Is it the same in RE as in other subject areas? At least there are some questions to work at here, which *may* be sound technique in the context of religious education!

2 Why should the modern RE teacher operate on a multi-faith basis?

What is so special about multi-faith religious education that it should become the universal pattern? Why (and how) is it different from other approaches to RE? Does it have distinctive aims and purposes, and if so, what are they and why are they distinctive?

The simple answer is that multi-faith RE is the ideal contemporary approach for the modern teacher because (a) it relates to the world community in which we all live; (b) it avoids the risk of indoctrination; and (c) it produces an ideal blend of description, insight and reflection as described in my answer to the previous question. It is neither too close to nor too far removed from its subject matter, and so avoids the twin perils of mistaking a single narrow viewpoint for the whole truth, and of developing a cold clinical objectivity that follows from the wrong type of detachment. The 'middle path' which I am recommending here is ideal, not because it is central, nor because it avoids extremes, but because its sense of balance offers a combination of description, insight and reflection that is appropriate to the aims of the subject and the world in which we live.

What are these aims? There will never be full agreement about them, even within a single approach. But for what they are worth, my own selection of aims would include the following: (1) to rivet the attention of the pupils by the regular use of effective method and exciting content; (2) to construct an accurate and detailed descriptive cameo of 'religious' life, ritual, tradition, belief and practice in at least two faiths; (3) to provide a series of insights into the meaning of faith in two or three traditions, and so to explore what is involved in being committed to a faith or to its various non-theistic alternatives; (4) to initiate a process of reflection about the material and the insights covered above, so that the pupils may learn to reflect on their own traditions, beliefs and practice in matters religious, and also on those of other people.

The modern 'multi-faith' teacher searches for an appropriate balance within these four aims. He is sufficiently removed from any one faith because he is involved in exploring two or perhaps three with his pupils. He is concerned with practice as much as with belief, so that his descriptions of ritual in several traditions affirm his impartiality. He covers enough 'theology' to stretch the pupils according to their age or ability. At the same time he is not seen as an atheist or a non-believer, because he finds something to enthuse about in each religion he covers (if he cannot, then perhaps he should leave the subject alone), and his personal commitment is never thrust at pupils, but equally it is not hidden from them. He is also known for his habit of raising controversial points for discussion or debate.

At a time when religious education in Britain appears to be polarising into a number of extreme viewpoints (theological, psychological and phenomenological), the approach I am suggesting may be seen as standing at a crossroads from which each of these other paths diverges. And yet it is not a neutral or negative approach, but one rich in positive affirmation and joyous exploration. This is why it is recommended to the teacher, whatever his teaching situation. To describe a selection of faiths is essential, to derive insights from them is natural, to reflect within oneself on these insights is the *sine qua non* of religious education.

In addition there is the possibility that through this approach the pupil may come to discover the true nature of religious studies. This may happen gently through a series of insights that build on each other like the ladders in a children's game; or it may occur suddenly in a flash of insight when perspective strikes home - like the moment of *satori* for the Buddhist monk as his meditation on the *koan* set by his abbot reaches its climax. This is not the development of an insight into religion or religious truth that will lead to a particular faith position, but an experience of understanding the logic and the nature of the subject (i.e. religious education): 'Now I see why we've been talking about the pilgrimage so much, Miss'.

3 How does one (a) start, (b) continue, and (c) finish teaching in the field of world religions?

The other three chapters in this section of *Approaching World Religions* offer ideas appropriate to this (and to my fourth and fifth questions) in some detail, so these comments need only be brief. The headings I would suggest for an answer include: (1) the provision of effective stimulus of a practical or insight-provoking nature (see aim 1 in question 2 above, page 40); (2) the use of this stimulus to excite and develop the children's interest (as well as to grab their attention) and then to organise the material into an intelligible and creative format (see aim 2 in question 2 above, page 40); (3) the elucidation by questioning of pupils' responses to this material as it affects them. This may take the form of insights into the nature of religious experience on specific topics or on issues of a more general nature (see aim 3 in question 2 above, page 40); (4) the opening of doors and windows for the type of reflection that would ensue after, for example the insight described by Eric Pain in regard to Mana and the Holy Spirit (see Chapter 2 page 22, and also aim 4 in question 2 above, page 40). Further examples will be mentioned later.

The essential point here is that these four headings, and each of the four aims to which they relate, are inextricably interwoven. Without this close relationship the development of a lesson or of a course is incomplete. And, in my opinion, a balanced diet of such material meets the needs of the child more effectively than any of the alternative lines of approach to contemporary religious education.

The following example may illustrate this point. An exciting introduction to an RE lesson was provided in an urban school by the display of yards and yards of a narrow band of coloured material in the classroom. An older Punjabi boy neatly folded and coiled this, swiftly producing a ready-to-wear turban. The teacher developed from this picturesque beginning a lesson on the distinctive features of the Sikh faith, and left the children with a question about what was distinctive for each of them in regard to their own faiths. The insights here emerged in the older lad's responses to the teacher's skilful questioning about why certain aspects of his faith were important to him, why these were generally (but not universally) observed in his tradition, why young people were less observant than previous generations about wearing the five Ks, and what it meant to go through the ceremony of joining the Khalsa and being initiated into the brotherhood of observant Sikhs. Around these responses a class discussion developed of a fragmented and disorganised nature. The purist would have welcomed a written climax or structured the discussion in some way, but the teacher let the pupils (third year secondary, medium ability, mixed sexes) react in their own manner and at their own level so that it was effectively a learning rather than a teaching situation. To round off the lesson he produced a copy of the *Japji* and invited the older boy to read some portions of his daily prayer.

Each stage of this lesson related naturally to the preceding and succeeding steps, so that there was never a loss of interest or relevance. To have changed the order would have produced a different type of lesson because the links from one section to the next were so natural and effective. Perhaps the unity of the lesson was more apparent to the observer than to the pupils, but it ensured that attention was retained and the pupils were 'stretched' and 'fed' to their individual limits. Was this good practice?

4 Where is a multi-faith approach possible?

In what sort of areas is it preferable and for which parts of the country, if any, is it unsuitable? It is often claimed that an approach of this nature is valid in any context, multi-cultural or mono-cultural (does the latter really exist?), but that there will be differences of approach, style and emphasis. Is this too superficial an answer? What are these differences and can one generalise in this way?

The short answer is that there are differences and that they are far-reaching, but that *some form* of multi-faith learning is viable – and even essential – in every area of the country. The differences, however, between such areas are considerable and we ignore them at our peril. RE will in fact take one form in a multi-cultural city centre, and a very different form in an urban school outside the city centre; a third style again will appear in an outer suburb, a fourth in a rural town, and a fifth in a country village.

The inner-city classroom, for instance, where representatives of many faiths are to be found, will approach each topic studied in a distinctive way. The earlier example of a turban as a way into Sikhism might well be extended by a study of clothing in various traditions. The sari in Indian culture is not quite so relevant to religious studies, but it still has near-universal interest, the yarmulka (or even the wig) in Judaism, the removal of shoes in Islam, the bared head in Christianity, the shaven head in Buddhism, all could offer an intriguing introduction to a single lesson or a series on the way people cover or uncover parts of the human form for religious purposes. In this inner-city situation not only can different pupils put on or describe what is familiar to them, but examples can be brought from home, photographs and illustrations are readily available, and interviews and tape-recordings on relevant issues are easy to obtain. Class response may also be well informed, but group interaction may prove rather tricky to handle.

In the outer suburbs of a city or a large town such a lesson would be theoretically possible, but it would be harder to obtain the services of a Sikh lad capable of introducing it and the presentation would often be less effective. The five Ks, for instance, could not be presupposed but would certainly have to be explained, and questions to individuals would be less effective unless previous study had taken place. A turban as an introduction could still be used, but a ready wound one would be a useful safeguard in case the winding proved clumsy or ineffectual. The descriptive content might be similar, but the reactions, insights and discussion would be very different and the pace slower.

There is in consequence a need here for the introduction of some sort of regular stimulus, such as a collection of artefacts on permanent display in the RE room,[6] a succession of visits to buildings of the different faiths,[7] the use of appropriate television series, or the development of relevant work experience opportunities and inter-school exchange schemes. Any of these will provoke and maintain the pupils' interest, so that they may become involved with each faith as a living reality for groups of people and not as a remote and intellectual set of ideas.

Between the inner city and this outer suburb lies an area where the situation is more fluid and flexible. It is often occupied by families from the inner city who have moved out from the city centre and progressed 'up the scale' into a comparatively settled and well established district. Many of these families are of Asian or Caribbean origin, though by no means all. In some areas they will arrive in small numbers; in others a school's population may become 'tripartite' in a variety of ratios. Tensions tend to be greater here as threats to housing standards and employment prospects are rumoured, and the role of RE is often that of keeping the peace. To this end a positive appreciation of what each culture has to offer may well be the indirect focus of many lessons. But the singling out of any one child as example or model in this 'middle-ring' area will call for understanding, skill and sound timing if one is to avoid disruption and conflict. The use in lessons of material that is on the one hand trivial or comic, or on the other particularly highly treasured, needs especially to be avoided here. In its place material from an overseas tradition that can effectively link up with what is already familiar in other cultures may prove more helpful. Bare or shaven heads might be tricky to introduce in this context, but the role of the sacred building or the use of the sacred scriptures could be a safe and acceptable choice.

In the average market town where only one or two members of minority ethnic groups are normally found the situation will again be different. Visitors are harder to import, contacts with 'different' types of schools for sporting fixtures are rarer, and multi-faith contacts can be hard to find. Here I shall outline three different paths, each viable in its own way. The first is to compensate through the introduction of artefacts, television, slides, posters, visits for a week-end to cities such as Coventry or Birmingham, school trips to exotic places, correspondence with pen-friends, and so on. The second is to capitalise on what is available from textbooks and to play to the strengths of the existing situation. A traditional course in two or three faiths along the lines of belief, ethics, ritual, scriptures, etc., is no bad thing, and many schools that take the AEB multi-faith, thematic O level syllabus are in areas where their local situation makes such an approach particularly desirable in preparation for life outside their immediate community. A 'Special Study' type of approach can of course provide another positive factor here – and the project can even be made the basis for one's whole approach to RE. The third path is to concentrate on Judaism and Christianity and still 'register' as a school with a multi-faith syllabus. As long as Judaism is treated in its own right and not just as an adjunct of Christianity, and as long as it is not restricted to Old Testament studies, there can be little objection to this course. Pluralism is present, the local communities are covered, the necessary insights and reflections are deepened, and a range of excellent educational support facilities is available. This is not in any sense an excuse for a diet which consists solely of (Christian) biblical content; but *a balanced course* of Judaism and Christianity is always preferable to a *sketchy* presentation of Asian faiths, offered because the latter is 'the done thing', regardless of the teacher's talents or the community's interests. And when these (or any) two Semitic faiths come to life in the classroom, the mixture is explosive.

In some rural areas even a market town is a metropolis, and a school may be extremely isolated geographically. For religious education here some of the problems relate to size (are there enough pupils to justify examination groups and a reasonable expenditure on resources?), some to the lack of contact with people of traditions other than the Christian, and others to the sense that multi-faith RE lacks immediate relevance to the community's life. Many teachers who work in this type of rural area find that the development of a learning bank, which includes artefacts, slides, cassettes and worksheets, can be a valuable asset, especially if it is coupled with the type of project in which pupils are motivated to find things out for themselves and to write up their own study files. Slide material is available from many sources, as are other types of resource.[8] It is amazing what richness can develop from such an initial step.

The use of a topic such as pilgrimage can prove a valuable focus here. Klaus Klostermaier's book, *Hindu and Christian in Vrindaban* will stimulate many teachers – and older pupils – in this direction.[9] The art of living in a pilgrimage centre and exploring the faith of those who visit it has a host of fascinating dimensions; and the insights into dialogue that such encounters throw up are essentially religious – an element all too often excluded from current religious education!

Another useful yardstick for distancing issues such as these may be found in the recent development of material on the Afro-Caribbean experience of religion, usually but not exclusively within the orbit of Christianity. Many RE departments have ignored this section of faith – even when it relates to their own school's community – because information is limited, or because it could be seen as divisive or even prejudiced to distinguish black Christianity from white, or because pentecostal and holiness churches tend to be fundamentalist and many multi-faith orientated teachers are liberals through and through. While it is recognised that many black Christians worship in traditional 'mainstream' churches, it is clear that description, insights and reflective material are all available here in abundance from a source as yet untapped, and several recent aids are now available to offer guidance and information.[10] In particular experienced teachers will find this material useful as a means of first distancing the subject and then analysing their own attitudes with regard to their receptivity, sympathy, and creativity where new material is concerned.

5 When (at what ages) is it appropriate?

At all ages. All the time. Chapters 1–3 spell out the different possibilities from the nursery to the sixth form. Only a few other comments are needed here.

These relate to the fresh work that is still waiting to be done as to what is best taught and how and when. The development of children's ability in relation to the Piagetian pattern has left certain gaps between the three main stages which are normally identified in descriptions of children's religious development. The implications of these gaps have yet to be worked out in a multi-faith setting. Are the ages of transition into concrete thought or into conceptual development the same in the different faiths? What affects these changes? Is the need for intermediate stages of circular thinking universal or not? And is there a right age for introducing pupils first to pluralism and secondly to non-theistic viewpoints, or should these normally be implicit throughout the child's schooling?

Perhaps the question of 'When?' is the most open, and, in the present situation, the most searching of the five I have posed here. But then time has always been the most intriguing problem to perplex the mind of man.

It raises more questions of an ultimate nature than any of the others explored above. The *reader who has the time* will do well to ponder how and when it is best to lead children from description of facts into the world of insights, and from insights into personal reflection. An opportunity lost may never come again, and there is no more important attribute for the teacher of religious education than sensitivity in timing.

Notes and references

1 *Stories of the Hodja* (written and published by Turgay Yagan, 1972), pages 64–5.

2 See the carefully arranged structure of the 1975 City of Birmingham Agreed Syllabus.

3 Associated Examining Board, Religious Studies O level, Alternative syllabus 155, multi-faith, thematic; and West Midlands CSE, Mode 3, Group Submission, based on Ladywood School, Birmingham.

4 For a summary account of a study tour of Israel by a group of 39 Birmingham teachers, see pages 13–14 of the 1980 *Shap Mailing*, available from the Shap Working Party, 7 Alderbrook Road, Solihull, West Midlands, B91 1NH.

5 This series has been revised several times. The current version retains individual programmes on the five faiths listed in the Birmingham syllabus but also introduces fresh material on Worship and Festivals, and expands the description of Christianity to give a more specific treatment of major traditions than was previously possible.

6 For a description of a central, library-based collection of a number of Project Packs, listing such artefacts, see the 1982 Supplement to *Living Together*, the City of Birmingham handbook for teachers of religious education.

7 For guidelines on the arranging of such visits, see the 1982 Supplement to *Living Together*, the City of Birmingham handbook for teachers of religious education.

8 See e.g. the sets of slides available from Bury Peerless, 22 King's Avenue, Minnis Bay, Birchington, Kent; the boxed kits of filmstrips, cassettes, booklets and reprographic masters available from Argus Communications, Plumpton House, Hoddesdon, Herts.; the Shap Working Party handbook, *World Religions: A Handbook for Teachers*, available from the Commission for Racial Equality, Elliot House, 10–12 Allington Street, London SW1E 5EH; and the annual *Calendar of Festivals* and the annual *Shap Mailing*, produced by the Commission for Racial Equality for the Shap Working Party, and available from 7 Alderbrook Road, Solihull, West Midlands, B91 1NH.

9 Klaus Klostermaier, *Hindu and Christian in Vrindaban* (London: SCM Press, 1969).

10 See the Southern Shap Conference book *Afro-Caribbean Religion* (Ward Lock, 1980), edited by Brian Gates; *Afro-Caribbean Religious Experience – a study in backgrounds and beliefs*, in the 1982 Supplement to *Living Together*, the City of Birmingham handbook for teachers of religious education; and Programme 1 (Worship) in the 1981 ATV school series, *Believe It or Not*.

Further reading for Chapters 1-4

The literature on world religions in schools is growing rapidly, so the following lists are selective. The suggestions for primary schools were contributed by Jean Holm. The other lists were compiled by Peter Woodward and the Editor. New books for schools on world religions are reviewed by the *British Journal of Religious Education* (published by CEM, 2 Chester House, Pages Lane, London, N10 PR), by *Resource* (published by the Institute of Education, University of Warwick, Coventry CV4 7AL) and by *Shap Mailing* (see note 4 above).

General

For exciting ideas turn to N. Smart and D. Horder (eds), *New Movements in Religious Education* (Temple Smith, 1975), a wide-ranging but still relevant symposium. *World Faiths in Education*, W. O. Cole (ed.) (Allen & Unwin, 1978) also puts together a number of Shap-orientated articles with some panache, and includes valuable chapters by the Editor on such topics as the use of ritual objects outside their faith context and the larger issues involved in the treatment of world religions in the multi-faith school. *Perspectives on World Religions*, Robert Jackson (ed.) (SOAS, 1978) includes chapters on teaching RE through art, world religions in public examinations, and the treatment of world religions in voluntary ('denominational') schools. The contrasts between these three books are creative and illuminating. The edited book seems to proliferate in this field today as opposed to the work of a single author, but Jean Holm's *Teaching Religion in School* (OUP, 1975) and *The Study of Religions* (Sheldon, 1977) are both replete with insights and sensitivity. The latter has a revised and expanded bibliography in the 1979 edition, as does the 1978 edition of *What Can I Do in RE?* by Michael Grimmitt (Mayhew McCrimmon, 1975). For information, creative ideas and reference material the Shap Working Party document *World Religions: A Handbook For Teachers*, W. O. Cole (ed.) (CRE/SWP, 1977) is particularly useful. It contains bibliographical material of an extensive nature, as well as general articles, ideas for project work, lists of audio-visual aids, and an annotated list of useful addresses. It is kept up to date by the annual *Shap Mailing*, available each Autumn from Shap Working Party, 7 Alderbrook

Road, Solihull, B91 1NH. ATV's booklet of teachers' notes on the series *Believe It or Not* also contains a useful bibliography of book material for teacher and pupil.

Syllabuses and handbooks

In recent years a number of local authorities have produced and published Agreed Syllabuses, usually consisting of short statements of policy, together with aims and sometimes an outline of content. For detailed classroom material teachers are often referred to handbooks designed to accompany and supplement the syllabuses.

Recent syllabuses include Birmingham 1975, Cheshire 1976, Avon 1976, Nottingham 1977, Hampshire 1978, Dorset 1979, Lincolnshire 1980, Humberside 1981, Northamptonshire 1981, Hertfordshire 1981. Others are currently in preparation, notably in Berkshire, Manchester and ILEA.

Major handbooks to note are those of Birmingham (*Living Together*, 1975), Nottingham (*Quest*, 1977) and Hampshire (*Paths to Understanding*, 1980). The contents of these three handbooks reflect the different needs of schools in the three authorities. The Birmingham one in particular contains extensive material and courses relevant to a multi-faith approach to RE. The 1982 supplement to the Birmingham handbook covers much new ground. The syllabus, handbook and supplement are all available from the City of Birmingham Education Department, In-Service Training Section, Margaret Street, Birmingham, B3 3BU.

Books for the teacher

The following list contains important books that have proved of use to teachers in a number of different ways: Ninian Smart's *Background to the Long Search* (BBC, 1977) is full of evocative material, excellent pictures and superb descriptive captions. Leo Rosten's *The Joys of Yiddish* (Penguin, 1968) combines linguistic study with anecdote, humour and a penetrating insight into Judaism that will enliven many an assembly, lesson and after-dinner speech. Lionel Blue and June Rose have produced *A Taste of Heaven – Adventures in Food and Faith* (Darton, Longman & Todd, 1977) which offers lively background information on customs, rituals and taboos related to food in various faiths and cultures. *Afro-Caribbean Religions*, Brian Gates (ed.) (Ward Lock, 1980) investigates fresh territory arising from a Shap course at Goldsmiths College. Another scholarly book is W. O. Cole and P. S. Sambhi's *The Sikhs – Their Religious Beliefs and Practices* (Routledge & Kegan Paul, 1978) which is basic for a serious study of this faith. Two beautiful books on Jerusalem are H. Stein and F. Jagodnik (eds), *Jerusalem Most Fair of Cities* (Armon, Jerusalem, 1977) and C. Thubron, *Jerusalem* (Time Life International, 1976). There is treasure too in J. Murphy-O'Connell's *The Holy Land: An Archaeological Guide from Earliest Times to 1700* (OUP, 1980). Richard Tames's *Approaches to Islam* in the present series is designed to guide the teacher through the religion and to suggest practical classroom activities.

Books for the classroom

(A) For primary schools: Books about children of different religious traditions, suitable for upper juniors, are *Pavan is a Sikh* by S. Lyle and *Nahda's Family* (Muslim) by M. Blakeley (both published by A. & C. Black), and the *Understanding Your Neighbour* series (Lutterworth): *Understanding Your Hindu Neighbour*, by J. Ewan, *Understanding Your Jewish Neighbour*, by M. Domnitz, *Understanding Your Muslim Neighbour* by N. and M. Iqbal, and *Understanding Your Sikh Neighbour* by P. S. Sambhi. Teachers should also use the books about the cultural and religious background of people of different faiths referred to on page 75. At primary school level children need a wide variety of resources (see pages 5-15). Materials on Judaism (including the Hebrew alphabet and books used for Jewish children, e.g. *The Children's Haggadah*, edited by A. N. Silbermann, and *The Passover Activity Fun Book*), can be obtained from The Jewish National Fund, Harold Poster House, Kingsbury Circle, London NW9 9ST, and on Islam (including Arabic calligraphy, pictures of mosques, and *The Children's Book of Islam*) can be obtained from Muslim Information Services, 233 Seven Sisters Road, London N4 2DA. A useful book of Christian symbols for juniors is *Saints, Signs and Symbols* by H. E. Pont (SPCK). Many children's stories make incidental reference to the phenomena of religions, for example the church figures in *The Bus that Went to Church* by J. Tomlinson (Faber) for infants, and in some of the novels by Philip Turner and William Payne, for older children. Fuller treatment of what is involved in helping children to understand religions can be found in *Discovering an Approach - Religious Education in Primary Schools* (Macmillan, 1977). Many books in the selection for use in secondary schools (below) will also be of value to teachers in primary schools. See in addition the reading list at the end of Chapter 11.

(B) For secondary schools: In the classroom pupils and teachers will find the following books useful. (1) Wide-ranging texts covering several faiths: S. Dicks (ed.), *The Many Faces of Religion* (Ginn, 1973), E. G. Parrinder, *A Book of World Religions* (Hulton, 1965) and W. O. Cole, *Five Religions in the Twentieth Century* (Hulton, 1981). Owen Cole's book is especially useful in preparing students for O level examinations in World Religions. (2) Surveys within one or two faiths: K. Klostermaier, *Hindu and Christian in Vrindaban* (SCM, 1969), J. Thompson, *The Christian Faith and its Symbols* (Arnold, 1979), R. F. Brin, *The Shabbat Catalogue* (Ktav, 1978), E. Guellouz, *Mecca, The Muslim Pilgrimage* (Paddington Press, 1977), G. Douglas, *Rivers of the World: The Ganges* (Wayland, 1978).

There are a number of valuable series of textbooks on world religions written for pupils of various ages. Note that some of those designed for children of junior age may be used profitably with younger secondary pupils. The quality of books within each series varies, particularly in the

Living Religions series (Ward Lock) and the *Way of* . . . series (Hulton).
Useful series of textbooks include the following:
For lower forms: *The Family in Britain* series – Hindu, Jewish, Muslim,
Sikh, West Indian (R.E.P); the *Strands* series – *Nahda's Family, Pavan is a
Sikh, Gypsy Family, Seven of Us, The Phoenix Bird Chinese Take-away, Shimon,
Leah and Benjamin, Rebecca is a Cypriot* (A. & C. Black); the *Understanding Your
Neighbour* series – Jewish, Muslim, Hindu, Sikh (Lutterworth); *The Way of*
. . . series – *The Buddha, The Hindu, The Jew, The Muslim, The Sikh* (Hulton
Education); the '*Joan Solomon*' series – *News for Dad, Bobbie's New Year,
Spud Comes to Play, Berron's Tooth, A Day by the Sea, Kate's Party* (Hamish
Hamilton).
For upper forms: the *Living Religions* series, now running to 16 titles on the
major faiths, denominations and sects (Ward Lock); the *Argus Major
World Religions* series – *African Primal Religions, Buddhism, Christianity,
Hinduism, Islam, Judaism, Religion in China* (Argus Communications) – to
link with boxed kits of filmstrips, slides and workbooks; the *Popular Judaica
Library* – the Synagogue, marriage, Passover, minor and modern festivals,
Shavuot, family, the high holy days, etc. (Keter, 1973–4); the *Thinking
About* series – *Buddhism, Christianity, Hinduism, Islam, Judaism, Sikhism*
(Lutterworth); the *Religious Dimension* series – *Islam, Meeting Sikhism, The
World of Jewish Faith* (Longman); *The Jewish Catalogue*, first, second and
third volumes (Jewish Publication Society of America).

Novel and story

The use of novel and story in religious education is currently receiving
considerable attention. Annotated lists of appropriate material appear in
World Religions: A Handbook for Teachers and in the Hampshire handbook
and the Birmingham supplement. The following list is a brief selection of
novels useful for secondary pupils, either to read in a class or at home or as
discussion starters:
Jonathan Livingstone Seagull by J. L. Bach (Pan, 1973). A delightful and
evocative parable of the urge to excel which is in all of us, with a messianic
feathered friend as the hero.
One More River by L. R. Banks (Penguin, 1975). An attractive, wealthy 14-
year-old, Lesley leaves the secure Canadian life she loves and settles with
her family in a kibbutz on the banks of the Jordan. Slowly and painfully
she learns to face a difficult new life, and builds up a strange friendship
with a young Arab boy across the river. Insights abound both into her
own torn self as a growing teenager and into her unusual situation.
Bilal by H. A. L. Craig (Quartet Books, 1977). The hero is a slave, black
Bilal, who is redeemed by Muhammad and joins his band of followers.
The story of Muhammad's life is told through the incidents Bilal describes
so vividly, and highlights relate to his own invitation to be the first
muezzin. Both pictures and story relate to the controversial Muslim film,
Muhammad – Messenger of God.
I Heard the Owl Call my Name by M. Craven (Pan, 1974). The

Tsawataineuk tribe of Canada live out the Christian faith while the main events of the tribe's life follow the customs and law of their forefathers. We glimpse them hunting and fishing, celebrating and mourning; we share their joys and sorrows; and all this against the background of a young Anglican priest who has been sent to minister to them. He does not know he is dying, but gradually as he learns from the tribe what it means to live, so in the end he is ready to die – when he hears the owl call his name.

The Bomber by Len Deighton (Pan, 1971). Implicit religion: a modern Tolstoy asks all the questions raised by war and leaves the pro-war party to face up to the implications. As an RAF bomber prepares for a bombing raid over Germany in 1943, we enter into the lives of all those involved – those on the airfield, their friends and their relatives; and those in Germany who, because of an infinitesimal computed mistake, will be the recipients of the bombs. The complete folly of the exercise is reminiscent of Tolstoy. There are no victors.

The Little World of Don Camillo by G. Guareschi (Penguin, 1970). The lovable and laughable Catholic priest, with his likable friend and enemy, the marxist mayor, live cheek by jowl in the north Italian countryside. Their adventures and encounters are recorded in ways that raise both laughs and questions, and the good Lord on his crucifix often has the last word.

I Am David by A. Holm (Puffin, 1969). David is helped to escape from the European concentration camp where he has lived all his life with strangers. As he travels across Europe he sees our world with freshly opened eyes, and at the same time is led to ask fundamental questions about his own nature and his identity. Sensitive, imaginative, compelling.

Friday the Rabbi Slept Late by H. Kemelman (Penguin, 1973). The art of the detective novel opens a door for us into the world of an ordinary (liberal) Jewish community in an American town, and of their ordinary (or perhaps not so ordinary) Rabbi. As the community prays and works, celebrates Sabbath and Yom Kippur, endures birth and death, and copes with the Rabbi's reactions to his first visit to Jerusalem, we gain a delicate and delightful insight into what Jewish life is sometimes 'all about'.

Walk-About by J. V. Marshall (Penguin, 1969). A plane crashes in the Australian desert, and the two surviving children who set out to walk to safety meet a young, black, naked aboriginal on his walk-about, the trial that precedes his initiation. The moral dilemmas all three face are recounted with simplicity and insight.

The Chosen by C. Potok (Penguin, 1970). Here is a story set in the traditional world of Hasidic and Orthodox Jews in post-war Brooklyn. We watch two Jewish boys from sharply contrasting backgrounds grow through adolescence to manhood. One is the son of an Hasidic Rabbi, the other of a less strict Orthodox teacher. Everything conspires to break up their friendship, but in the end without success. Through the story we explore what it means for a Jew to grow up in both a Jewish and a non-Jewish world.

Shanta by M. Thøger (Penguin, 1972). Shanta is 12 and lives in a peaceful village. Her father decides to take the whole family (and their beautifully decorated cow) to the Maharajah's city for the celebration of a harvest festival. Many frightening events were to happen before Shanta saw the procession, and she was glad to return at last to her home. One thread running through the story is the preparation for her marriage, and as she realises the implications of this – and copes too with the plague – Shanta grows towards womanhood.

Red Towers of Granada by C. Trease (Puffin, 1972). A thrilling adventure in the time of England's Queen Eleanor. A young Christian lad finds refuge with a Jewish family in Nottingham. He learns much about their way of life and their concern for the sick. Together they travel to Spain and there we meet the Spanish Jewish community and the Moorish Muslims of Granada. Finally at dawn three young men offer their prayers side by side – a Christian, a Jew and a Muslim.

Mila 18 by L. Uris (Corgi, 1961). A dramatic and unforgettable recreation of life and death in the Warsaw ghetto and of the final bitter destruction of the Jewish community there. We watch the characters live and die, argue about motives and action, love and hate; and in the end we remember not the horror of the atrocities, but a Jewish boy's poignant Bar-mitzvah during the last months of the siege, and a Passover meal for freedom on the last evening of the community's existence.

Part Two

Pluralism

Introduction

Two key factors should be considered in accounting for the growth in schools of a world religions approach to RE. One is the rapid development in universities and colleges of courses in religious studies rather than theology or divinity. The Department of Religious Studies at the University of Lancaster, under Professor Ninian Smart, has been particularly influential in changing the pattern of teacher education in religion, through its influence on the curricula of Colleges of Education in the 1970s and through the Schools Council Secondary Project on Religious Education and the second Schools Council Primary RE project, both based at Lancaster University. In setting up his department in 1966, Smart was concerned to broaden the scope of courses, partly through the introduction of studies in a range of world religions. This was seen to be appropriate in a secular university. He was also concerned to introduce what he called descriptive studies of religion (especially using phenomenology as a method), alongside theological, philosophical and textual studies, both to give students a better grasp of the nature of religion than might have been obtained on earlier courses and to begin the development in this country of studies already well established in Europe and North America.

Both of these concerns struck a chord with many RE teachers in schools, frustrated either by the biblical narrowness of old-style syllabuses or by the vapidness of newer ones which tended to identify certain moral, social and political questions as religious, while giving scant attention to the study of religion itself. For many teachers the publication of *Religious Education in Secondary Schools*, the working paper of the Lancaster-based Schools Council Secondary RE project – a document strongly influenced by Smart's ideas – was a landmark, indicating a major development in the establishment of RE as a subject whose place on the timetable was fully justifiable on educational grounds.

Further impetus was given to the world religions movement by the increasingly obvious plurality of religions to be found in our own society.

The various waves of immigration from South Asia, East Africa and the Caribbean – resulting from circumstances such as labour shortages in this country, and 'Africanisation' policies in certain East African states (culminating in the infamous deportation of Asians from Uganda in 1972) – brought to our cities large number of Hindus, Sikhs and Muslims, together with Christians of Afro-Caribbean background. RE teachers in inner-city areas such as Bradford, Birmingham and parts of London were among the first to teach significant numbers of children from religious backgrounds that were other than Christian. Among such teachers were many who became enthused by the presence of so much living religion that could be explored in the classroom. Coupled with the broadening of RE to embrace world religions was its revitalisation through school visits to temples, gurdwaras and mosques, through the participation in RE lessons of guests from the various ethnic communities and, above all, through the contribution in class of pupils from a variety of religious backgrounds (see Chapters 1–4 for examples of the contribution of ethnic minority groups to religious education).

Professor Smart's concerns and the insights of teachers from multi-ethnic schools were brought together in 1969 by the formation of the Shap Working Party on World Religions in Education whose first publication, *Comparative Religion in Education*, edited by J. R. Hinnells (Newcastle: Oriel Press, 1970), includes an essay by Ninian Smart on 'The structure of comparative religion' and a chapter by Professor Geoffrey Parrinder on 'The ethics and customs of the main immigrant peoples'. The Shap Working Party has continued to make an enormous contribution to the study of world religions in schools through the regular provision of short courses, through its books (including the periodically revised *World Religions: A Handbook for Teachers*, published by the Commission for Racial Equality) and through its annual *Shap Mailing*.

Despite these positive developments there are many parents and teachers who have reservations about the broadening of RE to include religions other than Christianity. Some of these reservations are specifically theological, and Raymond Hammer discusses them in Chapter 10. Some are pedagogic, representing a concern that RE should be neither overburdened with information, nor irrelevant to the experience of children and young people. Many chapters in this book discuss one or both of these concerns. Others are what might loosely be termed 'cultural' reservations commonly expressed in the following ways: first, a concern that a world religions approach to RE breaks the letter and the spirit of the 1944 Education Act; second, a fear that, in adopting a multi-faith approach to religious education, our cultural heritage is in some way compromised; third, an anxiety that by widening the scope of RE to include other religions, the study of Christianity – the historic religion of the nation –is threatened. The following chapters deal specifically with these last three concerns.

In Chapter 5 Dennis Starkings argues that the 1944 Act is essentially a management framework allowing agreed syllabus conferences to determine the aims and content of RE. Instruction and worship were made compulsory but the government deliberately avoided attaching the State directly to the teaching or practice of any particular faith or doctrine. The machinery allowed for the achievement of consensus on such matters in each local authority area. It was devised to include all those with a legitimate interest in the matter and not 'merely to decorate the mind of the church with secular laurels'. Starkings shows that the proper concern of the State was to arrange a place in education for the religious dimension of questions of value. It did not directly entrench the faith, doctrine or practice of any particular religious community, and it did not (in using the word 'instruction') imply any philosophical distinction between 'instruction' and 'education'. The first generation of agreed syllabus-makers thought otherwise – and that is how a 'mythology of the Act' has come to be commonly held even in our own day. Starkings is careful to observe that his argument is not an attack on the place of Christianity in RE or on Christian influence. Rather, he argues the legitimacy of a world religions curriculum where agreed syllabuses allow it.

In Chapter 6 Dennis Starkings responds to the suggestion of Professor John McIntyre that RE has become merely descriptive, contemptuous of truth-claims and thereby damaging to the dominant Christian culture. Rejecting his claim that RE should be reserved for the teaching of Christianity as true, Starkings takes issue with McIntyre's analysis of culture, his theory of cultural change and his characterisation of modern religious education. He anticipates Owen Cole and Raymond Hammer in Chapters 7 and 10 in arguing that Christianity stands to benefit more from being studied in the context of world religions than from being isolated in the curriculum. Truth claims, he maintains, receive better attention when religious education reflects the plurality of faiths and philosophies to be found in the adult world.

Owen Cole (Chapter 7) cuts the ground from under the feet of those claiming that multi-faith RE damages the study of Christianity in schools, by asserting that Christianity has *never* been studied adequately in our educational institutions. Traditionally, the school's role has been merely to supplement the nurturing activities of the family and the churches. Consequently, syllabuses have tended to give a partial and piecemeal treatment of the faith. A proper study of Christianity in the schools of a pluralistic democracy requires changes in aims, methods and content, and there must be no assumption on the part of pupils of any sympathy with or previous knowledge of the faith. In adopting the same kind of approach and methodology as specialists in the world's other religions, students are likely to gain a more balanced and complete understanding of Christianity than in the past. Cole also discusses practical problems concerning resources and examinations and he offers a tentative Christian studies syllabus for schools.

R.J.

5

World Religions and the Spirit of 1944

Dennis Starkings

Throughout the period of mass education religion has faced the challenge of historical criticism and scientific empiricism, while organised religion has shown a dwindling grasp on the loyalty of an urban and class-conscious society. In the same period too, the State has progressively separated itself from religious inspirations in framing social policies. Through it all, however, religion has kept its place in the curriculum. Indeed, the 1944 Act might be thought to have advanced and affirmed that place.

This chapter argues that there has been a broad tradition of public concern for religious education. It attempts to identify that tradition as something broader than the boundaries of any community of faith. It presents a view of the 1944 Act which places it within that tradition. Those who are attached to teaching one faith (and to teaching it as though teachers and pupils were alike believers) have shown their misunderstanding of the tradition by claiming the 1944 Act as a charter of their own convictions, when in fact it is little more than a management framework. Friends of the world religions approach have shown by their arguments an implicit concern for the perennial issues of religious education; but they have emphasised a discontinuity in their practices and so have tended to leave the tradition in the hands of those who wish to claim it. This has been unfortunate. It has left the case for a world religions approach incomplete – apparently careless of legality and neglectful of traditional concerns. This chapter tackles the questions of tradition and legality. In fact the tradition is alive and well, though living in comparative obscurity; and the world religions movement is potentially its most genuine fulfilment yet.

Searching the tradition

At first sight the survival of religious education is paradoxical – at least to those who are perhaps over-impressed by what is called 'secularisation'. Some have sought to explain it by pointing to a disproportionate influence on the part of committed believers. There is *some* truth in that:

the arrangements of 1944 were made in order to bring the largest possible number of inadequately equipped church schools into the orbit of the local education authorities, and a distinct place for religious education in state schools was from one point of view the price demanded and paid for that achievement. Others see religious education as an elite device for controlling the morals of a passive majority. Remove its cynicism, admit that there is still an inescapable moral role for the school, and there is some truth in that claim; but it does not tell the whole truth about the undoubted popular interest in religion. It would be better to look beyond both kinds of explanation and see that the religious provisions of the 1944 Act were widely welcomed for their own sake. In order to explain that, we need to understand that the community of interest in and concern for religious education has been far wider than the consensus of belief. Believers and unbelievers alike have sustained the concern for religious education and it is this social fact (rather than the concern for particular creeds) which has kept it alive.

The educational concern has its roots in a social concern. 'I am,' said John Stuart Mill, '. . . one of the very few examples, in this country, of one who has, not thrown off religious belief, but never had it.' Nevertheless, he sensed a certain difficulty:

> When the philosophic minds of the world can no longer believe its religion, or can only believe it with modifications amounting to an essential change of its character, a transitional period commences, of weak convictions, paralysed intellects, and growing laxity of principle, which cannot terminate until a renovation has been effected in the basis of their belief, leading to the evolution of some faith, whether religious or merely human, which they can really believe: and when things are in this state, all thinking or writing which does not tend to promote such a renovation, is of very little value beyond the moment.[1]

It hardly counts as an argument for teaching religion in school. But as an expression of social concern it falls into place with the religious concern of many ordinary men and women who have at the same time voted with their feet against institutional religion.

The Victorians had a strong sense that a crisis of values threatened the very fabric of society; and in our own times it is not easy to dismiss such fears. Until very recent times it was assumed that the 'decline of religion' was either the cause or the measure of that crisis. To say this is not at all to enter into argument with philosophers who wish to affirm a distinction between religion and morality. The point is that religion and morality have been *historically* interrelated matters and are still related in the lives of many people today. Two contributors to the magazine *The Nineteenth Century* could agree in making the distinction between morals and religion but still saw cause to lament the 'decline of religion' – Frederic Harrison because morality 'could no more suffice for life than a just character would suffice for any of us without intellect, imagination or affection and the power of fusing all these into the unity of a man'; and James

Martineau because 'morality would lose not its base but its summit'.[2] That has been and remains the social and historical sense of the matter, shared by many believers and unbelievers alike. Just such a sense of the social crisis was applied in turn to educational debate. It profoundly influenced the debate about 'citizenship' in the inter-war years, and it shaped the discussion which led to the 1944 Act.

In 1923 W. H. Hadow published his *Citizenship*. It was a work of social and political concern, reflecting on the competing claims of individualist and collectivist attitudes and applying the discussion to the process of education. It left the reader in no doubt that politics, morals and religion were profoundly interrelated matters. 'State and individual,' he wrote, 'co-operate in a real and personal sense to the divine purpose . . .' Putting it another way, he said, 'man and community are two powers appointed to carry on processes which pass beyond their limitations and to converge upon an end which is greater than their own.'[3] So high a view of the citizen's and the State's calling falls strangely upon our ears today, and it is not quoted now for any particular approval; but it is interesting as marking a stage in the tradition which emphasised a religious dimension in thinking about the well-being of our public life. Its roots were in the neo-idealist tradition of late nineteenth-century Oxford. Its branches extended through to the 1950s in the work of a man like R. M. McIver. T. H. Green, the founder of that tradition, has been presented by a distinguished commentator as seeking to impart a religious dimension to citizenship.[4]

The debate which preceded the religious provisions of the 1944 Education Act took place in the very special circumstances of a world war. In the columns of *The Times* it was made clear that the threat of Nazism was a threat not to persons and property alone but to the democratic political system and to the values on which it depended. From there it was easy to pass on to a concern for the source of those values in the national tradition, and to religion and religious education as respectively the inspiration and perpetuation of that tradition. It is important to see that it was a citizen's argument and not a theologian's argument. At no time did it include the assertion that any particular doctrine or belief was in fact true. Rather, it sought the widest possible support for what was essentially a historical and not a philosophical observation – that citizenship, values and religion were intimately related. At the time, it was well calculated to gain the maximum support. Clement Attlee had just pitched the justification of the war at a level designed to reconcile the pacifist and aggressively anti-fascist wings of his party. In the same issue which reported Attlee's speech, *The Times* hastened to affirm the consensus:

> Each month of the war shows its real nature more clearly. The issue lies between the fundamental precepts of Christianity, *shared as they are by millions in other lands and of other religions* [my italics] and a force which is consciously and resolutely vowed to their destruction.[5]

Once again, though in a form appropriate to the circumstances of a nation at war, religion had been proposed as a crucial issue in the crisis of values. The Archbishops were not slow to affirm their own adherence to this consensus. 'There is an ever-deepening conviction that in this present struggle we are fighting to preserve those elements in human civilization and in our national tradition which owe their origin to Christian faith.'[6] Even there it was an argument about a shared tradition and its religious roots, and thus more widely acceptable than an argument for specific religious beliefs would have been.

Against this background *The Times* argued 'that religion must form the basis of any education worth the name, and that education with religion omitted is not really education at all'. The persuasiveness of its argument can be seen if we compare the *Times* leader of 17 February 1940 with the White Paper of 1943. First, *The Times*:

> More than ever before it has become clear that the healthy life of a nation must be based on spiritual principles. For many years we have been living on spiritual capital, on traditions inherited from the past instead of providing for the future. Christianity cannot be imbibed from the air. It is not a philosophy but a historic religion which must dwindle unless the facts on which it is founded are taught, and such teaching made the centre of our educational system.

As for the White Paper:

> There has been a very general wish not confined to representatives of the Churches, that religious education should be given a more defined place in the life and work of the schools, springing from the desire to revive the spiritual and personal values in our society and in our national tradition. The church, the family, the local community and the teacher – all have their part to play in imparting religious instruction to the young.[7]

In appreciating the background to the 1944 Act we must realise that it sprang from a broadly based concern for the values of the national tradition. *The Times* did not demand more than a teaching of the facts on which the historic religion of Christianity was founded, and the White Paper had nothing more specific to say on the content of religious education. The subsequent debate in Parliament revealed all sorts of persuasions on the part of members, but the government's observations on the content and aims of religious education never exceeded the rather cautious statement of R. A. Butler drawn from an existing syllabus:

> . . . [that pupils] may gain knowledge of the common Christian faith held by their fathers for nearly 2,000 years; may seek for themselves in Christianity principles which give a purpose to life and a guide to all its problems.[8]

The consensus was not disturbed by so even an emphasis on factual knowledge and personal choice – especially since there was nothing in the Act to give statutory force to such a formulation of aims.

Law and mythology

The view is widely held that only an exclusively Christian education (taught from a standpoint of commitment) is consistent with the Act. Teachers are therefore continually confronted with a mythology of the law – one which claims the authority of the Act itself for what is (by Christian as well as by secular standards) no more than a partisan approach to religious and educational issues. It is necessary to explain the Act's relation to that broader spectrum of public opinion and suggest how more partial views came to predominate.

The Bishop of Chichester made the most important point quite succinctly:

> There is nothing to require that religious instruction according to an agreed syllabus should be in any particular faith. It is intended to be in the Christian religion, but intention is different from statutory obligation.[9]

Quite so; but perhaps if the intention had really been so clear there would not have been an issue. The government consistently opposed all attempts to specify the State's concerns as Christian within the framework of the Act. Agreed syllabuses were to be produced by conferences including not 'Christian' denominations but 'religious' denominations, and suggestions made in the House of Commons that school worship should be specified as 'Christian' were without effect. Lord Quickswood and Viscount Cecil of Chelwood failed to make regular church worship or the ultimate membership of a worshipping community into statutory aims of religious instruction. When Lord Selbourne replied to the Bishop of Chichester and others on the government's behalf he gave an assurance that it was the intention of the government (indeed, of Parliament) that 'the religious instruction required to be given shall be Christian instruction and that the corporate act of worship shall be Christian worship'.[10] But why then refuse to entertain the word 'Christian' in the Act itself? The answer was that it seemed extremely undesirable – in the event of any dispute – that the courts should have to decide who or what was admissibly Christian. His point was a reasonable one but it reflected a dilemma which applied not only to the courts but to the State itself – given the tendency of the State (over many years) to detach itself progressively from even that tenuous attachment to religion which establishment of the church represented.

Lord Selbourne's assurance of Christian intentions proceeded to take an interestingly circuitous direction. It was the job of the Act to provide machinery for giving effect to the government's intentions. The Act provided machinery which gave the Church of England a veto over the syllabuses; and the Church of England, he said, 'is not going to accept a syllabus which is not in accordance with the Christian faith'.[11] Doubtless so – as the bishops felt bound to agree. (No doubt also, they could see the advantage of turning religious disputes into disputes about machinery, and that in any legal dispute under the Act, controversy would be less likely to turn directly on matters of faith than on whether an agreed syllabus was valid, or whether classroom activities conformed to it.) But advantageous though it was, the emphasis on machinery put a limit to the cash value of Lord Selbourne's assurance. There was nothing in the Act to require that religious instruction according to an agreed syllabus should be in any particular faith – nothing, that is, apart from machinery. Against the plain words of statute – and Lord Selbourne's careful explanation that those plain words were indeed the government's intention – the courts would be very unlikely to regard the word 'religious' as conterminous with the word 'Christian'. In effect, Lord Selbourne's assurance could mean only that (so far as the government was concerned) any syllabus approved by a proper procedure must be regarded as Christian.

It is interesting to see what was and what was not a matter of machinery within the Act. Worship and instruction were clearly made compulsory – though subject to a conscience clause. By contrast all attempts to make statutory any precise notion of the aims and content of religious education were resisted by the government, and made a matter for subsequent decision by bodies set up under the Act. The difference is clear enough. Without compulsory worship and instruction there would have been no agreement on the part of the churches to surrender large numbers of their sub-standard schools to the local education authorities, and a consensus of opinion supported that much of the bargain – indeed, warmly welcomed it. By contrast it was by no means so clear that any precise notion of the aims and content of religious education would be so widely supported or that public policy made it desirable for the State to attach itself to such details. On the contrary, controversy over such details might imperil the Act and open to public questioning the State's attachment to particular religious policies or doctrines. That is why such issues were made a matter of machinery – consigned to special conferences to be convened by each local education authority for the purpose of producing a locally agreed syllabus of religious instruction. The State thus directly approved the machinery for making syllabus decisions; but it could thereafter be held to have approved the decisions themselves only in the sense that (and to the extent that) they were the product of a lawfully operated mechanism. Such an approach reflected not only the broad context of public opinion – a disposition to find religion both important and interesting provided particular commitments were not too closely questioned – but also a historical tendency for the State to make that mood the basis of public policy.

The parties to the syllabus conferences were carefully chosen to represent those with the clearest interest in what was done in the name of religious education – those whose exclusion might imperil the public acceptance of a syllabus. Each defined interest group was designated a 'committee' of the conference, and each committee had a veto over the decision of the conference as a whole. To balance the right of veto everyone had sure and certain knowledge that the Secretary of State (to use the modern terminology) would intervene to operate an alternative procedure if the veto reduced proceedings to a nullity. The composition of the conference was designed to bring together interests which had in the past been in open dispute (for example, the teachers' unions and the churches). Thus the local education authority was to provide one of the committees – and was in fact the only interest group with a direct and unqualified right to be represented. The Church of England provided a committee – but not in Wales and Monmouthshire, where it might hope only to be part of a committee representing religious denominations generally. Membership of the broader committee (as of another represent-ing teachers' associations) was everywhere to be at the discretion of the local education authorities 'having regard to the circumstances of the area'.[12] Such a balance of powers was not designed merely to decorate the mind of the church with secular laurels – though it would not prevent that outcome if the other parties had nothing of interest to say on the matter.

Compulsory worship and instruction are clearly requirements of the body of the Act itself, and not merely the product of applying statutory machinery. Both features were demanded by the churches very early in the negotiations, and both appear in sections of the Act which are grouped under the collective heading 'Religious Education'. Surely, then, they appear in the Act not only with a Christian pedigree but with the Christian intention to see worship and instruction as intimately related aspects of a common and Christian activity? Certainly that was the assumption of early syllabus-makers, but it may be challenged on lines similar to those argued above. It is open to an agreed syllabus conference to *make* worship and instruction into interrelated aspects of a common activity, and to make that common activity exclusively a Christian concern. Nevertheless, a conference which opens up a gap between them is not thereby in breach of the law, nor does it abuse the law or stretch a point. The fundamental mistake would be to turn a convenience of parliamentary draftsmanship into a philosophy of religious education. Worship and instruction had to be found a place in the Act. They were put together under the heading 'Religious Education' because they clearly did not belong in the preceding group of sections headed 'Secular Instruction'. The problem of draftsmanship was to find words to cover (a) school worship – though this was easy enough, (b) classroom teaching in religion, and (c) the two together. It was apparently solved by using the term 'religious education' to cover the two and as a heading for the group of sections dealing with them. Classroom teaching then became 'religious instruction' – partly because the term 'religious education' had already been used, and partly to *distinguish* it from worship. Even enthusiasts for a world religions curriculum have tended towards the same fundamental mistake by making misguided efforts to contrast their own 'educational' aims with the supposedly 'instructional' aims of the 1944 Act. Although it is wise and helpful to distinguish between the ideas of 'instruction' and 'education' it is probably wrong to supose that parliamentary draftsmen sought to draw that kind of distinction. They were not declaring that school religion must be indoctrinatory and instructional by contrast with some philosophical idea of sound educational principles. Whatever else it may be, the Education Act is not an exercise in the philosophy of education.

If we ask how the mythology of the Act has come about, the answer must be that it represents a view of the Act which was entertained by the first generation of agreed syllabus makers after the passing of the Act – and that those attached to those early formulations of a religious education have sustained the mythology in being. The imaginations of responsible churchmen did not in those early days run to anything more than a committedly Christian education for the state schools. Equally, however, no one else felt the need or the duty to question what the churchmen were essentially agreed upon. In 1944 it seemed that the supreme achievement of an agreed syllabus was that it produced educational peace between Christians: others were largely grateful to observe and to ratify that achievement. Aware that R. A. Butler had achieved the first major settlement of the religious question for some three quarters of a century, general opinion was content to regard compulsory worship and religious instruction as the just prize and property of the Christian denominations, their reward for the surrender of many sub-standard church schools to the local authorities. Thus the tendency of churchmen to see the children as postulants for a process of Christian initiation went largely unchallenged; while the aims of religious education were expressed in the language of Christian evangelism and piety. The Bampton Lecturer for 1944 attributed this not to the outcome of agreed syllabus conferences but to the Act itself. 'Parliament,' wrote Spencer Leeson, 'has declared the will of the nation that it shall be a Christian nation; and the State-aided schools are to do their part by teaching the nation's children to worship and to understand.'[13] This expressed an ecclesiastical view of the Act's significance, and the circumstances of the time conspired to make it the orthodox view.

World religions and the 1944 Act

The 1944 Act is a charter not for any one view of religious education but for the achievement of a consensus view within each local authority area. The hope is that when the local authority has agreed with the teachers and with the religious denominations, it will be possible to make educational progress in this important and contentious area of the curriculum and to reassure teachers that they are acting in accordance with a broadly based public understanding across a range of complex issues. The framework which the Act proposes does have certain implications for the sort of religious education we need to seek. It means that religious education (in the schools to which the agreed syllabuses apply) should be satisfactory to both religious and educational opinion. This chapter criticises not the Christian influence in religious education but what is taken to be a misguided view of the 1944 Act. A forthright secularism must be an unlikely product of such machinery as the Act provides – though that is not the same as saying that it will be wise to ignore the existence of such points of view. Nor will it serve the consensus on which religious education depends if communities of faith outside the Christian tradition are present in our society but are (without 'regard to the circumstances of the area') excluded from educational influence.

So far as the Act and its mythology are concerned, there remains one important issue arising from the move towards a world religions curriculum. When the Archbishop of Canterbury sought an assurance of Christian intentions from Lord Selbourne he was trying to prevent the agreed syllabuses from becoming syllabuses of comparative religion – 'there can be no comparative religion, there are only people who are comparatively religious'.[14] There need be no dispute over his chief concern. He rather cheerlessly equated comparative religion with the idea that adolescents should be invited to choose between a variety of faiths; and he was right to be suspicious of that. Religious education will not do justice to religion itself or to the personal education of its pupils by providing just a shop window or a package tour of the world's faiths. On the other hand religious education will be aiming wide of its target if it ignores the fact that most of its pupils are 'Christian' in only a residual and exiguous sense, inclined to frame their religious questions in terms that exceed the boundaries of any one faith.[15] The tradition on which religious education rests is truly compounded of belief, unbelief, and a sense that religion is fundamentally (though mysteriously) related to the quest for formulations of value in our society. As a consequence we have to *tell the truth* as we see it, but we must also be seen to be *seeking the truth*. A world religions curriculum is not in itself a formula for achieving that proper balance, but its arrival has for the first time put the issues into a proper perspective.

Notes and references

1 J. S. Mill, *Autobiography* (London: Longmans, Green & Dyer, 1873), chapter 2, p. 43 and chapter 7, p. 239.

2 Michael Goodwin (ed.), *Nineteenth-Century Opinion* (Harmondsworth: Penguin, 1951), pp. 135 and 133.

3 W. H. Hadow, *Citizenship* (Oxford, 1923), p. 205.

4 See Melvin Richter, *The Politics of Conscience, T. H. Green and his Age* (London: Weidenfeld & Nicolson, 1964).

5 *The Times*, 16 January 1941.

6 *The Times*, 13 February 1941.

7 *Educational Reconstruction*, White Paper Cmd. 6548, 1943, 111, p. 36.

8 *Hansard*, Fifth Series, Debates of the House of Commons, vol. 396, column 230.

9 *Hansard*, Fifth Series, Debates of the House of Lords, vol. 132, column 46.

10 *Hansard*, Fifth Series, Debates of the House of Lords, vol. 132, column 366.

11 *Hansard*, Fifth Series, Debates of the House of Lords, vol. 132, column 367.

12 The Education Act, 1944, Fifth Schedule.

13 The Rev. Spencer Leeson, *Christian Education* (London: Longmans, Green & Co., 1947), p. 194.

14 *Hansard*, Fifth Series, Debates of the House of Lords, vol. 132, column 43.

15 The second chapter of Harold Loukes, *New Ground in Christian Education* (London: SCM, 1965), contains much that is relevant here and to the understanding of the Act in general – though the understanding of the law and its context is restricted, as the title of the book indicates.

Further reading

Spencer Leeson, *Christian Education* (London: Longmans, Green & Co., 1947), states and comments upon the traditional view. Understanding was advanced by Harold Loukes in the second chapter of his *New Ground in Christian Education* (London: SCM, 1965). John Hull vented serious Christian and educational concerns in *School Worship – An Obituary* (London: SCM, 1975), while Edward Norman protested all such novelties in his article, 'The threat to religion' in C. B. Cox and Rhodes Boyson (eds) *Black Paper 1977* (London: Temple Smith). More recently Leslie Newbiggin in 'Teaching Christianity in a secular plural society', *Christianity in the Classroom* (London: CEM, 1978) and Angela Tilby, *Teaching God* (London: Fount Paperbacks, Collins, 1979) have with varying implications tended to underline what the chapter in this present book calls a 'mythology' of the 1944 Act. Two important studies of the general background are Marjorie Cruickshank, *Church and State in English Education* (London: Macmillan, 1963) and James Murphy, *Church, State and Schools in Britain, 1800–1970* (London: Routledge & Kegan Paul, 1971), while P. H. J. H. Gosden, *Education in the Second World War*

(London: Methuen, 1976) provides a thoroughgoing administrative history. A flavour of the times can be savoured in W. Kenneth Richmond, *Education in England* (Harmondsworth: Penguin, 1945). Edward Norman's *Church and Society in England, 1770-1970* (Oxford, 1976), is a mine of relevant information and analysis on the key figures and the issues. Some insight can be gained from Lord Butler's memoirs, under the significant title, *The Art of the Possible* (London: Hamish Hamilton, 1971). Approaches to statutory interpretation and construction are considered in A. S. de Smith, *Constitutional and Administrative Law* (Penguin, 1971).

6

Pluralism and Truth in Religious Education

Dennis Starkings

Are we perhaps so sensitive to the claims of immigrant cultures and religions that we neglect the native tradition of Christianity? Are we so obsessed with fairness and impartiality that we become merely descriptive and neutral in our teaching – pushed by a misplaced sensitivity into passing on a cultivated agnosticism or indifferentism as today's message in religious education? More bluntly, has the study of world religions made religious education into an instrument for a dismantling of the culture and a neglect of the truth? These are questions which teachers may well ask themselves about their own professionalism and they are questions which Professor John McIntyre has explored and articulated systematically in an important paper.[1] If this chapter takes the trouble to disagree with much of Professor McIntyre's analysis it is all the more a tribute to the way in which he has formulated the issues as questions about culture and about truth.

Truth and values

Professor McIntyre's indictment of contemporary practice is serious indeed.

> Truth claims must under no circumstances be raised, or if the question of truth is asked it has to be answered in the terms that all religions are equally true, or that the truth is a compendium of them all. This view has become canonical in some circles in Britain, and I have seen a redesigned curriculum for religious education which proceeded upon it as an unexamined assumption.

That would be bad enough, but the grave charge leads on to an even graver one:

> We must be one of the few generations in history which has failed to feel sufficiently strongly about our own values, moral standards and religious convictions to secure their transmission to the next generation. A widespread support for descriptive religious education coupled with failure to construct an effective system of moral education has come to ensure a minimal adoption by the next generation of the values, beliefs, attitudes which our fathers and mentors passed on to us.

But McIntyre does not confine himself to expressing fears and concerns. He offers an analysis of culture which points to an alternative policy.

A new policy

Perhaps some readers will not have seen Professor McIntyre's paper. For that reason a very skeletal summary of his argument may be helpful, offered on the understanding that it may be checked against the paper itself. The argument appears to take the following form:

1 'There is at least an historical case for saying that in western society, it is religion, and in particular, the Christian religion, which has been the source of the values and concepts from which the culture has sprung.'
2 Education is 'culture perpetuating itself'. Or, in other words, 'the relation of culture and education is co-implicative'.
3 Britain is a multicultural society only in the (relatively weak) sense that there is a dominant Christian culture alongside various subordinate but independent cultures. The values and vitality of the dominant culture guarantee the independence and vitality of the subordinate cultures – which may to that extent be said to depend on the dominant culture.
4 If all this is true (that is, if the three propositions above are taken together) then religious education should perpetuate the religion of the dominant culture by teaching Christianity as true and therefore worthy of the pupils' commitment. This would benefit both the dominant and the subordinate cultures.
5 The world as a whole is multicultural in the strong sense that 'there are many equal, independent and alternative cultures existing side by side'. Pupils must be prepared for the encounter which the world will inevitably bring, and so the religions of Britain's subordinate cultures must have a place in the curriculum. This will not, however, count as 'religious education', for that is reserved for the teaching of Christianity as true. It would be a separate study of religions in their cultural context.

This summary shows an argument based on the analysis of *existing* cultural conditions. It omits the analysis of cultural *change* by which Professor McIntyre further supports his policy – an omission which will be remedied at a later point in the discussion. It is omitted from the summary because it serves largely to dramatise the need for (and possibility of) the kind of policy recommended by the rest of the argument. The policy is clear enough: religious education is to be reserved for the teaching of Christianity as true.

Religion, culture and education

'There is,' says McIntyre, 'at least an historical case for saying that in western society, it is religion, and in particular, the Christian religion, which has been the source of the values and concepts from which the culture has sprung'. The case is urged in terms of a particular culture and a particular religion; but in fact the historical case is rather highly questionable. It is at least as likely that the reverse is true and that culture has been the source of values and concepts from which religion has sprung. It is likely, for example, that the very structure of Christian theism owes as much to the world Hellenic thought (through which it passed) as to its Hebrew origins. More recent times have shown influential Christians to be more than anxious to adjust their own understanding of religious concepts and values to those of the surrounding and largely secular culture. As for concepts, consider the Christian teaching about Jesus Christ. 'Somewhere between Liddon and Gore,' writes Don Cupitt, 'a view of Christ which took shape in the fourth and fifth centuries began to collapse; and to collapse, not just in the minds of rationalist critics, but in the minds of the leading churchmen of the day.'[2] He goes on to attribute both rise and fall 'at least in part' to social and political causes. In the world of values Christianity has shown even clearer evidence of its adaptability to impulses deriving from the surrounding culture. Church leaders have been only slightly slower than the British Parliament to adopt established formulations of value - as witness, the changing attitudes to divorce and to sexual morality. Religion is capable not only of inspiring the culture but of being subject at even a very fundamental level to impulses provided by it.

It is only with some equivocation that we can affirm religion as being the bedrock of culture and then make an educational policy out of that affirmation. Clearly there is a relationship between religion and culture; but the relationship is subject to many levels of ambiguity. There is clearly a gap between popular and official religion. There can clearly be a gap between the concepts and values of the culture and those of its institutionalised religion: from time to time culture may or may not depend on the values of even its dominant institutionalised religious forms. If education is 'culture perpetuating itself' it is by no means clear that any particular religious concepts or values (from among the range to be found within the culture) should be perpetuated. If we decided that the full range of them should be perpetuated, not all of these could be true or fundamental to the culture. The policy of supporting the culture by teaching a religion as true therefore collapses at several points of theory and practice.

An educational policy might, however, be justified if we adopt a softer version of the theory - urging not that religion is a cultural bedrock (or the source of culture's values and concepts) but that there is an interaction or dialogue between culture and religion. The importance of each to the other would be that each becomes better known by our examining their relationship. (Indeed, Professor McIntyre explicitly approves the proposition that religion should be studied in the cultural context.) In so far as education was 'culture perpetuating itself' it would seek to perpetuate the living cultural situation in all its dynamic and capacity for development. To tell the truth about religion in its cultural context would be to show encounters between religions and encounters of religions with secular values and concepts. But these realities could not be shown unless religions were treated *together* in the curriculum – while conversely it would tell an untruth about the nature of religion if it (or rather, its favoured and fashionable form) were preserved in educational apartheid.

A sense of crisis

Professor McIntyre's theory of cultural change tends to dramatise choices which a more subtle appreciation would put in a different light. He regards traditionally dominant cultures as withstanding all sorts of shock from even 'sharp criticism' of their basic values. Indeed, protest and disaffection (manifested in what he in any case calls 'expressions of the culture') are in general allocated a place at what he calls 'the negative pole of the cultural field' – that is, they are contained by the cultural field in which they occur. A 'new culture' is said to emerge when 'the values and concepts of the community are no longer either accepted or rejected, but simply ignored; when the imagery which has sustained the several expressions of the culture of the community becomes irrelevant and then, new values with the attendant imagery take over'. Or perhaps not even then, for so much is preserved for the continuity of the established culture: 'At that point we have a new culture, or, depending on the magnitude of the expression, a new form of cultural expression'. We may say that this is a kind of cultural catastrophe-theory. Its bearing on the general argument is that it puts teachers of RE into the position of courting a cultural catastrophe, or averting it by teaching Christianity as true. Presumably all sorts of protest and disaffection from the pupils will testify to the vitality of the tradition that is being defended before them. It will not do. Cultures are not uprooted only by the onset of catastrophe. Developments cannot be assessed one by one for the profundity of their attack on the existing culture. Teachers cannot be put into the artificially contrived position of defending a citadel until it has finally fallen about their ears. And they cannot be put into a position which makes them arbiters of complex processes of change by the adoption of policies which prefer one pattern of change to another. However we characterise Britain's multicultural situation, the impact of religions upon each other – and the impact of the godless upon all of them – will remain. And a religious education which fails to reflect the continuity of this process will fail the dominant and the subordinate cultures equally.

But even if this catastrophe-theory were correct, a decision to avoid the catastrophe must be essentially an act of preference and will. It cannot count as a decision to be deemed appropriate in consequence of the analysis of culture, for the imminence of cultural catastrophe might be held to point just as much to the degeneracy of the culture as to its endangered vitality. There is nothing in the analysis (apart from the fact of a previous cultural dominance) to require that we should protect either the degenerate or the endangered. In such a situation we could not know with any security whether the emergent 'new culture' was less desirable than its predecessor. Indeed, the balance of judgement might properly lie with a support of the emergent 'new culture' on the grounds that we should be taking the facts of the cultural situation the more seriously. Of course it might not. The argument is only that there is a choice of policies and that a preference has to be exercised for which the cultural situation offers but ambiguous guidance. One extraneous factor may however be relevant. A choice in favour of the established culture would contain the currently subordinate cultures in their position of subordination. The person McIntyre calls 'the stranger within the gate' would stay at the threshold.

Truth

The concern for truth and for the treatment of truth-claims in the classroom is indeed something to be taken very seriously. In urging that we should teach Christianity as true, Professor McIntyre does not show that any Christian doctrine, value or concept is specifically true. He argues only that Christianity is the religion of Britain's dominant culture and that to teach it as true fulfils the responsibility of education towards the culture. It is at best an indirect argument for the purpose. The weight of tradition and the size of a following suggests that a religion's truth-claims merit serious consideration, but neither factor can be decisive of the truth. The truth of Christianity is indeed compelling for the Christian, and it is to be hoped that pupils gain some sense of this as well as the opportunity to make their own response. What teachers cannot do is to institutionalise what most people would regard as a judgement or conclusion by requiring that any religion be taught as the truth. The appropriate institutional framework will be one that requires the pursuit of truth, the propagation of an inquiry, and not merely the transmission of received conclusions.

In a tribute to what he calls 'the old-fashioned method of religious education' Professor McIntyre finds it to have had a right instinct in seeing 'that somehow it had to elicit from the educands commitment to the faith, or at least awareness that commitment was of the essence of the matter'. But awareness that commitment is 'of the essence of the matter' is something more than a pale shadow of commitment itself. It is something to be valued on educational grounds. It teaches something that is true about the nature of religion and what it means to take a faith seriously. The unbeliever who appreciates this has gone some way in a process of religious education. The committed believer who appreciates it goes some way to making commitment a conscious and educated achievement. A possible indictment of 'the old-fashioned method of religious education' is that its pursuit of commitment was known by the pupils and by the general public to be at the expense of relevant challenges presented by other world faiths and by secularist and humanist opinion. It did not meet the range of opinion to be found in the breadth of the traditional culture, let alone the perceptions of other cultures and faiths; and to that extent it was felt to be a propagandist and infantile offering. If we are inclined to think nostalgically about the old-fashioned religious education, we should consider the evidence (which is all around us) that it produced an adult public whose understanding of religion remains markedly immature, if not positively infantile. If we would have a religious education to remedy that situation, there must be a framework of reference which is demonstrably related to the adult world of opinion and belief. It must comprehend a range of faiths. If it does so, and if it reflects something of the range of disciplines by which religion is understood in the adult world, it will be the more likely to meet the range of questioning which will in any case come from the pupils.

So far the demand is for an inquiry into truth and a world religions frame of reference. That does not mean the prohibition of truth-claims as an issue in the classroom. Nor does it lend the teacher's authority to the belief that all religions are equally true (or, for that matter, false), or that the truth is a compendium of them all – though distinguished opinion may be cited for all those points of view. Nor does it mean that pupils or teachers should suspend their commitment (or pretend that they have none) in the classroom. It means that, as in the study of any controversial subject where the teacher is likely to hold strong personal opinions, the professional duty will be to uphold the values of rational enquiry and to indicate the paths on which it may be pursued. That cannot be done without putting the questions or without being prepared to say what one's own opinion is. There may be educational danger in an authoritative opinion from the teacher but chiefly so where the values of rational enquiry have already been made subservient to dogmatism or propaganda. Our position as teachers will not be *neutral* in the sense that we are careless of our own convictions or cynical of the very possibility of truth. It will however be *impartial* in the sense that we are as prepared to countenance rival conclusions as well as those to which we are personally attached, and in the sense that our concern for truth is just sufficiently larger than our love of the self. The distinction is an important one, with significant bearings on the value of classroom discussion.[3]

We must expect that this will lead to a *range* of decisions and judgements on the part of our pupils: it will be so whatever our programme of religious education, and our primary responsibility is to see that their growth is towards an informed and judicious capacity to defend whatever their conclusions may be. In asking our pupils of varying faiths and philosophies to approach *together* some of the most exciting and important questions – questions of meaning, significance, value and (indeed) truth – we shall hope to establish for their maturity the attitudes which may make adult interactions better informed and more constructive. Truth-claims certainly do matter – though it is to be understood that we should expect ordinary good manners and a concern for the feelings of others in their consideration. What may be readily agreed is that none of this is possible in a merely descriptive religious education.

But where is this offensive descriptivism? As a reference to the 'phenomenology of religion' or to the six dimensions of religion which the Schools Council derived from Professor Ninian Smart and passed on with its recommendation[4] – surely two of the major influences of recent years – it would at the very least be ill-considered. Professor McIntyre does not specifically cite the offending 'redesigned curriculum for religious education' or attribute the offensive descriptivism to anything more precise than 'some circles in Britain'. The most favourable explanation must be that Professor McIntyre regards a neutrally descriptive religious education as the only alternative to teaching a religion as true. Now, this is simply not the case. Description of course there must be, but it should not be assumed that the art of accurate and appropriate description by-passes the critical intelligence or makes no contribution to the apprehension of truth. It is no necessary assumption of a multi-faith religious education that truth-claims should be avoided, and it is not widely assumed that *mere* description is the essence of religious education. In that case any descriptivist 'Rake's Progress' (McIntyre's description) from neutrality through subjectivism and indifferentism to humanism, agnosticism and atheism, cannot be laid at the door of multi-faith religious education. There is something rather odd about that list, anyway. Humanism, agnosticism and atheism would seem to be fairly well-defined and conscientious positions, hardly the further outposts of subjectivism or indifferentism.

Christianity

A concern for the Christian tradition must be close to the heart of religious education in Britain. We may reasonably expect to give to Christianity a more extensive treatment than we give to other faiths, for it has in our society a more substantial presence. For many of us it has been the all-important framework for perceptions of value and meaning. For all of us in western society it is the tradition which has embodied a dialogue between fact and value, between the actual and the transcendent. The possibility that an encounter with this tradition should be diminished or even withdrawn from our children is indeed deeply shocking. What we have to understand is that a multi-faith religious education offers advantages for the appreciation of the Christian tradition which were denied in the days when its primacy was unique in religious education. As

Owen Cole points out in the next chapter, the question of teaching Christianity was not seriously and critically faced until more imaginative ways of teaching other faiths were a matter for debate. The old teaching of Christianity suffered more than anything from its assumption that it was informing young Christians about their own faith – ignoring the probability that God died (so far as our society is concerned) not with the writings of Harvey Cox and Paul Van Buren but slowly and progressively from the rise of scientific empiricism in the seventeenth century, and ignoring the alternative schemes of concept and value which derived from urbanisation and the facts of class-consciousness. In the multi-faith context I have seen students learning something about the meaning and value of faith which had previously escaped them in the predominantly secular atmosphere of British society. To teach Christianity among the world religions will be in part to teach it afresh and as though to the unbelieving and the uninformed. Effective religious education will be more likely for the achievement of at least that much realism.

Notes and references

1 John McIntyre, *Multi-Culture and Multi-Faith Societies: Some Examinable Assumptions*, Occasional Papers No. 3, Edward Hulmes (ed.), (The Farmington Institute for Christian Studies, Oxford).

2 Don Cupitt, 'The Christ of Christendom', in John Hick (ed.), *The Myth of God Incarnate* (SCM, 1977), p. 137.

3 See Charles Bailey, 'Neutrality and rationality in teaching', in David Bridges and Peter Scrimshaw (eds), *Values and Authority in Schools* (Hodder & Stoughton, 1975), especially pp. 126–7.

4 *Religious Education in Secondary Schools*, Schools Council Working Paper No. 36 (Evans/Methuen, 1971).

Further reading

That pluralism was an excuse for secularisation of the schools and the demotion of Christianity was but one of the claims made by E. R. Norman in 'The threat to religion', *Black Paper 1977*, C. B. Cox and Rhodes Boyson (eds) (Temple Smith). The chapter in this present book responds to the more temperate and systematic argument of Professor John McIntyre, *Multi-Culture and Multi-Faith Societies: Some Examinable Assumptions*, Occasional Papers No. 3, Edward Hulmes (ed.) (The Farmington Institute for Christian Studies, Oxford). Something of the significant and positive contribution to religious education made by ethnic minorities can be seen in *East Comes West*, Peggy Holroyde (ed.)

(Commission for Racial Equality, 1970); Alan James, *Sikh Children in Britain* (OUP, 1974); D. G. Bowen (ed.), *Hinduism in England* (second edn, Duckworth, 1982); and Brian Gates (ed.), *Afro-Caribbean Religions* (Ward Lock, 1980). There are sections on Islam and Hinduism in Britain in companion volumes in the present series: Richard Tames, *Approaches to Islam* and Duncan Macpherson, *Approaches to Hinduism*.

7
Christian Studies in Schools

W. Owen Cole

A number of factors have influenced the writing of this chapter and it might be helpful to the reader if these are mentioned at the very outset. First, my original training in theology and teaching experience were traditional and Christian. Secondly, an interest in learning about and teaching other religious faiths developed, accompanied by a methodology which was multidimensional and phenomenological; though only once in my professional career has a year gone by without my teaching Christian studies in one form or another, usually under the heading of Christian Origins, sometimes as Church History. Thirdly, I have never forgotten the comment of one of my students on returning from a very successful teaching practice in a middle school. She said that the children enjoyed learning about Islam and Sikhism, but found Christianity dull and boring. As a Christian she was upset by this. As a Christian and a teacher I share her disquiet. Fourthly, there has been an upsurge of interest in teaching Christianity in schools which, whilst it is to be welcomed, needs to be greeted with caution. My purpose in this chapter is to consider some of the issues raised by teaching Christian studies in schools in the United Kingdom in the hope that those producing syllabuses, or, more especially, those teaching Christianity next Monday morning will have cause to reflect.

We have never taught Christianity in our schools, colleges, and universities, so for most teachers the challenge is not to reinstate it but to begin teaching it for the first time. The reasons for this situation are not difficult to find. The 1870 and 1944 Education Acts were based on the assumption that England and Wales were pluralistically Christian. The clauses governing school religion, therefore, were taken to encourage, or even enforce approaches to worship and study which inhibited a multidimensional exploration of the phenomenon of Christianity even supposing some visionary had proposed it. The Bible, supplemented by stories of Christian pioneers who transcended denominationalism, provided teachers with the raw material for their lessons.

The school's role was to supplement what was supposed to be happening elsewhere in society. As recently as 1960 the Reverend

Michael Bache, the secretary of the Institute of Christian Education, spoke to the newly opened Harlow branch on the theme of religious education being a three-legged stool of parent, church and school supporting the child. Knowledge and a sound understanding of the Christian faith was the school's task in this learning and nurturing partnership. For these and other reasons, not least the diet of biblical studies which had been the staple education of most teachers who had some qualification for teaching the subject, Christianity in school really meant the Bible, supplemented by an act of worship. For some pupils who reached the sixth form there might be an added element of theology, sometimes Pauline, more often Johannine (one suspects the influence of William Temple's *Readings in the Fourth Gospel*).

Now the situation is different. We cannot assume that children are receiving Christian nurture at home or are coming under the influence of the churches. The three-legged stool has become a shooting-stick. Coincidentally, there has also been much questioning of the nurturing function of maintained schools and surprisingly a broad consensus of opinion that they should not be places where children are subjected to Christian evangelism or upbringing. In 1969 the British Council of Churches observed, 'It should be clear that the aim of religious education in county schools is to deepen understanding and insight, not to proselytise.'[1] The Church of England *Durham Report* of the following year made the same kind of assertion.

> The aim of religious education should be to explore the place and significance of religion in human life and so make a distinctive contribution to each pupil's search for a faith by which to live . . . To press for acceptance of a particular faith or belief system is the duty and privilege of the Churches and other similar religious bodies. It is certainly not the task of a teacher in a county school.[2]

This view is the one accepted by the writer in his attempt to place Christianity in the context of religious studies. It is not easy to pick representative quotations out of the important essays edited by Norman Richards for the Association of Christian Teachers under the title *Aims in Religious Education* (1976). The authors are naturally eager to defend the teaching of the Christian faith in schools (incidentally I know of no one who opposes this wish, save the extreme secularist fringe of the British Humanist Association and the National Secular Society), but they are also aware of the pluralistic context in which they are operating. Mr Richards' own chapter analyses very carefully the real situation of the Christian teacher in a society which is post-Christian and does not, for the most part, support any wish that he may have to use the classroom for evangelism. Eric Bramhall sums up his thoughts on the aims of secondary school RE as follows:

Two main aims have been dealt with in this chapter. The importance of an understanding of Christianity has been recognised, and the view has been argued that there is a sense in which the concept of 'evangelism through education' may be valid if evangelism is seen in very broad terms. This would derive from the fact that Christianity (like other major religions) has an affective area which includes commitment and personal involvement. But it has to be recognised that to concentrate on Christianity alone could hardly be seen as justifiable for an RE which aims to initiate into the religious mode of awareness. Hence the teaching of Christianity must be part of the wider aim of initiating pupils into religion as an activity which tries to make sense of and find meaning for life and man's place in the scheme of things. Such teaching would recognise the variations given by the different religions in their answers to these questions, and the whole exercise would come under the general educational desire to establish truth.[3]

That the justification for RE must be educational seems to be a matter upon which there is little disagreement and it is only those outside our classrooms and staffrooms who appear to expect teachers to undertake burdens which many parents and society at large have repudiated. Professional teachers, however optimistic and inspired by the Holy Spirit they may be, know that there are practical limits to what they might wish to attempt and hope to achieve in schools where colleagues and pupils represent the variety of values found in the world outside.

Besides the repudiation of nurturing or evangelising as aims proper and possible for the teacher of RE five other factors exist which should not be ignored by those hoping to teach about Christianity.

Firstly, we cannot assume any sympathy with Christianity on the part of teachers or pupils. In fact the church on the corner often represents something which they no longer respect or find relevant, though they may feel guilty about it. (Here Christianity in Britain faces the kind of problem which Islam might face in Turkey or Buddhism in Burma.) Teacher and child are emotionally attached to or alienated from Christianity in a way that is not true of Judaism, Islam, Hinduism, Sikhism, or Buddhism – perhaps in that order. The enthusiasm for teaching about Buddhism found among many secondary school specialists in RE may be related to the fact that in almost every respect it stands furthest away from Christianity and therefore presents no emotional embarrassment to teacher or child. We all know the warts of Christianity as a phenomenon, but not those of Buddhism; and whether the Buddha ever lived or is only the personification of a particular Indian philosophy will not worry us as the questioning of the historicity of Jesus might. Let it be noted, however, that he who sharpens the tools of scepticism for use against the miracles of the Buddha or Guru Nanak must not be surprised when they are turned against those of Jesus; children tend to be less discriminating than their teachers. The reply I once heard, that Jesus was the Son of God, cannot be expected to convince all teenagers, even in Ripon or Wells. In Britain, as in France or New Zealand and the United States, the teaching of

Christianity is attended by emotional problems not encountered in teaching about Buddhism or Islam.

Secondly, we cannot any longer assume a cultural general knowledge of Christianity. Perhaps we never should have done for it is possible to hear middle-aged and well-educated men and women on radio or television programmes demonstrating a woeful ignorance of biblical fact accompanied by very peculiar theological notions. However, teachers are now also aware of children arriving in school at the age of five who have never heard the name Jesus. Most syllabuses of past years seemed to assume some kind of working acquaintance with the faith. Now we must start from scratch – but with a potentially hostile bias in mind.

Thirdly, we are also aware of the considerable theological pluralism which exists within Christianity, not between the denominations but within each. Dare anyone say what the Christian view on euthanasia or divorce is – or even what the Anglican position is? The Roman Catholic Church may appear more monolithic but those near it are aware that it has many voices which do not always sing in harmony. This pluralism has always been one reason for my doubts about the wisdom of those wanderings through the ethical wilderness discussing drugs, sex, abortion, violence, crime and punishment and the other topics which constitute courses masquerading as religious studies in so many schools. The Christian ethics element in a Christian studies syllabus must not ignore this pluralism, pretending that it does not exist. It is an essential ingredient of any real study of Christianity, distinguishing that religion from Islam, for example.

Fourthly, the approach to the study of religions is changing. Textually based theological studies may still be the diet in some universities but to an increasing extent theology is only part of a wider examination which explores religious phenomena comprehensively ranging from mysticism, worship, sociology, to scriptures, beliefs, and historical developments. This broader approach has long been applied to Judaism, Islam and other faiths. Students and school children find it stimulating and it would seem to be a methodology suitable for studying Christianity.

The fifth factor is the world religions context of Christianity. This is particularly important with regard to Judaism. Once in our ignorance many of us believed that the New Testament concept of Messiah was the only one which any sensible and fair-minded person living in the first century could accept. The problem of the early church was that the Jews were not fair-minded, they did not wish to face the truth which was staring them in the face. Some of us are now aware that the Handel's Messiah or Matthaean picture of the Old Testament as a document pointing to Jesus is partial and not Jewish. We realise that the New Testament is polemical, that it certainly does not present the whole truth about the Judaism of Jesus' day, and perhaps (dare we admit it) the writers were not interested in providing a true picture of Judaism at all. The New Testament conceals the rich variety of first century Judaism of which the Christian community was a part, under a thick lacquer of legalism. John's gospel especially, and to some extent Matthew's, are seen to be potentially anti-semitic, as anyone who teaches Jewish students will soon discover. Those of us who have also studied Islam may no longer believe Richard the Lionheart to be a hero; much more important, we may now know that it is possible to accept the Virgin Birth and his messiahship and still deny the divinity of Jesus. Islam teaches both but regards Jesus only as a man, though as a great prophet.

There is another side to this particular coin, namely that when we see the New Testament as a reinterpretation of the Jewish Torah or Tenakh we become aware of the genius of the first-century Church for the first time. It and its Lord can be appreciated in the context of a real, live, and dynamic movement attempting to demonstrate that Jesus was the one promised in the Hebrew scriptures. The New Testament emerges as a kind of oral Torah intended to explain sacred texts of Judaism. Something of the distinctiveness of Christianity starts to emerge, perhaps for the first time, as we look at the over-familiar in a new way. By doing so we have begun to be fair to both Judaism and Christianity.

Added to all these considerations is the final deterrent, the dauntingly rich variety of Christianity. Teaching biblical studies has helped us to escape this challenge, but once we regard the religion as a phenomenon we are confronted by a mystery at once tremendous and fascinating.

All these difficulties may probably be reduced to one, that of distancing ourselves from the religion which is closest to our hearts, most accessible to our scrutiny, and most familiar to our experience. The problems raised are no less acute in reality for the person who would study Hinduism or Judaism, and probably Buddhism and Islam, but we see them as being less formidable because the accident of birth has naturally distanced us from these faiths. Also the scholars who have transmitted them to us have often already decided what is most worthy of our attention and we are compelled to accept the précis which they offer. The summaries may correspond to the essence in the case of studies of Islam and Sikhism, but Hinduism has clearly been less well served. It is still almost impossible to enter the ritual dimension of Hinduism guided by western writers, for their interest has invariably been in the texts and the philosophical systems. One has to turn to the anthropologists to find out what the religious practices of Hindus are, only to discover that these scholars generally have little interest in the religious meaning of the actions or the myths upon which they are based. Judaism seems to have fared better, and significantly its interpreters have often been Jews. They give the student of Christianity hope that he can successfully describe and analyse the tradition of which he is also a member. It may not be necessary for us to call in Jews or Muslims to achieve the balance and perspective which eludes us. This is not to say that such men as Klausner, Montefiore, Sandmel and Vermes do not have much to teach the student of Christianity;[4] as Jews they can discern niceties and essentials which the

Gentile or the believer immersed in the traditional interpretations is likely to miss. However, it would appear obvious that the distancing problem can only be overcome if teachers and students of Christianity are willing to adopt the same kind of stance and methodology as those who specialise in the world's other religions.

When we turn our attention from the phenomenon of Christianity to the classroom a new range of issues confronts us. Teachers are notoriously, but very properly, down-to-earth. They will quickly point out that the resources for teaching Christianity in the way suggested in this essay are lacking. Most textbooks assume belief, they are written from an 'our Lord' standpoint, and they also presuppose considerable general knowledge on the part of the reader. Slides and filmstrips are obviously more open but the notes that accompany them are not. Often it is assumed that pictures of the familiar – parish communion, a baptism, or a wedding – are unnecessary, yet these are important starting points, especially for the teacher of younger children, and many children are growing up in a secular family which has contact with organised religion only at times of bereavement. In terms of resources Christianity stands where other religions were at the start of the 1970s. Then the challenge which teachers made to people like myself was to provide materials which they might use in the classroom. That need has been met; in the eighties we must provide equally well for Christianity as a world religion.

Another response of the seventies was the introduction of some O and A level syllabuses in world religions. Here again Christianity has lagged behind, keeping to a diet of monotonous biblical studies and highly predictable examination questions, relieved just a little by courses in Christian responsibility which may be more relevant but are also, if anything, less religious. It is astonishing that most children who leave our schools, especially those who have taken an O level course in religious studies, are likely to have little idea of what Christianity is, in terms of beliefs and practices.

Another issue is academic and has already been touched on, but there are one or two matters which the schoolteacher must consider which the university teacher may view differently. First, there is the need to be fair to Judaism and to Christianity. Sufficient may have been said already about the problem in general terms, but more specifically there is one A level course in Judaism which begins effectively with the destruction of the Temple in the year 70, with the result that I receive students who have taken it successfully and are surprised to learn that Jews do not accept the Handel's Messiah interpretation of their scriptures. I gather that the syllabus to which I refer omitted a study of the Jewish Bible to avoid overlap with an existing Old Testament syllabus! It must be a ground rule of religious studies that one does not misrepresent one faith in order to present another. In a society which is still inclined to antisemitism the teacher of Christianity has a special responsibility.

It is also necessary to ask how much attention should be given to biblical criticism and especially to the problem of the historical Jesus. This analytical approach to the study of religion is perhaps a distinctive feature of Christianity and as such cannot be ignored. It can have the value of liberating the essential message of Jesus from its cultural milieu, but often the exercise is misunderstood by teacher and pupil with the result that the historical Jesus becomes the object of scepticism and the Jesus of faith is ignored. In approaching the person of Muhammad we tend to concentrate on attempting to appreciate his place in Islam; perhaps we should do the same for Jesus. If children leave school knowing what the place of Jesus is within the Christian tradition perhaps we have achieved as much as we can and should.

The sheer volume of Christianity presents problems which are not going to be overcome by giving it more time. More than once an adviser has complained to me about a teacher who gives a whole term to Hinduism, especially as there are no Hindus in the school; more than once I have pointed out that this presumably means thirty-two terms of Christianity, and that somewhere the balance seems to have gone wrong! In my experience to give Christianity less time and consequently to be compelled to bring it into sharper focus is one step towards making it more interesting and more intelligible. By having to be selective we may be able to distinguish between what pupils need to know in order to understand Christianity as a living faith, and what we as theologically trained adults think they should know. By allowing Christianity to take its place in a syllabus which includes other faiths and stances for living its distinctiveness may become apparent to the teacher as well as to the student for the first time. That at any rate has been my experience.

The relationship of Christianity to other faiths is an academic issue which the teacher cannot shirk, especially in the multi-faith classroom, and I would want to argue that television, if not the settlement of Sikhs in our particular area, has made the whole world multi-faith – and that includes Norfolk and Sussex villages. Apparently universities can mount courses in Islam, Judaism, and Christianity, without considering the truth claims and personal problems which may perplex the students. The sensitive teacher cannot. Biblical views of Christianity's relationship to Judaism (far more complex than we suppose), and its traditional relationships with Judaism and Islam (and Hinduism to a lesser extent), would seem to require consideration.

There is also a group of issues which might be called religious which ought not to be ignored. These range from interfaith dialogue on the one hand to mission on the other and encompass liberation theology, the growth of indigenous churches in Africa and India, and pluralism in matters of morality. The Latin captivity of the churches is being shaken off, the Constantinian mould is being broken. It would be tragic if the Christianity syllabuses devised by schools and examining bodies were as colonialist and reactionary as some history and geography syllabuses continue to be. Christianity is neither western nor white and WASP syllabuses (White Anglo-Saxon Protestant) will not serve it or our children well, bearing in mind the speed at which the world is changing.

Having reached the end of this long catalogue of caveats the teacher may feel like leaving the ranks of the religious studies specialist for a deputy headship or some other non-RE post. I hope this will not have been the effect of what I have written so far, but I believe there is a need to challenge those who make simplistic pleas for the reinstatement of Christianity in our schools. We must not pretend that we once used to teach Christianity, and we must be wary of those who ignore the changed social, educational, religious, and theological circumstances in which we find ourselves now as compared with the 1940s and 1950s.

For those continuing to attempt to follow my arguments I must express my gratitude by suggesting, however tentatively, the form that a Christian studies syllabus might take. By the time a pupil leaves school I would hope that he or she had some understanding of the following:

Jesus: one of many Jewish teachers in a richly varied political, social, and religious milieu; what Christians believe about the meaning of his life and work; what he means to them – commitment.

Issues in early Christianity: interpreting Jesus to Judaism as Messiah (fulfilling Judaism in Matthew, replacing it in John's Gospel, but continuing to live within it in Acts); interpreting Jesus as Lord and Saviour to a Gentile world where the concept of Messiah was meaningless (for example Acts and I Corinthians); attitudes to society and the Roman State.

The Canon: what the New Testament is; its relationship to the Old Testament; its purpose.

Why Christianity is a missionary faith: its expansion, the growth of indigenous churches, current attitudes to mission; attitudes to other religions.

Authority: through examining the question 'where does authority lie?' to try to give some meaning to the divisions of Christianity but without embarking on a tedious journey through the denominations.

Worship, sacraments and festivals: the forms of worship and its purpose; the role of the clergy; the significance of baptism and the Lord's Supper; the festivals of Christmas as combinations of Christian theology and practices taken from other religions.

Christianity and the Arts: the influence of Christianity on art, architecture, music and literature.

Christian responses to political, social, scientific, and ethical questions: the criteria Christians use to make their responses; the way of personal discipleship and the way of obedience to church discipline.

The approach to such a course might be based on a number of issues, for to a large extent Christianity as a phenomenon is the sum of responses to a number of issues. For example, Jesus faced the issue of deciding how to explain himself and accomplish his mission. The apostles had to face the issue of a Judaism which rejected the claims of Jesus. There were the issues of how to worship, and whether to celebrate the nativity of Jesus –

and if so, how. There are the present issues of how to respond to moral questions like euthanasia, or to the presence of faiths which we know too well for us to dismiss them as parodies of Christianity. Their spirituality and social responsibility challenge us to take them seriously. One could go on, for the list is endless. However, beyond the detail, about which there will be disagreement, there exists the need to teach Christianity in such a way that pupils can recognise it to be a faith by which reasonable men and women can find meaning in life and in death and enter a spiritual world which they believe exists and transcends that of space and time. If this chapter has encouraged teachers to believe that this is a proper and possible though difficult task, and has invited them to address themselves to it as they are already doing to Islam, Sikhism or some other religion, it will amply have achieved my purpose. Their skills must then make the study interesting and enjoyable.

References

1 Interim Statement submitted to the Secretary of State for Education and Science by the British Council of Churches, July 1969.

2 *The Fourth R* (SPCK, 1970), p. 103.

3 *Aims in Religious Education*, Norman Richards (ed.) (Association of Christian Teachers, 1976), p. 28.

4 The most recent contribution is the new edition of Emil Schurer's *History of the Jewish People in the Time of Jesus*, Vol. 2, by Geza Vermes (T. and T. Clark, 1979). Teachers of New Testament studies should know this book and *A Jewish Understanding of the New Testament*, by S. Sandmel (New York: Ktav, 1974), though the latter work has not been without its critics.

Further reading

It is not easy to direct the reader of this chapter to other articles or books for the simple reason that it is the author's thesis that the world religions approach to Christianity has yet to begin. There are a number of items, however, which might be mentioned, starting with *Christianity in the Classroom* (CEM, 1978), a booklet containing the papers delivered at the Christian Education Movement Easter Vacation Course, held at Lincoln in 1977. This conference was probably the first of a number having Christianity in the title rather than Bible, Church, or Life of Jesus. The papers are worth reading for the important comments they make about a number of issues. However, the speakers do not appear to have considered the implications of treating Christianity as a world religion in a country where it enjoys cultural dominance. The *Shap Mailing* of 1978 contains a number of articles which begin a reappraisal, especially 'Old Testament studies – a new look', by Rabbi Douglas Charing, and 'A Jew looks at Christian biblical studies', by Hyam Maccoby. The 1979 *Shap Mailing* contains an essay entitled 'Christianity as a world religion', by Dr Frank Whaling. In *World Faiths in Education*, edited by Owen Cole (Allen & Unwin, 1978), the present writer and others frequently touch upon the task of teaching Christianity in a world religions context. The issues become apparent at a practical level in Marilyn Thomas's chapter 'World religions in a comprehensive school' in *Perspectives on World Religions*, edited by Robert Jackson (SOAS, 1978). *World Religions: A Handbook for Teachers*, edited by Owen Cole (CRE, 1977), includes an examination of resources for teaching Christianity as a world religion. Since its publication two other aids have appeared. Argus Communications have produced a resource kit on Christianity which taken as a whole is extremely useful, though Dr Howard Clark Kee's book *Christianity* adopts a historical approach which neglects areas of the faith which are related to practice. For a comprehensive survey one may now turn to Ninian Smart's *The Phenomenon of Christianity* (Collins, 1979), but this is not the kind of volume to hand to a Sikh friend who has no previous knowledge of Christianity. At CSE and O level, as well as bearing in mind the general needs of the classroom, the Chichester Project is producing materials for teaching Christianity in the open and comprehensive manner outlined in this chapter. The first four books were published by Lutterworth Educational in February, 1982. Further details may be obtained from the publisher or the director of the project, John Rankin, at West Sussex Institute of Higher Education, Bishop Otter College, Chichester. To help pupils studying Christianity alongside other religions in multi-faith syllabuses such as AEB, the present writer has produced *Five Religions in the Twentieth Century* (Hulton, 1981). This covers messengers of God, scriptures, worship, festivals, and pilgrimage. Blandford Press is publishing *Comparative Religions*, which includes a study of Christianity together with Hinduism, Judaism, Islam and Sikhism. This should also be helpful to secondary school pupils and their teachers. It will be available shortly. The recently approved JMB A level syllabus, which will be examined from 1984, is likely to draw attention to the need for more advanced books to be written on Christianity having the kind of approach and range that is to be found in books on Islam, Judaism, or Sikhism published in the last decade.

Part Three
Commitment

Introduction

The relationship between religious commitment and religious education is of perennial concern to many teachers, pupils and parents. Over the last twenty years or so there has been much debate about changing aims in RE, with many educationalists – from both inside and outside religious bodies – arguing that RE in county schools should be concerned not with the transmission of religion, but with giving pupils an understanding of religious beliefs and practices and their significance for believers. Insufficient attention has been given, however, to the question of the commitment of teachers and pupils – whether religious or not – in relation to the subject-matter of RE, and literature exclusively devoted to the topic has appeared only in the past few years. In reaction to the evangelistic tendency of earlier religious instruction, some teachers have chosen to conceal their personal views in an attempt to achieve a degree of objectivity, while others have continued in their attempt to foster faith. A few, however, have experimented in order to find educationally accept-able ways of discussing their own or their pupils' commitment in the classroom.

The growth of a world religions approach to RE has highlighted and complicated the issue of commitment and RE, not least in multi-faith schools, and there is a need to help teachers and parents to clarify it. This is what the next three chapters attempt to do.

In Chapter 8 several issues concerned with commitment are tackled. A reply is made to those who argue that in order to understand a religion a person must be committed to that faith. Next the view is advanced that many teachers, having a wide range of commitments – religious and otherwise – are capable of the sympathetic treatment of world religions in schools. Finally it is maintained that there are appropriate occasions in the classroom when the commitment of both teachers and pupils can be used as a valuable teaching resource. Note that the commitment of pupils is also discussed by Brian Gates in Chapter 11.

In Chapter 9 John Hull attacks the simplistic view that those RE teachers who are also religious people will, as a matter of course, wish to pass on their beliefs to pupils. There are *some* religious RE teachers, says Hull, who will encourage in their pupils a mixture of responses to religions being studied precisely *because of* their (the teachers') religious commitment. In developing his argument he classifies teaching processes into two types – convergent and divergent. The convergent teacher assumes that his or her personal faith and the content of lessons are the same, whereas the divergent teacher makes no such assumption. Convergence occurs only in certain kinds of teaching – nurture, evangelism and indoctrination being examples of convergent teaching processes. Readers will find John Hull's careful definition of these terms helpful in distinguishing kinds of teaching that may be morally acceptable or even desirable in certain contexts – for example, within faith communities or families – from those that might be more generally considered to be unethical. Education (in contrast to nurture, evangelism and indoctrination) is a divergent teaching process, involving no fixed attempt to transmit religious beliefs to children.

The key question for Hull is whether the divergent RE teacher who is also religiously committed should suppress his or her commitment: 'Must religious education teachers, in having open minds, also have empty hearts?' Hull's answer is that religious commitment *can* illuminate good educational practice, but only if there is a consistency between the teacher's *religious* commitment and his or her *educational* commitment, that is commitment to the values which underpin the notion of divergence. Such educational values include a concern for all pupils, irrespective of their views or beliefs, a desire that pupils should be encouraged to think for themselves and the promotion among pupils of a sense of critical inquiry.

It is likely that within each of the major world religions there will be *some* varieties of religious belief that will facilitate divergence. Religiously committed teachers who want to be religious educators, argues Hull, must explore such areas in finding theologies which permit the coherence of religious and educational commitments.

Raymond Hammer, in Chapter 10, offers an example of the kind of theology that would permit the Christian RE teacher to teach divergently. He sympathises with the committed Christian who feels perplexed in the face of a diversity of faiths, but also discourages him from burying his head in the sand; there can be no shirking the fact of pluralism, either in the world at large or in our own society. In arguing that the Christian must come to terms with other faiths, Dr Hammer asserts first that the study of world religions should emerge from the Christian's understanding of God and the world, and second that the study of different faiths can illuminate the Christian's own faith.

Hammer supports his first assertion by reference to the Christian notion of God's universal love for all mankind. He does not claim that all religious faith is essentially the same, but rather that Christians have a double loyalty, to what is distinctive about their faith and to the generality of the human race.

Such a double commitment enables the Christian to learn from other faiths, whether about prayer, spirituality and religious experience or about moral and political values (note that *learning from* religion is a notion explored further in the context of RE by Michael Grimmitt in Chapter 12). Learning from others, however, should not be confined to an academic search for understanding. It should involve *meeting people*, exchanging ideas and experiences with them. In this respect our plural society, and multi-faith schools in particular, have a great deal to offer Christian teachers, pupils and parents.

Further issues relevant to an analysis of the relationship between religious education and commitment – especially the question of treating the truth-claims of religions in RE and the important distinction between neutrality and impartiality (in relation to the role of the teacher) – are discussed by Dennis Starkings (Chapter 6).

R.J.

8

Commitment and the Teaching of World Religions

Robert Jackson

Commitment and aims

One of my former students, let us call him Peter, made a visit to a state secondary school as part of his preparation for a spell of school practice. Peter was greeted by the head of religious education - we'll call him Trevor - with the words 'Are you for Christ? If you're not you've no place here.' Heated discussion followed which resulted in Peter applying to go to a different school for teaching practice.

We appear to have here a straightforward disagreement about religious commitment: 'Should the RE teacher be a committed Christian?' But we also have a dispute over *aims*. Trevor had a frankly missionary aim, and he still preaches his version of the Gospel in a way many have increasingly recognised as unproductive. Peter's basic aim, however, was more in line with the 1978 Hampshire syllabus which states that 'the principal aim of religious education in schools within the public sector is to enable pupils to understand the nature of religious beliefs and practices and the importance and influence of these in the minds of believers'.[1] Peter would claim that this is a reasonable aim in a democratic society embracing a diversity of non-religious and religious views, and that there is no convincing reason why it should not be adopted by teachers of RE whatever their own personal commitment.

Commitment and understanding

Peter shares with the writers of such recent Agreed syllabuses as those of Hampshire, Avon and Humberside the assumption that people are capable of understanding religious beliefs regardless of their religious commitment or lack of it. There have been, however, challenges to this assumption. The challengers do not attack recent Agreed syllabuses - indeed the main critics published their material in or before 1973, several years before the new wave of Agreed syllabuses appeared in print. But if their arguments are valid then many widely used syllabuses are based on questionable assumptions. There are two different viewpoints that assert a very close relationship between 'understanding religion' (or 'religious beliefs') and 'commitment to religion' (or 'religious beliefs'). Variants of these positions are sometimes formulated by those with a vested interest in evangelism in the classroom or by opponents of the study of world religions in schools.

Understanding religion, according to the first viewpoint, involves participation in theological reasoning and religious worship. The second, and stronger, position claims that religious understanding presupposes religious commitment.

In advancing the first view, W. D. Hudson argues that since education is a process of initiation into certain pursuits, each characterised by a concept or set of concepts, religious education (as distinct from the scientific or historical study of religion) is initiation into religious belief in its two aspects of theology and devotion.[2] Further, in emphasising the performative function of religious language – that is that religious utterances are not merely *descriptive* of acts such as worship, but are themselves the *performance* of such acts – Hudson claims that in order to understand it the pupil must engage in theology and worship.

One objection to Hudson's argument lies in an ambiguity in the notion of initiation into a pursuit or discipline. Initiation into theology could involve practice in elucidating one's own religious ideas, but it could also involve the sympathetic study of the writings and pronouncements of theologians in order to understand their ideas and their arguments. The former interpretation of initiation into theology involves the student's religious commitment, but the latter does not.

A second objection concerns Hudson's claim that the only way to understand the performative nature of religious language is through doing theology or participating in worship. Here Hudson underestimates the human capacities of imagination and empathy. As Peter Gardner drily remarks, 'Bachelors and spinsters can understand what the bride and groom are doing in a marriage ceremony, the calm and shy can recognise the speech acts of the politician without ever having stood on the hustings, and you do not have to be a fast bowler to know that an appeal can be much more than a question'.[3]

In fairness to Hudson it should be said that in advocating participation in theology and worship he takes pains to avoid the charge of indoctrination by distinguishing between the 'form' and 'content' of theology and devotion. 'Form' refers to the logical form of thinking constituted by the concept of God while 'content' refers to specific religious beliefs and devotional practices. But it is difficult to see how this distinction could be maintained in the classroom and Hudson does not indicate how the teacher can initiate children into theology and devotion without their becoming committed to particular beliefs.

The second viewpoint is strongly influenced by the later writings of the philosopher Ludwig Wittgenstein and it proposes that we cannot understand, even in principle, the claims of someone from a belief system radically different from our own. It is argued that since our 'world' is determined by the concepts that we have, by the language that we use, it follows that those committed to a particular way of life or 'form of life' with its own religious language – say Hinduism – may be unable, as a matter of principle, to understand the beliefs of those who belong to another way of life – say Christianity – except insofar as the two ways of life may overlap to some limited degree. So D. Z. Phillips, a supporter of this position, writes: 'Religious language is not an interpretation of how things are but determines how things are for the believer. The saint and the atheist do not interpret the same world in different ways. They see different worlds.'[4] This view presupposes that a 'form of life' such as a religion can be understood only by a person who is committed to it. A similar philosophical position is adopted by Roger Marples in an article discussing the possibility of religious education.[5] Marples argues that since, in his view, religious understanding presupposes religious belief, it is not possible to pursue an approach to religious education in which children are expected to understand religious beliefs from the point of view of the believer, while at the same time remaining free to reject those beliefs.

The view of religious language shared by Phillips and Marples has certain consequences which are likely to turn away many of those superficially attracted to it, whether they be theists or atheists. Firstly, it appears to confine God to the way of life in which the concept of 'God' is used: as D. Z. Phillips says,

> The religious believer must be a participant in a shared language. He must learn the use of religious concepts. What he learns is religious language; a language which he participates in along with other believers. What I am suggesting is that to know how to use this language is to know God.[6]

God exists, it seems, only within the 'form of life', and hence within the minds of believers.

Secondly, this view of religious language implies that truth is relative to each 'form of life'. There are rules for truth and falsity *within* religions, but since members of different forms of life use different concepts – indeed, says Phillips, see 'different worlds' – there can be no disagreement, for instance, between atheist and theist. Marples' view that there is no distinction between understanding religious beliefs and recognising them to be true also implies that the believer's religious concepts are different from those used by the unbeliever in rejecting religious claims and leads to the same conclusion, namely that the theist and the atheist cannot disagree with each other about religious matters.

An alternative view is that we see the same 'world' in different ways, and that our various commitments involve beliefs which may turn out to be true or false. A person may be committed to theism, and this commitment involves that person's belief in God's existence; but it may be the case that God does not exist. This position also allows for intellectual doubt; a committed Christian, in the face of personal suffering, may have doubts about the omnipotence and benevolence of God. But those doubts do not necessarily indicate a change in that person's beliefs. Further, although it may be difficult in practice, for various reasons, to understand the concepts, beliefs and rituals of someone from another religion or culture, such understanding is not ruled out in principle. Commitments are not entirely self-contained within any particular way of life, be it religious or not.

On this view there can be degrees of understanding; understanding is not an all or nothing affair. Thus the atheist, in principle, can have a formal understanding of Christian concepts in so far as he or she can give examples of what constitutes, say, sin, grace and faith within Christianity.[7] Likewise the Christian can have a formal understanding of such Hindu concepts as *dharma* and *karma*. Similarly an atheist can have a formal understanding of religious beliefs, and of the relationship between various religious and other – for example moral or political – beliefs that may be encountered within a particular religion or sect. In so far as religious rituals and ceremonies are linked with beliefs (say, the Muslim postures for prayer or the baptism of an infant in Christianity), these too can be understood by an atheist.

Difficulties arise when one begins to talk of understanding the emotional side of religion – what it *feels* like to be a worshipper for example. There are obvious difficulties in attempting to understand how Christians feel when receiving communion, or how Hindus feel when engaging in *bhakti* (loving devotion) since followers of a particular religion do not necessarily share the same beliefs nor do they all take part in the same ceremonies and rituals. Further, emotional responses, even within a tightly-knit group of like-minded people, may vary considerably from person to person. Thus, although it *may* be possible to empathise with a body of worshippers feeling an emotion such as awe, it makes more sense to attempt to understand how a particular *individual* feels during an act of worship, a mystical experience or whatever. The student needs not only to understand the relevant concepts and beliefs but also needs an account from the worshipper or mystic of his or her feelings and experiences. On the basis of this information many students will be able to empathise with the believer, will be able to use their faculties of imagination in putting themselves in another's shoes, and in so doing will achieve an understanding of that person's feelings. If the student's own religious commitment is close to that of the believer being studied this may be a help in understanding the believer's feelings, but there is no guarantee that this will be the case.

The critic might respond by suggesting that RE teachers are less ambitious than other educators in expecting their pupils to achieve a less than full understanding of their object of study. In the words of Roger Marples,

> If those who call themselves religious educators are concerned with anything other than full understanding they are unique in this respect, for it is, or should be, the goal of all those concerned with the education of the young to try to bring about the fullest kind of understanding possible.[8]

In reply one might say that educators certainly should want to develop 'the fullest understanding possible' but it does not follow that they delude themselves into thinking that full understanding is always a possibility. The RE teacher can be no more certain that a student has fully understood a believer's religious feelings than the teacher of art can be sure that his or her students have a total understanding of a painting or the teacher of literature that his or her students completely understand the emotional life of a character in a novel or play.

Varieties of commitment

I have argued that some understanding of a religion, whichever it is, is not conditional on or identical with commitment to the beliefs of that faith. Thus I would conclude that RE syllabuses which aim to foster an understanding of a variety of religions are workable in theory. But what sorts of teachers are likely in practice to be able to teach successfully to such broad aims? Will the teacher's own religious commitment be a help or a hindrance in developing in pupils an understanding of a number of religions? It might be useful to make a few distinctions before attempting to answer this question.

Firstly, there is an ambiguity in saying that someone is committed to a religion or faith such as Christianity. In one sense, 'Christianity' is the name for a whole family of religious positions. This ambiguity sometimes leads to a facile distinction being drawn between the deeply committed person and the believer whose commitment is shallow. Turning back to our earlier example, it may appear superficially that Trevor, the teacher, was a deeply committed believer while Peter, the student, was not. As a matter of fact, *both* are committed Christians. The key difference lies in the range and generality of the beliefs to which each is committed. Trevor, on the one hand, has a very specific view of divine revelation. God's commands are revealed in the scriptures as a set of rules which are to be followed to the letter. Peter, on the other hand, has a much more general view of revelation – God reveals himself to humanity in many and various ways – and Peter is much more interested in general principles derived from biblical sources than in specific commandments when trying, for example, to work out a Christian position on some current moral question. One could list Trevor's and Peter's beliefs. There would be some overlap but there would also be some contradictions, for example, over whether there is anything of God in Hinduism that is not derived directly from Christian influence. But we would also find that both Peter and Trevor are *equally* committed to their respective beliefs.

Christians like Peter, it should be said, are not the only liberal religionists mistakenly regarded by some of their conservative counter-parts as lacking genuine commitment. In their book on Liberal Judaism, rabbis John Rayner and Bernard Hooker affirm their commitment to the Jewish faith in the following way:

> The fact that we are reformers of Judaism does not make us less devoted to it. On the contrary, it is an earnest of our devotion to it. You don't bother to reform what you despise; you just leave it alone. You don't expend time, thought, energy and money on something you don't value. You don't build synagogues and schools, train rabbis and teachers, hold services, organise meetings, produce journals, write books and pamphlets, and perform the countless other tasks involved in conducting an active Jewish communal life, unless you are for Judaism. Still less do you incur hostility and ostracism for its sake, as has often been the experience of Liberal Jews, unless your concern for Judaism is above the ordinary.[9]

Of course, there may be believers of any religious persuasion, whether they be liberal or conservative, who are less committed to their beliefs than the authors of the above passage or Peter or Trevor. There is no necessary correlation between the variety of someone's theological position and that person's degree of commitment to his or her beliefs.

We have so far distinguished between different objects of commitment and degrees of commitment. Both of these, in turn, should be distinguished from the varying extent to which different committed people feel charged to broadcast or promulgate their views. Trevor is a person who feels such a charge, while Peter does not. Although, on empirical grounds, it seems that theologically conservative believers are more likely to want to transmit their own beliefs than religious liberals, this is by no means a universal rule. There are theological conservatives who are professionally committed to openness in religious education, just as there are theo-logically liberal teachers who are intolerant of conservative religious views held by certain pupils and colleagues.

Clearly there are certain varieties of religious commitment that would prevent people holding them from teaching about commitments which they do not share with any degree of sympathy. For example, the believer whose urge to pass on his own beliefs to children is stronger than any professional commitment to a sympathetic study of a variety of belief systems would be unsuitable as a teacher of world religions. A person whose theological stance included beliefs entailing the blasphemous nature of alternative religious positions would find the task of elucidating those beliefs extremely difficult. There is a range of theological views, however, that may be very deeply held that would not inhibit teachers committed to them from treating a variety of religions. In certain circumstances – say if a faith being studied and the teacher's own religion both emphasised mystical experience – a teacher's religious commitment could even enhance his or her capacity to foster an understanding of another faith.

But what of the teacher who is not committed to religious beliefs? Is that person more or less likely to give a sympathetic treatment to a variety of religions than the religiously committed teacher? Like the religious believer, the atheist is a committed person and we can make the same distinctions regarding his commitment as we did with the religious believer: between his beliefs and the degree to which he is committed to them; between these and the extent to which he feels charged to propagate his own point of view. On this basis the deeply committed atheist who also feels that he must convince pupils of the truth of his own beliefs would be an unsuitable teacher of religions, as would the atheist holding that religious beliefs are not only false but harmful. An atheist who does not feel charged to transmit his beliefs and who appreciates the value and functions of religion in personal and social life, however, might make a competent teacher of a range of religious views.

At this point something should be written about agnosticism and the agnostic teacher. Although the term 'agnostic', coined by T. H. Huxley, was originally used in a strict sense – holding that the truth or falsity of religious claims *cannot* be known – it has become used more widely. In particular it is commonly used of the person who considers the question of God's existence to be important and in principle answerable, but who finds the evidence presently available for and against religious belief ambiguous and confusing. Agnostics of this kind are generally well disposed towards religion and are often committed to some form of religious search or quest, without having a commitment to any particular religious stance. Some agnostics of this type, should they be convinced that faith is possible where knowledge is not, may be religious believers but the majority find that the most rational course to take in assessing evidence for and against religious belief is to suspend judgement until more convincing evidence is available. Since many agnostics do not demand publicly specifiable evidence for religious belief, being impressed with the conviction gained by many religious believers through personal religious experience of various kinds, they are unlikely to want to foster agnosticism among others, especially those who themselves have arrived at religious belief through some form of religious experience. Agnostics of this type, being open-minded and interested in the exploration of religious ideas, are likely to make sensitive teachers of religious education.[10]

Commitment and the classroom

I have written about the commitment of the teacher, but it has to be remembered that *pupils* as well as teachers have different religious and non-religious commitments. Further, if pupils are to study world religions at first hand they need to encounter material written from a committed standpoint or to meet committed believers during the course of their RE lessons. Such encounters may provide students with opportunities to encounter directly religious views that their teachers are unlikely to embrace. The number of possible encounters between different types of commitment – of teachers, pupils and religious believers who may take part in RE programmes – is enormous and each provides an educational opportunity. I can perhaps characterise some of the numerous ways in which commitment may be one of religious education's resources by recounting three stories.

The first story suggests one way in which the teacher's own commitment can be a positive resource in the classroom. A former student of mine, a committed Liberal Jew, had tremendous imaginative flair for presenting faiths other than his own. He had integrity, accuracy and something of the actor's art. Having, with great skill, done some work on Hinduism with a class of 14-year-olds, he was asked if he believed in *avatars* – 'incarnations' of the deity, usually of the god Vishnu – and had no hesitation in saying that as a Jew he did not. But he also pointed out some different Hindu views on the subject, and opened up a general and wide-ranging exchange of views with the class.

This student's attitude to RE teaching is, to some extent, a consequence of his liberal theological position. He had the honesty to give a straight answer about his own views, but also the flexibility to use his reply to stimulate further reflection by his pupils, drawing on theological positions from inside and outside the class in order to do so. He also showed skill both in letting a religion speak for itself, and in judging when it was appropriate to encourage some corporate reflection on what had been studied.

The next story, from a teacher in a multi-ethnic comprehensive school, illustrates one of the ways in which the commitment of a pupil can enhance an RE lesson.[11] She writes:

> Last year I had a very weak fifth year CSE class. Some class members were of very limited ability, one hardly able to read, and some had 'turned off' school. We follow the Middlesex CSE syllabus. One section of this is on *Beliefs* and I had left 'the Holy Spirit', with its Biblical references, to the end, not having the courage to tackle it with them – because it *is* difficult and because *I* find the concepts worrying. I went into the class with a traditional lesson on *Acts* chapter two, not really looking forward to the double period. The whole situation was changed by Gwen, a Jamaican girl very much involved in an all-black Pentecostal church. She suddenly joined in with a very vivid description of a service at her church and her own experience of speaking in tongues. She fascinated the Greek Catholic contingent in the class whose church experience is mainly of baptisms and weddings. The questions and comparisons came from a deep interest and the discussion was very controlled. Gradually everybody became involved, with me becoming part of the class, and being in no way a leader or prompter. Nobody took any notice of the lunch bell when it went and the students all moved off about five minutes late, still talking. It was one of the most exciting lessons in which I have taken part, but not one I could have planned and organised. It worked because all the initiative came from Gwen's commitment. My saying something about the Pentecostal church would not have prompted her to make a contribution.

Of course there are likely to be cases in which it is completely inappropriate to draw upon a pupil's commitment in the classroom, but this story illustrates how, in the care of a sensitive teacher, a pupil's faith can both deepen and enrich work in RE.

The third story illustrates how a committed person outside the school community can play a valuable part in religious education. The first religion other than Christianity that I attempted to teach was Judaism. I had devised a course for first-year secondary pupils (all boys) involving some study of worship and festivals, and I hoped that the climax of the course would be a visit to a synagogue. Through a Jewish friend I was introduced to the local Orthodox rabbi who seemed, initially, defensive and suspicious about my motives in wanting to bring a party of non-Jewish pupils to the synagogue. After I explained, however, that our main objective was to increase our understanding of Judaism he agreed that the visit could take place. For my part I was very keen that the visit should be a success and discussed my reasons for this with the class. I was delighted with the response from the pupils, who buckled down to learning as much as they could in preparation for the occasion. On the day of the visit we walked to the synagogue and were greeted by the rabbi. 'Come on in,' he said. 'We can't, sir', came the reply, 'we aren't wearing our *yarmulkas* – that's Hebrew – *cappels* in Yiddish.' A smile appeared on the rabbi's face. He came out with a box of paper *cappels*, and having donned these we went in. There was an atmosphere of both reverence and industry, as the students made notes on their worksheets and jotted down questions they wanted to be answered. The discussion which took place towards the end of the visit was relaxed and uninhibited. 'You know more than my Sunday school class!' declared the rabbi. At this point someone asked, 'Why do the women sit in the gallery and not down here with the men?' I began to feel less comfortable. 'Well, if a man is praying,' said the rabbi, 'he doesn't want to be distracted by attractive ladies.' A pregnant pause was interrupted by 'But sir, you can get a much better view of the ladies if they are in the gallery instead of down here!' With this priceless and relatively innocent remark rabbi, boys and all collapsed with laughter. The questions kept coming and the rabbi told anecdotes and stories which gave the pupils something of the flavour of Judaism that could only have come from a Jewish source.

After the visit we kept up our contact with the rabbi, and were delighted when he agreed to accept an invitation to conduct an assembly for first- to third-year pupils. It was explained that this was not an act of worship, but an opportunity for the children to hear an account of the Passover festival as it might be celebrated in a Jewish home. He gave a brilliant, witty and highly committed account of Passover and what it meant to him and his family, and then he answered questions from the floor.

This story illustrates two ways in which children can encounter at first hand a deeply held religious commitment through the involvement of a person in religious education from outside the school. Note that this particular rabbi, splendid though his contribution was, would not have made a good RE teacher. He would have been the first to admit the immense difficulty he would have found personally in teaching about Hinduism or the doctrine of the Trinity. But as a 'living resource' for religious education the rabbi was magnificent. Secondly, the pupils' understanding of Jewish beliefs and practices was greatly increased through his contributions, and some of the significance of these in the rabbi's own life was grasped. In addition, the work done stimulated some reflection on our own experiences of religion. For example, one boy was very impressed with the involvement of children in the Passover celebrations and thought that children ought to be included more in the activities of his local church. Another contrasted the seriousness with which Passover seemed to be taken by Jewish children and adults with his own experience of Christmas.

Conclusion

In this chapter I have argued that formal understanding of religious concepts, beliefs and rituals is not dependent upon religious commitment and that, given certain background information, students can achieve varying levels of understanding of a believer's religious feelings. In view of the diversity of emotional responses to worship or mystical experience even within a single religion, prior religious commitment on the student's part will not necessarily help him or her to achieve that understanding, though in certain cases it might aid understanding. The student's degree of understanding will depend on his or her capacity to empathise with the particular worshipper or mystic being studied.

There are believers whose religious commitment need not inhibit their ability to teach world religions sympathetically. In certain cases their religious commitment may be an advantage in elucidating a position which is in some way related to their own. Similarly, there are atheists who may become competent world religions teachers. Those agnostics who are favourably inclined to religion are likely to approach world religions teaching with openness and sensitivity.

Among all these teachers is to be found a wide variety of theological or philosophical positions about the relationship between the truth claims of different religions. What they are likely to have in common, however, is a mind that is open and receptive to diverse systems of belief and practice. They are willing to let others tell their own stories as fully as possible before wanting to concur, to modify or to respond.

Within the classroom there are occasions when both committed teachers and committed pupils can become valuable teaching resources. The use of material written from a committed standpoint, and the involvement in religious education lessons of committed believers other than RE teachers and their pupils, provide further opportunities for exploring religions and furnish opportunities for the consideration of religious views that may not otherwise be encountered directly in class.

Notes and references

1 *Religious Education in Hampshire Schools* (Hampshire Education Authority, 1978), p. 8.

2 W. D. Hudson, 'Is religious education possible?' in G. Langford and D. O'Connor (eds), *New Essays in the Philosophy of Education* (London: Routledge & Kegan Paul, 1973), pp. 167–96.

3 Peter Gardner, 'Religious education: in defence of non-commitment', *Journal of Philosophy of Education*, vol. 14, no. 2, 1980, p. 163.

4 D. Z. Phillips, *Faith and Philosophical Enquiry* (London: Routledge & Kegan Paul, 1970), p. 132.

5 Roger Marples, 'Is religious education possible?', *Journal of Philosophy of Education*, vol. 12, 1978, pp. 81–91.

6 D. Z. Phillips, *The Concept of Prayer* (London: Routledge & Kegan Paul, 1965), p. 50.

7 Formal understanding involves the ability to give an account of the things to which a concept applies; see J. P. White, *Towards a Compulsory Curriculum* (London: Routledge & Kegan Paul, 1973), pp. 26–7.

8 Marples, op.cit., p. 91.

9 J. D. Rayner and B. Hooker, *Judaism For Today* (Union of Liberal and Progressive Synagogues, 1978), pp. 4–5.

10 A very good exploration of agnosticism and an agnostic view of religious education is *What It Means To Be Agnostic*, an essay by Edwin Cox published in booklet form by The Resource and Technology Centre, Back Hill, Ely, Cambridgeshire, 1977.

11 This story is from Marilyn Thomas, Head of Religious Education at Hornsey Girls' School.

Further reading

In addition to the books and articles referred to in the notes above, the following writings deal with commitment and religious education. A useful and practical discussion is Jean Pardoe and Michael Lavender, 'Problems for the committed believer', in Robert Jackson (ed.), *Perspectives on World Religions* (London: SOAS, 1978). This chapter is especially interesting in that it is written jointly by a Christian teacher and a Jewish RE student. Edward Hulmes, *Commitment and Neutrality in*

Religious Education (London: Geoffrey Chapman, 1979), emphasises the need in RE 'for a recognition and use of the creative and liberating potential of the teacher's commitment'. This is an important contribution, though the author's characterisation of a world-faiths approach to RE in schools as neutral to questions of truth seriously underestimates developments in rationale and methodology that have occurred at the grass-roots level in RE (see, for example, Chapters 2–4 of the present volume and the examples cited towards the end of the present chapter). Further, the author's assertion that a neutral stance slides into relativism and indifference to religion, and that these in turn support the claims of agnostic humanism, is highly questionable (see Dennis Starkings' reply to a similar claim made by John McIntyre in Chapter 6 of the present book). A shorter piece on commitment by Edward Hulmes is 'The problem of commitment', chapter 3, W. O. Cole (ed.), *World Faiths in Education* (London: Allen & Unwin, 1978). A valuable symposium of fifteen short articles on commitment (including pieces by June Jones and Marjorie Freeman relating specifically to primary schools) appears in the *1982 Supplement* of the City of Birmingham Education Department's *Living Together: A Teacher's Handbook of Suggestions for Religious Education*. Another relevant article on this subject is Michael Grimmitt, 'When is "commitment" a problem in RE?', *British Journal of Educational Studies*, vol. xxix, no. 1, 1981.

9
Open Minds and Empty Hearts?

John M. Hull

It is often taken for granted that a religious person will want to pass on his faith to others. In the case of teachers of religion who are themselves religious, the assumption is that they will be obliged by their faith to try to pass their own religion on to their pupils in their religious education lessons. This assumption is perhaps stronger when we think of the great missionary religions like Islam and Christianity. But even with religions such as Hinduism and Judaism which are for various reasons not usually regarded as being so obviously committed to universal evangelisation, it remains odd to many people that a member of such a faith should be happy and at ease, with no sense of hypocrisy or unfaithfulness to his own commitment, when he is teaching some other religion. But is this widespread assumption justified? Is there indeed something about commitment to a religion which logically and psychologically compels a believer always to seek to convert others to his faith? Or might it be the case that there are at least some religions or some types of religious commitment in which the believer, if he is an RE teacher, will be compelled to encourage a variety of responses to a variety of religions from his pupils? In the following pages we will discuss these two types of teacher, calling them either 'convergent' in their approach or 'divergent'.

Convergence and divergence

Some teachers of religious education simply teach what they believe. This one, for example, believes that the Bible is the Word of God, teaches that it is the Word of God, and hopes and intends that his pupils will form the same view. Another teacher believes that Islam is the most noble faith, teaches this, and hopes and intends that her pupils will come to see this. We may describe this situation as one of convergence, since the personal faith of the teacher converges with the content of his lessons and with his hopes for the pupils. Convergence may take a negative form, as when a teacher believes that the Bible is not the Word of God, teaches this, and expects his pupils to form the same conclusion. Convergence should be regarded as a general pattern of identity between faith-commitment, classroom work and teaching aims, which may not be apparent in every scheme of work. A convergent teacher, say a Catholic teacher in a Catholic school teaching Catholic pupils, may teach a course on world religions, having a content which he may see as diverging from his own commitment to Catholicism. His pattern of convergence may be shown in that he may treat the world religions objectively and from the outside, while Catholic teachings are taught from the inside and with the assumption of faith in his pupils. It may also sometimes happen that a convergent teacher is not very consistent, being, perhaps, naively convergent rather than self-consciously and deliberately convergent.

We may find another teacher who is a Christian but is teaching Islam as part of the worthwhile educational experience of the pupils, intending neither to deepen their faith in Islam nor to discourage it. Similarly, when this teacher teaches Christianity, although his or her faith and the lesson content do now in fact converge, the religion is similarly taught only for its educational value, without the intention of either fostering Christian faith or making it more difficult. In situations like these, the personal faith of the teacher diverges from the content and the aims of the teaching. Like convergence, divergence is a pattern which will be sharper or less sharp according to the particular syllabus, the pupils, and so on. It is a divergence in principle, which will actually appear more or less frequently. Divergent teachers, like their convergent colleagues, may be inconsistent or naive, and there may be some teachers of religion to whom questions like these have never occurred, and who could not be clearly diagnosed.

Convergence is a simpler situation than divergence. There is an immediate and obvious unity of life and work. Simple descriptions, however, can be oversimplifications, and before we can understand what is at stake between convergent and divergent teachers we must distinguish several kinds of teaching, and see that convergence occurs only in certain *kinds* of teaching. For the nature of teaching itself changes when viewed from converging and diverging perspectives.

A group of convergent teaching processes: nurture, evangelism and indoctrination

Religious nurture, the teaching activity which intends to foster or deepen the commitment of those who are already believers or already inside the religious community, is clearly a convergent process. Only a Muslim can nurture a child within Islam. The faith of the nurturer, the content, and the goal of his nurture are identical. This unity finds expression in a unified religious community, and nurture is a domestic activity of that community, taking place within the home, the church, mosque, synagogue or temple. Because it is specific to a community of faith, we should speak of *Christian* nurture, *Hindu* nurture and so on, and the theory and practice of religious upbringing will vary from one religion to another. Not only can nurture be offered only by a teacher whose own faith is also being nurtured in the same process, but it can be received only by a child or adult already inside that faith. The Christian nurturer deals only with children being brought up by their parents as Christians. Moreover, the goal of the nurture process is identical with the content and the learners – the Sikh teacher nurturing faith in the Sikh religion fails as a nurturer if his Sikh pupil forsakes Sikhism.

We can distinguish religious nurture from general encouragement. A Christian pupil may be encouraged by the understanding attitude of any patient and wise teacher who treats Christianity with respect although not himself a Christian believer. Indeed, teachers should encourage all noble commitments which their pupils possess, just as they should encourage virtue and discourage vice. This is quite different from the active process of Islamic upbringing, or the definite practice of Christian child-rearing.

This convergence of personal commitment on the part of the teacher with his lesson content and his teaching aims is seen still more clearly when we turn to evangelism and indoctrination. You do not sincerely evangelise someone with beliefs you do not hold yourself. There are cases where professional public relations firms are engaged to spread religious and political opinions, but they are merely agents of the evangelists and not evangelists themselves. In a similar way we might think of a teacher who imagines himself employed to teach religion in order to persuade children to go to church, and who might conscientiously do his best in that direction, although not a church-goer himself. But leaving such cases on one side, evangelism seems a pretty clear case of a convergent style of teaching. Of course, it differs from religious nurture in that it is addressed to anyone. Far from being confined to the existing members of the religion, it is usually directed towards non-adherents. But like religious nurture, it certainly seeks to establish convergence, in that the evangelist is not successful unless at least some of his hearers commit themselves to his message. He might not have failed in his *duty* if they do not respond. Nevertheless, his hope and intention is that some at least and all if possible shall respond. We can see then that the evangelist tries to establish the unity of convergence and the nurturer tries to deepen it.

The indoctrinator is prepared to sacrifice almost everything for the sake of convergence. Divergence and the freedom and variety of opinion which it entails are repellent to him. He does not want his pupils or subjects to think or choose for themselves but wants them to be conformed to his own likeness. Indoctrination can be offered both to those already committed and to those uncommitted, and in this sense it straddles nurture and evangelism, but it differs in that it is an assault upon the person of the hearer. Instead of displaying the reasons for choice, as happens in good evangelism, reasons are concealed and reason is by-passed. Differences between religious nurture and religious indoctrination will be more subtle, and will vary widely from religion to religion, but it is enough for our present purposes to say that there are certainly some religious child-rearing patterns in which to indoctrinate would be to deny the very ideal of life into which the child is being nurtured. Be that as it may, the central point is that in indoctrination a particularly rigorous or even ruthless attempt is made to secure convergence.

Education and divergence

The remarkable thing about education, and the feature which distinguishes it most vividly from the other teaching processes we have been considering, is that this convergence of the commitment of the teacher, the content of the teaching, and the commitment or desired commitment of the pupils, does not exist. A teacher can educate a pupil with respect to Islam whether he (the teacher) is a Muslim or not. Such education may be good or bad, sensitive or insensitive, skilful or crude. Such an education will not necessarily deepen the Islamic faith of the pupil (should he be a Muslim) although it certainly should not discourage him; it will not seek to convert him, although what will actually take place in the heart and mind of any pupil can never be known for sure beforehand by any teacher; it will certainly not indoctrinate him. But if it is good and successful it will educate him.

Moreover, just as good teachers can educate pupils in a religion whether they themselves are believers in that religion or not, so pupils can receive and benefit by such education whether they are members of the religion or not.

The reason why the 1975 *City of Birmingham Agreed Syllabus* was such an important landmark in the development of religious teaching in Britain was because this was the first new Agreed Syllabus which was addressed to divergent teachers. It is a syllabus which can be taught by any well-trained and well-informed teacher, regardless of his faith, to any pupil whose interest can be caught, regardless of his faith. But the move from convergency to divergency which this implied became a thorny problem for many teachers, for the idea that they should teach something which was not identical with their own personal faith came as a shock to the naive convergent teacher and as a challenge to the shrewd one. The simple link between faith, content and aims was broken, for, to take an example, a successful piece of education about the resurrection of Jesus is not necessarily one after which the pupils come to believe that Jesus did indeed rise from the dead (that is, their commitment becomes identical with the obvious content of the lesson); it is, rather, a lesson after which the pupils come to know the accounts, stories and traditions of the resurrection, have a degree of insight into the ideas, feelings and actions inspired by these accounts, and have acquired some skills in studying and evaluating them from various points of view. Such evaluation might result in the pupil's forming the judgement that Jesus did, after all, rise from the dead, although it would not be in the formation of that judgement *per se* that his education would lie. He might, on the other hand, evaluate the stories as probably unreliable, but again, his education would lie in the way this judgement was reached and not in the opinion itself. Education does not seek or assume convergence. Any convergence there might be is the result of accident or individual psychology and not a matter of principle or intention. But with religious nurture, evangelism and indoctrination, divergence, if it occurs, is exceptional and accidental while convergence is assumed or sought as the pattern and the norm. For the convergent teacher, a divergent pupil represents a failure, but for the divergent teacher a convergent pupil does not necessarily represent a failure, for being educated is not simply a matter of what views are held but has to do with the way in which views are formed.

Must RE teachers have empty hearts?

If we were to see a lesson on the joy of Lord Krishna as he played his flute in the forest, and we knew that it was intended to be an evangelistic lesson (perhaps the teacher had told us so), we would then know what was in the heart of the teacher, assuming his sincerity: the joy of Krishna. And if we saw a lesson on Jesus as Lord given as part of a programme of Christian nurture in a Christian church or school, then also we would know what was in the heart of the teacher – Jesus as Lord. But if we saw an educational lesson on Lord Krishna or Lord Jesus or both, and knew that it was intended to be an educational experience, then, no matter how seriously we believed in the sincerity of the educator, we would not have an obvious way of knowing what, if anything, was in his heart. So we come to our central question. Is divergence a situation without commitment? Or (to put the same point more vividly) must RE teachers, in having open minds, also have empty hearts?

It is *possible* that the teacher who seeks to be a true educator *will* have an empty heart as far as any religious commitment is concerned. It is possible that such a teacher may be able to teach several religions without any problem of religious commitment simply because he is equally indifferent to all of them as concerning his personal faith. Where there is no commitment of a specifically religious kind, there can be no convergence of religious commitment and lesson content, and such teaching will meet the bare requirement of divergency. That will be sufficient to mark it off from religious nurture and evangelism. But there is, as we have seen, both good and bad education. It is perfectly possible that children would be able to learn more (let us think now of children learning rather than adults teaching) from sincere and interesting evangelism than from such bad education. This would not justify school evangelism; it would point to the need for improved education.

Heartless or uncommitted education, education in which the heart of the educator remains a mystery, has been a particular problem for the RE teacher in recent years in Britain. Part of the blame must lie with the false distinction between confessional and non-confessional teaching of religion, a distinction made popular by the 1971 Schools Council Working Paper 36: *Religious Education in Secondary Schools.*[1] Confessional or neo-confessional teaching was that teaching which sprang from the teacher's personal confession of faith whilst its opposite was that teaching which did not spring from personal faith but was professional. This shallow and harmful distinction has led to the view that there is and should be a gulf between having a personal faith and being a professional teacher of religion, suggesting that personal religious faith does not and could not illuminate good educational practice. The Working Paper was right in regarding *what it called* confessionalism as being other than education, but wrong in *calling it* confessionalism in the first place.[2] Good education can be *as confessional* as good religious nurture and good evangelism, and the belief that it cannot leads to the teacher with the open mind and empty heart.

So far we have spoken of the teacher without a heart as the one whose lack of religious commitment made him a mystery to his pupils, or the one who felt that his duty required him to ignore his own religious commitment because of the assumption that religious commitment can lead only to convergence. There is another sense in which we might think of a teacher without a heart, namely, one who not only lacked a religious commitment but who also thought that being a good teacher was possible without deep commitment of any kind. The teacher who lacks religious commitment may still be a perfectly adequate RE teacher and even an excellent one, but it is hard to see how the teacher who does not see that teaching itself demands beliefs, values and commitments could be a successfully divergent teacher.

The reason why teachers with empty hearts in this second sense are likely to be bad educators is that divergence is itself a value, or a bundle of values. If divergence is to be expressed in good education in the classroom, it must be realised that it springs from commitments as deep as the commitment which is expressed in convergence.

Education and passion

The values expressed in divergent teaching are easy to identify. First, this truly educational teaching is directed to all pupils alike, since no distinction is made in divergent education between Christian pupils, Jewish pupils and pupils of no religious affiliation. This value is unique to the teacher who is an educator. The Christian nurture teacher is only dealing with his Christian pupils. The teacher who is an evangelist is speaking to all his pupils *except* those of his own faith, and in this way, the nurturer deals with one section of the class and the evangelist with the other. But who is to teach *all* the children? Moreover, although the teacher as evangelist is concerned with all the pupils except those who share his own faith, he is not concerned with them *as* Hindus, Jews or as secular young people. If he is a Christian evangelist he is concerned with them as *non* Christian, as those who do *not* follow his way. They are, to him, the unconverted. Far from offering them encouragement in their own commitments, he would see his task as to win them to his own.

This availability of the teacher who is a true educator to all his pupils is part of what is meant by the neutrality of education. It does not mean that the teacher does not care but that he cares for them all, accepting them as they are. It does not mean that he is not committed, but that he is committed to them all. He recognises his responsibility as a teacher to give equal support to all. It means that each child has the right, just because he is in the school and in the charge of the teacher, to expect that the teacher shall be *his* teacher. The teacher as religious nurturer *per se* cannot consistently express this value. His convergence prevents him from doing so. Possession of this value, availability to all, is the first mark of the superiority, in the pluralist schools of a democratic society, of education over all the other teaching processes. The others may be superior in other situations for which they are intended (for example the church or in the media) but education rules in the county school.

But this availability of the teacher to all his pupils is a belief which must be felt in the heart, a conviction which must illuminate classroom practice, which makes education warm, personal and self-giving. When teaching in schools where potential divisions along social, ethnic or religious lines appear, the teacher as educator, committed to every child, must possess this commitment as a passion.

Secondly, the teacher as educator seeks certain kinds of lives for his pupils. His divergence does not mean that he does not have ideals for them. He wants them to learn to think for themselves. In this also he is unusual. The instructed pupil thinks what he is told to think. The socialised pupil thinks what others think. The evangelised pupil comes to think what the evangelist thinks. The indoctrinated pupil does not think at all, but merely conforms or echoes. The educated pupil thinks for himself.

But thinking for yourself is a value. It is difficult to attain, difficult to maintain. It is precious. It involves respect for the personality of the pupil. It requires great patience on the part of the teacher, and his constant vigilance. The teacher who teaches in this way must believe that the autonomous man or woman possesses a greater value than the merely pleasure-seeking man or woman, or the person fitted for life in the consumer society, or the one merely trained for the needs of industry. In a society where group pressures, consumer delights, and the daily appeal of a mindless acquisitiveness are all around us, belief in the dignity and value of the person who thinks for himself must be held with passion if it is not to be swallowed up.

The third value of divergence is inquiry. The teacher as religious nurturer, the evangelist and the indoctrinator seek to create or deepen their pupils' commitment to the content of their lessons, but the teacher as educator seeks to make his pupils critical of the content of his lessons. He asks many questions. It is not true that he gives no answers; he gives many answers, and more questions spring from every answer. There is no end to this process; indeed, one of the purposes of this teacher is that his pupils shall not cease their education simply because their schooling is over. They are to go on asking questions and finding answers which lead to more questions all their lives.

But is this not confusing for children? Yes, it is confusing, and not only for children. Choice is confusing. Democracy is more confusing than dictatorship and thinking for yourself is more confusing than being told what to think. Nothing could be more secure and simple than accepting indoctrination. This is why the teacher as educator takes an interest in developmental psychology, and in the idea of 'readiness' for various kinds and levels of educational content and method. Children, like all people, must be prepared for education, educated into education. Education is dangerous, but the danger and the confusion are acceptable not only because of the skill and the patience of teachers who handle them so as to benefit children, but because without them the values of independent thought and inquiry might never be found by the growing child. If we are teaching in schools where the value of inquiry is subordinate to the idea that we learn mainly in order to pass examinations or mainly to get a better job, then belief in the value of asking questions can only be maintained by the teacher for whom it has become a passion.

Divergence as a theological problem

These then are some examples of the commitment which lies in the heart of the teacher as true educator. The divergent quality of religious education is only a symptom of these deeper causes. But many teachers of religion will need to press deeper yet. What is the relation between *religious* commitment and commitment to the values which lead to divergence? Unlike the simple, convergent situation of the religious nurturer and the evangelist, the religious beliefs of the divergent teacher are mediated *through* the intervening values, and are not intruded directly into the teaching content and aims. Now it is easy to see that a religiously committed person would want to evangelise. But why would he *on religious grounds* want to educate? So it is that divergence, which stands between religious faith and the lesson content and aim, becomes a problem in theology.

But this is only a *possible* situation. The theological problem *need* not arise. It is quite possible for a teacher to educate his pupils in religion, expressing through divergence the educational values discussed above but combining these with his own non-religious outlook. A humanist, a non-religious existentialist or a secular liberal democrat might well have such values (although such teachers may be equally tempted to adopt convergent styles), and passionate possession of such humane and educational values expressed through divergence is not only necessary but sufficient for educational work in religious teaching as far as the question of commitment is concerned. Still, it is possible in theory and probable in practice that the religious educator may and will in fact possess religious faith.

Let us then consider the situation of these two kinds of teachers of religion, both kinds having religious faith, leaving aside the equally good teachers who lack religious faith. First, we have the religious nurturers, the evangelists and the indoctrinators. Their problem is that their commitment to convergence prevents them from becoming educators. Second, we have the religiously committed religious *educators*. Their problem is to see whether (and if so how) their religious beliefs support and even generate their educational work, that is, how to be confessionalist and (for that very reason) divergent and thus educational. The problem of the first group of teachers has no solution. They must simply resign themselves to not being true educators. They may find other teaching work. In the case of the religious indoctrinators, this will be other bad teaching work. In the case of the religious nurturers and evangelists, this will probably be other good teaching work, if what they are nurturing and evangelising into is itself good.

For the second group, the religiously committed religious *educators*, the problem seems to be soluble in at least some cases. Finding the solution will depend on the kind of religious beliefs to which the teacher is committed, and we may suppose that within each of the major world religions there will be some varieties of religious belief which will hinder divergence and others which will facilitate it. The essential questions are: Does my religion help me to think for myself or does it require me to submit without question to authority? Does my religious commitment cause me to discover questions and do the answers provided by my religion lead me to further questions? Is this how being religious actually makes me live? And if the answer is yes, is this for merely psychological reasons connected with my temperament or is it a result of the beliefs themselves? Are the ideas of learning, autonomy and inquiry actually an integral part of my theological system?

There are religious systems, theologies, which meet the test of these questions, and which actually give rise to such questions. Religiously committed teachers who want to be religious educators must find such theologies. If they do not, they need not, like the convergent group, abandon their teaching since they will still be educators. But they may become those with open minds and empty hearts, unable to connect their deepest religious values with their work. Those on the other hand whose educational work is richest because their hearts are full, who are committed to divergence on religious grounds, will probably be those from whom young people will have most to learn about the life which is both open and passionate.

Notes and references

1 Schools Council Working Paper 36, *Religious Education in Secondary Schools* (Evans/Methuen, 1971).

2 See my article 'From Christian nurture to religious education: the British experience', in *Religious Education* 73 (1978), pp. 124-43.

Further reading

For an influential (and fully justified) attack upon 'confessionalism' see *Religious Education in Secondary Schools*, Schools Council Working Paper 36 (Evans/Methuen Educational, 1971), pp. 30ff. Chapter 13 of the Working Paper, 'The Christian as RE teacher', pp. 92ff, is quite unsatisfactory in that it merely highlights the problem, offering no Christian reasons for the Christian's participation in teaching faiths other than his own. Professor Paul Hirst rejected the idea of an education springing from religious belief in his article 'Christian education: a contradiction in terms', *Learning for Living*, vol. 11, no. 4 (1972), pp. 6-11, and I have attempted to discuss his claims in 'Christian theology and educational theory: can there be connections?', *British Journal of Educational Studies*, vol. 24, no. 2 (June 1976), pp. 127-43. The position of the Christian Education Movement on a Christian rationale for participation in a critical, exploring religious education was discussed in the Editorial 'Are you a Christian?', *Learning for Living*, vol. 16, no. 4 (Summer 1977), pp. 146ff, and for an interesting denial of this possibility ('a Christian can *only* seek the cause of his own party') see the letter from John Herbert in *Learning for Living*, vol. 17, no. 2 (Winter 1977), p. 97. More recently, Richard Wilkins has discussed the convergent/divergent distinction in his letter to the *British Journal of Religious Education*, vol. 3, no. 3 (Spring 1981), p. 108, and I have tried to show how Christian believers are required by their faith to enter into critical inquiry in my article 'Christian nurture and critical openness', *Scottish Journal of Theology*, 1981.

10
The Christian and World Religions

Raymond Hammer

Changes in the relationship between religions

Twenty years ago, when writing of Eastern religions, I happened to quote the opening lines of Kipling's famous stanza:
'Oh, East is East and West is West, and never the twain shall meet.'
It was my concern to indicate the great divorce between Eastern and Western thought and culture. A reader, however, reminded me that I was misquoting Kipling's meaning, if I did not go on to read him further:

'But there is neither East nor West, Border nor Breed nor Birth,
When two strong men stand face to face, though they come from the
    ends of the earth.'

Here we may see a parable of the relationship between religions. Whereas, at one time, religions had existed almost in isolation from one another and any minority grouping could be conveniently enclosed in a ghetto, the picture is now different. Formerly it was as if every religion had its own territory and, apart from a few travellers, the adherents of a particular faith were to be found there. You confronted Buddhism only if you went east. 'Hindu' and 'Indian' were seen as terms describing the same people. We tended to associate Islam with North Africa and the Middle East. Sikhs were to be found in the Punjab . . . and so on.[1] All this has now changed. Not only has the world shrunk and intercommunication become possible, but movements of population have created the phenomenon of religious pluralism: isolation is becoming a thing of the past. Religions now stand 'face to face' and, no longer feeling oppressed by Western superiority, some Afro-Asian faiths have shown signs of revival and, what is more, have become the basis of a strong sense of self-identity. We live indeed in a time when 'strong men' confront one another.

Here in Britain it is reckoned that we have over 1,000,000 Muslims, more than 400,000 Jews, 250,000 Hindus, 200,000 Sikhs and 100,000 Buddhists – not to mention minor groupings of Zoroastrians, Jains and many others. But, further, we are not speaking simply of the inter-mingling of different ethnic groups. Many of these religions have found adherents among westerners. One can find western Buddhists in Nepal and most of the countries of East Asia, as well as in Britain, America and Europe generally. I have myself witnessed the dancing of Hare Krishna groups in London, Frankfurt, Toronto, California and Texas! A committed Christian can be excused, therefore, for feeling somewhat perplexed and wondering what attitude he or she is to adopt in the new situation. There is also the possibility of feeling threatened which, in turn, creates the desire to withdraw within the boundaries of one's own particular religious tradition. Are Christians involved in the teaching of RE to concentrate on the Judaeo-Christian tradition, arguing (with quite a measure of justification) that this has been, at the very least, the normative influence in British culture? If, however, world religions are incorporated into the curriculum, what are the implications of this for personal faith and for the children's growing understanding of the place of 'religion' in life?

Changes in the curriculum

It is the actual presence of so many religions among us that has been the major factor in the creation of new-look multi-faith RE. We certainly no longer live in the age of the Butler Act, when religious education could be understood in terms of Christian education and when an 'act of worship' would be automatically understood to be a Christian act of worship. As recently as 1965 a group of us met in Birmingham and put out a 'Memorandum on the Teaching of Comparative (*sic*) Religion', in which we noted that there was 'a great and growing demand for information about world religions' as well as an 'attempt to rethink the principles of religious education in schools'. The word 'comparative' was used because, up till then, this was the name used for any wider study of religious traditions. It was also pointed out that newer universities contemplated the incorporation of 'the study of religion' within the broader umbrella of liberal or general studies. (It is not without interest that Professor Ninian Smart, one of the 1965 Birmingham group, was to head a new Department of Religious Studies in the University of Lancaster from 1966 and to be a leading instigator in the formation of the Shap Working Party.) The Memorandum went on to recommend that 'some teaching of world religions should form a component of the curriculum in religious education in schools, *chiefly for the higher age-levels*' (my italics) and that the then Colleges of Education should include them as 'part of the curriculum in religious studies'. It was indicated that such study would help in creating 'a better understanding of the different cultural backgrounds of African and Asian people resident in this country'. It is probably because of this last-named motive that there has been so speedy and so general an acceptance of the study of world religions in more recent syllabuses, although the drift away from an establishmentarian Christianity has been a contributory factor.

Much of the study (which has, of course, been applied to *all* age groups and not simply to higher age levels)[2] has followed the phenomenological approach, advocated by Professor C. J. Bleeker in the International Association for the History of Religions since its Marburg Meeting in 1960. The question, however, still remains of whether RE in schools is simply to be an introduction to the varying religions (naturally including Christianity as the religion which has been normative in the development of British culture) as phenomena within society or whether *truth values* are also to be involved. The problem is particularly acute for the teacher who is a convinced Christian or for those voluntary aided schools where the children may realistically be said to belong to a single religious community; in such schools nurturing in the faith may be seen as one of the objectives (if not the chief one) of RE within the general school curriculum.

Other chapters in this book have already considered religious commitment and its impact upon patterns of teaching and Owen Cole discusses, in Chapter 7, the place that Christianity is to have within a pluralist curriculum. It will be the aim of this chapter to assert first of all that the study of world religions, far from being a threat to Christian faith, actually emerges from the Christian's understanding of God and the world, and, next, to consider ways in which the very study provides a lead-back into the Christian's own faith, illuminating those facets of his faith which may be implicit within it, but which are not always clearly enunciated. This may sound somewhat conceptual, as though religion (and religions) were an abstraction from life and not something which is inextricably bound up with the whole of life. We must be constantly reminding ourselves that religions are *not* to be seen as abstractions, but as the living faiths of practising believers. But religious values are also bound up with cultural heritage, so that a cultural renaissance may have religious revival closely related to it. It also happens that dissatisfaction with the results of secularisation brings religionists together, when they feel that, at the very least, they are in contact with those who are convinced that truth- and value-judgements are important. It may be that the demands for community-building bring them together, as in the case of AFFOR (All Faiths for One Race) in the West Midlands. The more it can be seen, therefore, that the study of world religions belongs to the area of *people* meeting one another, the better. A mere concentration on religious *concepts* is inadequate. Too often a religion is assessed in the area of its ideas, as though a religion were to be identified with its creeds. In the classroom we may be primarily concerned for an informed understanding, a critical appreciation and a well-considered assessment – but this all needs supplementing by *actual contact* and the kind of interchange (perhaps in the context of multi-racial/multi-religious grouping) which makes for mutual respect and empathy.[3]

Christian attitudes to other faiths

In speaking of 'attitudes' I am already suggesting that there is no single approach. In fact, the same individual may not always manifest consistency of approach.

For long the majority of Christians have tended to emphasise the exclusivism of grace – the limitations of 'revelation' and 'truth'. This underlay the dictum of Cyprian, *'extra ecclesiam nulla salus'* ('there is no salvation outside the bounds of the Church'), but such a statement goes counter to those emphases (already present in the Biblical tradition, as we shall see) upon God's universal love for the totality of his creation. To take a hard exclusivist line would almost suggest that God had ignored all other peoples and only shown his love first to Jews and then to Christians. Roger Hooker (who studied for many years at the Sanskrit University in Varanasi and engaged extensively in Christian-Hindu dialogue) asks pertinently: 'Can we really worship as *universal* Lord [my italics] a God whose writ only runs among Christians?'[4]

If we take seriously this relationship of God with all mankind, it would follow that adherents of other religions are confronted with the 'living God' of Christian faith and worship and that the Christian must show humility and expectancy, as he looks at the religious experience of others – humility because he has not 'cornered' truth, and expectancy because he may find in the heritage of others the revelation of God. This, then, would be a case of our faith itself providing the incentive for a broader examination of mankind's religious heritage. As Dr Samartha put it (in commenting on a World Council of Churches-sponsored inter-religious exchange), 'A full and loyal commitment to one's own faith did not stand in the way of dialogue. On the contrary, it was our faith which was the basis of, and drawing force to, intensification of dialogue and a search for common action between members of various faiths.'[5]

But there may still remain the niggling doubt that to take other religions seriously is somehow to compromise one's own faith and go counter to the long-standing Christian standpoint that there is finality and ultimacy in Christ to whom all Biblical history is seen as pointing and that any form of religious syncretism is anathema. Let us, therefore, take a closer look at what the Bible has to say on the subject. This, however, is no easy task, as there is no commonly accepted interpretation of the scriptures. Furthermore, their evidence is often ambivalent or inconclusive and their application to present-day eventualities unclear.[6] The Biblical approach to religion and nationhood is often quite different from our own; politics, economics and culture are all integrated with religion (see Deuteronomy 7:1-6), and the harshly exclusivist position might suggest to some that Biblical religion is simply one of the many religious phenomena of that age and area. But since that was the cradle out of which Christianity developed (and this is seen not so much as man's creation as God's provision), Biblical attitudes are regarded by most

Christians as having a relevance for present-day assessments. Perhaps crucial to our investigation is the Biblical estimate of humanity. Mankind is seen as created in the divine image, and both the search for God and relationship with God (how the Bible understands 'religion') are seen as essential, constitutive elements in what it is to be human. But this is seen as true of *all* mankind (see Ecclesiasticus 17:1-8) and mankind, from the first stirrings of civilisation, is seen as turning to the true God (Genesis 4:25). It is only the 'fool' who denies the existence of God (Psalm 14:1) and experience of the world as such is understood as the basis of the conviction that God is active in the world (Romans 1:19-20). This perception of the divine in nature and history is seen as true both for individuals and for nations (cf. Acts 17:26-27). Persian kings are understood as provided with the knowledge of the 'God of heaven'. When the prophets attack the surrounding nations, it is not so much in terms of their religious imperfection or deficiency as in terms of their social crimes, cruelty and overweening pride.

But there are harsh words as well. The Gentiles are said to sacrifice to demons and not to God (1 Corinthians 10:20). It is likely, however, that the religions are not condemned *qua* religions, but because of the aberrations from truth and goodness which may be present in them. The worship of Moloch is accompanied by child sacrifice; the Canaanitish High Places are centres of orgiastic cults. The condemnation of the 'throne of Satan' (in the Book of Revelation) is made of a state which was substituting itself for God. The creature is not to assume the role of the creator and sin can lead to ignorance of the truth (see Acts 17:23).

None the less God's positive action in history is seen as having its impact on all mankind. After all, Israel is called to be a Light to the Gentiles (see Genesis 12:1-3); God's blessings are for all the world (Deuteronomy 7:6-7).

But truth comes through the door of particularity and so the Bible shuns the vagueness of generalities. Israel is called to be faithful to her covenant and vocation. There *is* the duty to follow a certain pattern of moral behaviour because only in this way can God's glory and the knowledge of God be mediated. It is in the New Testament that exclusiveness seems to give way to inclusiveness – although, basically, the New Testament is simply reaffirming the more universalist elements in the Old Testament, and it would be wrong to draw hard and fast lines between the faith of the Church and the faith of the Synagogue. After all, the goal of history is universality and unity. *All* nations share in table-communion with Abraham. There is to be *one* fold and *one* shepherd – *one* body of which Christ is head. It is not a matter of a takeover bid – with Christianity absorbing everything else – but of a common heritage, a common participation in blessing.

But, even now, have we really avoided exclusivism? Does not Acts quote the apostles as saying: 'There is salvation in no one else, for there is no other name under heaven given among men by which we must be saved' (Acts 4:12)? Is not this a claim for uniqueness? It has been so interpreted and has been regarded by adherents of other faiths as a sign of Christian intolerance and bigotry. If, however, it is read in context, it can be a claim that 'salvation' (in this case to be understood in terms of 'wholeness' or 'healing') is the work of the Messiah whom the Jewish rulers had rejected.[7] It is, moreover, difficult to see how any faith-commitment can avoid all charges of exclusivism. A complete relativism is a mental abstraction rather than the attitude of a religious adherent at the point when he commits himself. John Hick[8] or Wilfred Cantwell Smith[9] may take the standpoint that faith is always in essence one and the same thing irrespective of the ritual patterns followed or the symbols and language used. According to them it is unimportant whether the faith is expressed in Christian, Jewish, Hindu or Buddhist terms. Eric Sharpe, however, is surely right, when he points out that you cannot get at the essence apart from its manifestations. He would hold that Christians and Hindus are 'the human beings they are in part because of the explicitness of their faith *in* Christ or *in* Krishna'. 'It is this explicitness,' he says, 'which must be accepted, and which an attempt must be made to understand.'[10] But it is inherent in the Christian understanding of *love* that there should be this attempt to understand. When Raimundo Panikkar stresses our solidarity with the whole human race, he is but echoing Paul's emphasis on our common humanity – 'And he made from one every nation of men to live on the face of the earth' (Acts 17:26), and we begin to realise that we cannot be open to others and remain unchanged ourselves. A strict logical correlation of our double commitment may not be possible, but the messages of the other faiths – whether it be the primal vision present in African religions, the note of joy and abandon (or, again, contemplation and discipline) in Hinduism, the notes of comprehensiveness, detachment, mystery, zeal and quietude in Buddhism, the rejection of racialism and class in the Muslim brotherhood, the passionate prophetism of many a new cult, the sense of history and law in Judaism or even the notes of critical judgement in modern agnosticism and Marxism – do not leave us unchanged. They leave us with an echoing note that rings out from within our own Christian tradition, but, were it not for the others, we might not hear it. The spontaneity of the festival in another religion may remind us that it is children who are to enter the kingdom and the note of quietude in many an eastern faith presents a challenge to 'poor talkative Christianity' which may have forgotten that 'the Lord is in his holy temple . . . let all the earth keep silent before him' (Habakkuk 2:20).

Roger Hooker states the dilemma which confronts the Christian towards the end of *Journey into Varanasi*: 'I am gripped by two loyalties: to the Christian tradition and all that it has given me, which means supremely Christ himself . . . I am also held by loyalty to my friends of other faiths.' He would stress, however, that his loyalty to Christ must be 'open-ended', because Christ is '*not a formula* of which the exact words must be preserved inviolate, *but a person* in whom I can discover ever new dimensions, not least through my meeting with men of other faiths . . .' (op.cit., p. 70 – my italics). He is accordingly assured by his own Christian understanding of what God is like that God influences the lives of adherents of other faiths 'in countless ways, hidden and unrecognised, in the stirrings of conscience, the striving after excellence in their daily work, the growth of compassion for the poor and needy, in the provoking of new questions' (ibid.).

Bishop George Appleton (formerly Archbishop in Jerusalem), in the second edition of his book of prayers,[11] includes a section which he calls 'Praying with Others'. One of the prayers that he has composed speaks of 'God's creative love . . . seeking for people everywhere', and of God 'showing (himself) in ways they can understand.' His prayer for the Christian is that he may *'learn more of [God] from the experience of other communities of faith'* (my italics) and so live and act as to share his own religious experience and insights with others. There are petitions for the opening of our eyes, the enlightening of our minds and the enlargement of our hearts.[12] Bishop Kenneth Cragg reminds us of the element of transcendence in religion, the impenetrability ('dark without excess of light') and the mystery which 'escapes or denies our comprehension'. It is a Persian Muslim mystic whom he quotes to affirm this truth:

> Jalal al-Din Rumi asked:
>   Why this oft repeated Naught?
> and replied:
>   Naught brings you first upon the track of aught.
>   Though idle air may seem the Negative
>   It wafts faint odours of the Positive.[13]

Do we not find this highlighting Paul's own words: 'For now we see in a mirror dimly, but then face to face. Now I know in part; then shall I understand fully, even as I have been fully understood' (1 Corinthians 13:12)?

> From the unreal lead me to the real;
> From darkness lead me to light;
> From death lead me to immortality.

So run some oft-quoted sentiments in the Upanishads, and, despite all the difference in the respective Hindu and Christian interpretations of 'deliverance', Bishop Stephen Neill asks: 'Is there not . . . some element of yearning after the ultimate which is common to the Hindu and the Christian?'[14] And one may well add that it is the haunting plea within Hinduism, which brings us face to face with the Christian quest as well: 'Not that I have already attained or am already perfect . . . but I press on toward the goal . . .' (Philippians 3:12–14).

Notes and references

1 There was also a strong sense of western superiority which was applied to religious and cultural traditions. Bishop Stephen Neill illustrates: 'In the nineteenth century missionaries had entertained a sanguine belief that, under the impact of the Gospel and western science, the ancient religions would quickly collapse and leave a vacuum into which Christianity would triumphantly enter' (S. Neill, *Salvation Tomorrow*, Guildford and London: Lutterworth Press, 1976, p. 9). He stresses the meeting of the World's Parliament of Religions in Chicago in 1893 when, for the first time, 'the ancient religions made audible their claim to be received on an equality with the newer religions of the west' (op.cit., p. 10). Bit by bit, there has been a movement towards the 'dethronement of Christianity' and towards 'the renaissance of the ancient faiths of the east' being seen as the liberation of their adherents from Western dominance.

  Professor Joseph Needham confirms the Western attitude of superiority: 'We westerners are still the slaves of this idea that our culture and our religion is in some way "superior" to those of our brothers and sisters in the great countries of Asia' (*Within Four Seas*, London: Allen & Unwin, 1969, p. 203). It is difficult to find a Christianity *sans plus* –i.e. pure and uninfluenced by 'westernism'! Stanley Samartha also speaks of the main obstacles to a real encounter between Christians and adherents of other faiths as being, on the one hand, a feeling of superiority and, on the other, the fear of losing one's identity.

2 See Chapters 1 and 11 for educational arguments that support this wider application.

3 In this context readers will be interested in the work of the Standing Conference on Inter-Faith Dialogue in Education. SCIFDE was formed in 1973 'to convene, or encourage the convening of national and regional inter-faith conferences concerned with education in school and community, including religious education, and to circulate or publish reports of the proceedings or findings of those conferences.' The conference includes representatives of the various world faiths and of organisations concerned with inter-faith and race relations.

4 *Journey into Varanasi* (London: CMS, 1978), p. 68.

5 *Dialogue between Men of Living Faiths* (Geneva: WCC, 1971), p. 21.

6 The present writer, in trying to sort out the use of 'God' and 'god' or 'gods', once indicated that, if we accept the truth that God relates himself to all, it follows, then, that the 'god' (or some other symbol of the transcendent) within another religion would not 'necessarily describe objects other than "God" – but would indicate . . . a mistaken or inadequate view of the ultimate reality which we indicate by the

word "God"'. There was, however, the added caveat that 'the Christian, too, is limited in his apprehension of the "truth"' and 'is also unable to express that which he has apprehended', so that the use of the word 'God' is no guarantee that we have dismissed the 'god' or 'gods' of our own creating (see R. Hammer, *Japan's Religious Ferment*, London: SCM Press, 1961, p. 20).

7 Bishop Cragg emphasises that 'we moderns can never precisely know what apostles would have done in our situation' and that even Paul, 'for all his travail about Torah and Israel, did not possess the perspective on Judaism which must be ours these centuries on' (Kenneth Cragg, *Paul and Peter: Meeting in Jerusalem*, London: Bible Reading Fellowship, 1980, p. 84).

8 John Hick, 'Whatever path men choose is mine', in the collection *Christianity and Other Religions* (London: Collins Fount Paperbacks, 1980), pp. 171-90.

9 Wilfred Cantwell Smith, *The Meaning and End of Religion* (New York: Mentor Books, 1964) (London: SPCK, 1978).

10 Eric J. Sharpe, *Faith Meets Faith* (London: SCM Press, 1977), p. 150.

11 George Appleton, *In His Name* (Guildford and London: Lutterworth Press, 1978).

12 See also Kenneth Cracknell, *Why Dialogue?* (London: BCC, 1980), p. 24.

13 Kenneth Cragg, op.cit., p. 85.

14 Stephen Neill, op.cit., p. 138.

Further reading

Klaus Klostermaier, *Hindu and Christian in Vrindaban* (London: SCM Press, 1969) is still the most exciting and challenging book to come out in the area of inter-religious dialogue, where Krishna-worshipper and Christian rub shoulder to shoulder in the sweltering heat at festival time. Like Raimundo Panikkar, *The Unknown Christ of Hinduism* (Darton, Longman & Todd, 1964), it sees Christ operative within Hinduism, but refrains from imposing traditional Christian categories upon the other faith. 'Christ,' he says, 'meets the Hindu – not from the outside, but with his own thought and faith.' One may add that the Christian, in meeting the Hindu, is surprised to find that he, too, has met with Christ in him. Professor Eric Sharpe in *Faith Meets Faith* (SCM Press, 1977) looks at Christian attitudes in the nineteenth and twentieth centuries, but Roger Hooker's *Journey into Varanasi* (London: CMS, 1978) once again introduces us to the existential demands in person-to-person encounter.

Face to Face (London: CMS, 1971) contains some thought-provoking essays on inter-faith dialogue, three by men who are now Anglican bishops, but who have had intimate contact with African religions, Islam and Buddhism respectively. The essay from the late Dr Max Warren is entitled 'A theology of attention'. The Christian-Communist dialogue also has a chapter.

John Hick and Brian Hebblethwaite have provided us with a useful selection of attitudes in *Christianity and other Religions* (Collins, Fount Paperbacks, 1980) – from Troeltsch early in this century through to Bishop J. V. Taylor. Bishop Kenneth Cragg, *Paul and Peter: Meeting in Jerusalem* (London: BRF, 1980), asks some searching questions on Christian-Jewish-Muslim relations.

Two small pamphlets are to be recommended highly – Kenneth Cracknell's *Why Dialogue?* (BCC, 1980) and *With People of Other Faiths* (URC, 1980). Both consider the challenge to be faced by Christians as they find themselves in relationship with people of other faiths.

The Secretariatus pro non Christianis in the Vatican puts out a valuable journal, and its other publications, notably *Meeting with African Religions, Guidelines for Dialogue between Muslims and Christians* and *The Meeting with Buddhism* (2 vols), are all of use. So, too, are the WCC reports, put out by Stanley Samartha and John Taylor, both very much involved in inter-faith relationships.

The present author's chapter, 'The theological perspective in the encounter of religions', in Robert Jackson (ed.), *Perspectives on World Religions* (London: SOAS, 1978), provides a complement to the present chapter.

Part Four

Personal Development

Introduction

The desire to make religious education relevant to the questions, dilemmas and problems of young people in school is a recurring theme in the history of the subject. One of the principal reasons for the move away from the post-1944 diet of biblical studies in schools was the need felt by pupils and teachers for 'relevance'. With the growth of interest in a world religions approach to RE some have detected a tendency to return to an over-emphasis on content, though it is clear from the opening chapters of this book that this trend is not general. The chapters which follow seek to place pupils at the centre of a religious education which draws on their own insights and questions as well as on material from world religions. At the same time the contributors endeavour to maintain a balanced, accurate presentation of the religions themselves, and a lack of prescription over what pupils should believe.

Brian Gates reminds us of the Plowden report's emphasis on education beginning with the experience of children. He rejects, however, both the Plowden committee's majority view that children 'should be taught to know and love God' and its minority view that religious education, because it involves the difficult intellectual activity of theology, is better left until the later years of the secondary school. The former view does not take account of the secularising and pluralist nature of our society, while the latter fails to make a distinction between children's developing intellectual capacity for handling religious concepts and their ability to understand before they can think in an adult fashion. Even young children are aware of some of the raw material of religion, a few of them through their attendance at places of worship but many more through their explicitly religious beliefs and their potentially religious feelings and questions. The task of the RE teacher – and Gates is thinking especially of the primary school teacher – is to translate the raw material of religion (whether from children's experience or from institutional religion) into terms that children can comprehend. Story, ritual, verbal and visual imagery, music and silence, as well as social and individual patterns of behaviour, may all be employed by the imaginative teacher as vehicles for conveying religious meaning.

Gates goes on to distinguish between the school's role in educating children in religion – turning them out religiate as well as numerate and literate – and the task of the various faith communities in nurturing their children in religious belief and practice, though he points out that the two processes need not be mutually exclusive. Each is a provisional activity, for the growth of religious understanding (in either context) is not confined to the years of childhood. Both processes too are concerned, in their different ways, with commitment.

Michael Grimmitt (Chapter 12) is critical of certain features of the RE of both the 1960s, typified in the work of Ronald Goldman, and the 1970s, influenced by the phenomenological approach of Ninian Smart. He maintains, however, that important insights can be gained from both in relating religious data to the personal development of children and young people.

Just as the theological assumptions underlying Ronald Goldman's idea of RE are idiosyncratic and therefore unacceptable to many believers and unbelievers alike, so the presumption of a dichotomy between the sacred and the profane made by phenomenologists of religion is considered to be equally problematic. In addition, maintains Grimmitt, the phenomenological approach to religious studies has led to a heavily content-centred RE little related to the personal lives of pupils. There are, however, certain perceptions from the RE of the 1960s and 1970s which, together with insights from phenomenology and from world religions, suggest an approach to religious education which is non-prescriptive, which draws on a variety of religions and yet which is concerned with each pupil's personal development.

Grimmitt offers a definition of education as 'a process in and through which pupils may begin to explore what it is, and what it means, to be human'; RE's contribution to this process of education consists in both learning *about* and learning *from* religion. The phenomenology of religion provides a methodology for learning *about* religion, but learning *from* religion involves helping pupils to apply insights gained from their study of religion to their own lives.

Grimmitt points out that what has become known as the phenomenology of religion is but one branch of a wider discipline and argues that this discipline's emphasis on the 'life world' of the individual – particularly on the phase in which the individual has a 'personal' and individual rather than a 'public' understanding of his experience – gives insight into how pupils learn and reveals a need for a pedagogy which, in the case of RE, encourages pupils to reflect on the ways in which beliefs and values shape the lives of individuals.

From world religions pupils can learn what each faith understands by the notion of the religious or spiritual quest, and can especially learn how individuals give personal accounts of what it means to be a believer. The pupil may thus encounter a whole range of 'models of the human' upon which he or she can reflect. In this way the study of religion makes a distinctive contribution to the personal development of pupils.

The author's views on the negative effects on RE of the phenomenology of religion will appear to some readers as too pessimistic. Many teachers have successfully employed phenomenology as a tool for understanding religion while also encouraging pupils to reflect upon and to criticise views that have been learned. The opening chapters of this book add weight to this suggestion. Grimmitt's definition of education and his account of RE's role in the educational process, however, offer radical and challenging ideas which support Robin Richardson's plea (in Chapter 16) for more vital theories of learning than those traditionally associated with religious education.

Like Grimmitt, Simon Weightman (Chapter 13) is particularly concerned with the relevance to pupils of material from world religions. While upholding the teacher's responsibility to present religious material accurately and regarding the aim of understanding the pupils' various religious traditions as basic, Weightman is concerned that pupils should learn about *themselves* from world religions; this, he maintains, is the distinctive opportunity offered by the study of world religions in schools. A diet of too many facts or negative experiences resulting from cynical or narrow-minded teaching can kill the possibility of children learning from religion and of having fundamental human questions awakened in them.

Weightman uses the word 'realisation' in his title to convey the necessity of making religion 'real' to pupils. Through doing this something is 'realised' in what he calls children's 'essential natures'. In explaining his use of terminology he distinguishes between the actual and the real. To actualise is to make knowable. The word 'actual', like the words 'existence' and 'existential', are associated with the factual side of things. 'Realisation', or to make real, however, is concerned with making abstract values concrete and it is associated with the words 'essence' and 'essential'; 'essence' Weightman defines as 'the intrinsic possibility of being real that resides in every entity'.

The educational process, argues Weightman, is concerned with achieving the right balance between existence and essence. Specifically within religious education the existential should meet the essential in a number of ways, and Weightman illustrates these by means of a model. One point he makes is that a balance between the existential and the essential should be struck in the teacher's selection of suitable 'content' from the religions and appropriate resources for teaching that material.

On his model Weightman posits a Goal or Ideal which is distinct from the aims of RE; it is elusive and indefinable, but 'has to do with the aspirations of education itself, with the personal development of children and . . . with the awakening of some form of inner awareness, of essential values, and with the implanting of questioning about the meaning and purpose of life'. This Goal interplays with the aim of RE (seen as the understanding of religions or of religion) in the teacher's capacity to see whether an understanding of a particular feature of a religion will help a child's inner life to awaken or grow. In requiring the teacher's integrity, especially in respecting each child's individuality, the Goal or Ideal interacts with the activity of teaching. The teacher's skill and sensitivity are also needed in balancing children's questions about themselves and the world in which they live with the highest aspirations and ideals represented by the Goal.

In summary, in the presentation of material from the world's religions, teachers should aim to bring out the immediate questions, awarenesses and experiences of children while at the same time implanting and awakening in them ultimate questions.

R.J.

11
Children Prospecting for Commitment

Brian Gates

It is not that many years since the Plowden report on primary education was published[1] yet many of its comments on RE seem more remotely dated. The report itself was considered by many to be progressive, but it insistently cautioned against any deviancy from Christian nurture in the infant and junior years of schooling.

> . . . young children need a simple and positive introduction to religion. They should be taught to know and love God . . . children should not be unnecessarily involved in religious controversy. They should not be confused by being taught to doubt before faith is established. (para. 572, p. 207)

A minority disagreeing with this view argued rather differently that RE involves theology, which is 'too recondite and too controversial' for primary-age pupils, and therefore is better left until later secondary years. Neither of these views is consistent with the changes in RE that have taken place in the meantime. In connection with the first, the assumption of a practising Christian norm is increasingly perceived as inappropriate in a country which, while remaining Christian in heritage, is also secularising and multi-faith. In regard to the second, religion is recognised as involving more than intellectual abstraction; religious behaviour, belief and belonging express themselves in many different forms.

Whilst taking issue with any presumption about the need for Christian instruction in the content of RE in schools, we may still appreciate the Plowden emphasis on starting with the children themselves. What do we know about religion in childhood and adolescence? What are children and young people capable of understanding? Where, if at all, does commitment come into their experience? In attempting to answer these questions, this chapter offers a foundation for RE in children's experience and explorations of where their lives might lead.

Religion in childhood and adolescence

Religion is never easily defined, and yet any judgement about the degree and depth of contact that boys and girls have with it will depend largely on what range of knowledge and experience is considered relevant. This is a problem facing social scientists and theologians generally: any working definition needs to be broad enough to reflect the variegated experience of humanity, yet sufficiently discrete to prevent blur and distortion.

One activity commonly associated with religion is that of regular attendance at a place of worship. In our own society it is clear that only a minority of boys and girls is involved in such attendance. The 1979 census of the churches conducted by a 'nationwide initiative in evangelism' registered a typical weekly attendance figure at church or Sunday school of 14 per cent of the available child population under 15 years.[2] This compares with over 30 per cent in 1950. Even allowing for some limitations in the sampling (74 per cent of English churches were drawn on, half directly, the others via their central offices), there is little reason to judge this a gross under-estimate. Comparable figures for the children of Buddhist, Jewish, Muslim, Sikh and other faiths are not available, but though the parent communities might wish it were otherwise, the total number involved is unlikely to add much more than 1 per cent to the over- all total.[3] Evidently, more than four-fifths of boys and girls in England are not regularly involved in attendance at a local place of worship.

It would be wrong, however, to assume that these figures represent the full extent of formal religious association. The practice of 'occasional conformity' still persists amongst adults, and their children, especially at Christmas and Easter. On a smaller scale a similar phenomenon may be observed on the part of the Jewish and other minority religious communities. The involvement of children with the familiar rites of passage still persists – baptisms and naming ceremonies, and weddings, if not funerals. The proportion of boys and girls who have such occasional contact with the local places of worship is significantly higher than 15 per cent, though actual figures are not available.[4]

What meaning such occasional associations with institutional religion have for the children concerned is difficult to ascertain. At worst there is little more than a superficial familiarity with the outward vestiges of an otherwise eccentric inheritance; at best, a sense of being part of a communal tradition which, along with family, region and nation provides another frame within which personal identity is forged. Self-ascription as Catholic, Church of England, Muslim, Rastafarian or whatever by a boy or girl may derive from either frequent or infrequent attendance, but in any case more often than not it will have been picked up from parents and grandparents.

An alternative or additional characteristic is that of explicit religious belief. Survey data regarding the adult population have consistently indicated a very high percentage of persons professing belief in God, a percentage which becomes higher with age.[5] Such evidence as is available pertaining to those under 18 years would suggest that among younger boys and girls belief in God is as commonplace as belief in Father Christmas, but that both are increasingly questioned during junior school years. Although the balance of belief and unbelief may in fact be shifting amongst young people[6] (and in any case there are regional variations[7]), belief in God appears to persist for the majority, often accompanied by continued questioning. The content of beliefs may well be intellectually confused and reflect much ignorance, as illustrated by Loukes[8] and more recently by the General Synod Board of Education's report *A Kind of Believing*.[9] However, on the basis of my own research I would claim that, generally speaking, boys and girls do all work towards a 'beliefs equation' of their own, one which is internally consistent and a key ingredient in their total attitude to life.[10] Irrespective of the degree of belief or unbelief, it is also true that virtually all acquire some everyday connotations of the word God; that is to say, a concept of God, however simplistic, or even sophisticated, is part of their mental furniture. Intensity of religious belief varies, but exposure to it is constant.

Alongside all the explicit contact with religion in terms of belief and belonging, certain spontaneous musings on the part of the individual child may also count as relevant to his or her association with religion. Boys and girls from time to time experience certain feelings and are moved to ask particular questions, any of which may be potentially religious. A sense of wonder and awe provoked by some sound or sight of great beauty, feelings of trust and security, of gratitude or joy prompted by some act of kindness or playful merriment, or grief and sadness at some loss—these can all be the occasion for Wordsworthian sensations of mystery or presence, of greater purpose or meaning. Such experiences are now widely attested in adults[11] and it seems from children's talk, personal writing and playground lore that they abound also with them. Without presuming that the truth claims of religion are publicly proved by such stirrings, it is important to recognise that they are commonly human and religious.

The questioning referred to is typified by the young child's pressing 'Why?'. It looks for relationships, causes, connections to explain anything and everything. In so pressing towards final explanations, the boy or girl is engaging in that realm of exploration and inquiry which is not satisfied with instant or interim solutions, but seeks as well for fully comprehensive cover, as ultimate as can be. Of course, such meaning may not be available, or may sometimes arise from confused thinking or mistakes in logic. Nevertheless, religion has itself been traditionally very much occupied with the question of whether there is rhyme or reason in life and death, whether there is any justice in the face of innocent suffering, and children with their questions move unwittingly into the territory of religion.

Children's capacities for religious understanding

According to A. J. Ayer and his professional and head teacher colleagues in their minority statement on RE in the Plowden report, religion is too difficult an area for boys and girls to cope with, because it involves theology.[12] This has been taken by some as the conclusion also to be drawn from R. Goldman's examination of the development of children's religious thinking between the ages of 6 and 17.[13] The responses he received to questions he had put to boys and girls regarding three episodes from the Bible and three pictures of children with reference to praying, bible reading and church-going, lead him to talk of their general unreadiness for religion. Until the age of formal operational thinking in secondary schools when they become capable of hypothetical reasoning and abstract analysis, children are largely 'sub-religious'. Premature exposure to theological concepts will only encourage misconceptions and subsequent alienation. Goldman's research was extensively reported and had widespread impact on syllabus makers throughout the country; it has been widely replicated, most notably by J. Peatling in North America,[14] and comparable claims have been advanced independently by others.[15] As a result, the inference may very easily be drawn that on psychological grounds RE provision should be deferred until 13+ when a stage of more advanced intellectual sophistication will have been achieved.

It is one thing to admit that children's ability to handle religious concepts develops gradually and through a series of well-defined stages, as does their handling of, for instance, number, space and time. It is quite another to underestimate how much boys and girls are able to understand about religion before they can think in an intellectually elaborated way. Much may still be refracted through to them via earlier modes of thinking – intuitive and fanciful, or concrete and circumstantial. The solution for the teacher will be to engage in more imaginative translations into terms that the children can cope with. This is preferable to waiting for a stage which may only arrive after school has been left behind. Given the extent of children's exposure to religion, whether in its institutional manifestations or their own wonderings, the raw material is already there.

Just as boys and girls, if read aright, provide their own resources for effective RE, so too there is much in religious tradition to which they can respond, in spite of their intellectual limitations. Theology, in the Plowden dissenting sense, is not ignored; it is instead expressed through a variety of media designed to convey its meaning at the appropriate level.

1 *Story* or *myth* is a basic medium for expressing religious meaning, but it also has a basic appeal to children of any age. The good story lends itself to understanding at different levels, and involves imagination and feeling as much as intellectual comprehension. It is well worth exploring as a form for work with all abilities. To this end, each teacher may wish to develop his or her list for story telling, separated into different categories, as illustrated in the table.

2 *Ritual* or symbolic gesture is no less a basic medium for expressing religious meaning than story. It too may have a counterpart in the child's own heritage of ritual play – in the school playground, or with friends, or in connection with his or her support for a favoured team. Whether in the

TYPE OF STORY	IMPLICIT	EXPLICIT		
		Biblical	Christian	Other Religions
Archetypal	J. L. and W. K. Grimm, *Hansel and Gretel* (Dobson, 1974)	Noah's Flood	The Grail, e.g. Cavendish, *King Arthur and the Grail* (Paladin, 1980)	African creation stories, e.g. E. G. Parrinder, *African Mythology* (Hamlyn Mythology Series)
Fantasy	A. P. Pearce, *Tom's Midnight Garden* (OUP, 1958)	Jonah	C. S. Lewis *The Lion, the Witch and the Wardrobe* (Collins, 1974)	Ramayana, e.g. B. Thompson, *The Story of Prince Rama* (Kestrel, 1980)
Moral	*Aesop's Fables* (Dent, 1972)	Naboth's Vineyard	Charles Dickens, *A Christmas Carol* (Allen Lane, 1979)	M. Iqbal, *The Guiding Crescent* (Pakistan, 1973. Available from Dr M. Iqbal, The Polytechnic, Queen's Gate, Huddersfield, HD1 3DH)
Exemplary	A. Holm, *I am David* (Methuen Magnet, 1980)	Temptation stories	S. M. Hobden, *Mother Teresa*, 'People with a Purpose' series (SCM, 1973)	G. M. James, *The Bodhi Tree* (Chapman, 1971)

form of non-verbal communication ('body talk') or role-play and enacted story, ritual can reverberate with any age or ability of pupil. Again, each teacher may wish to develop an assortment of ritual acts which their pupils may be encouraged to try out, whether individually or in groups. In both cases their acts might include gestures of gratitude, affection, awe, quietness and pleading, and in groups they might also include those of trust, sadness, celebration, pledging and sharing. The power of simple action to promote a new awareness and to convey a special meaning is quickly felt. And again this is true of acts which are either implicitly or explicitly religious.

3 *Verbal and visual imagery.* Imagery in verbal or visual form is vital to religion. Taboos against making images warn us that they must be deliberately interchanged with other images or avoided altogether, to prevent any confusion between them and the reality they purport to represent. As an aid to understanding, children's picturing with words or paint is a welcome means of conveying ideas which might otherwise remain beyond anyone else's grasp. In a culture in which the media constantly multiply the images to which a child is exposed, it is well worth the RE teacher's time to devise opportunities for sharing, exposing and inventing images that people live by – from Christmas cards to cigar adverts!

4 *Music and silence*. Music manages to be both earthy and sublime – its rhythm and beat are instantly communicable, so too is its mood; with both it can move beyond surface feeling. On occasions, it may lead to silence followed by newer appreciation. The RE teacher would do well to look to musical resources; whether as a result of listening to music or of making it, the children's responses may be surprising.

5 *Social organisation and individual life-style*. The different shapes – ages, sizes, sexes, colours – of clubs or gangs, as of families, schools or whole nations, are quickly registered by children growing in the midst of them. The sense of belonging to one or more such grouping develops fairly early in life. There are parallel experiences here for exploring the sense of belonging that accompanies membership of a church or the *khalsa* and, perhaps, for asking about the value of membership to an individual. Social horizons can easily be restricted, but class or year/ability group labelling may itself prompt the pupil to a greater awareness of the networks of administrative and teaching arrangements that affect others. How people organise their own lives and those of their communities can be very real questions, made the more answerable by reference to the sense of social belonging and casual copying of others, already begun at home or in school.

With the aid of such vehicles as these many of the intelligibility problems that religion might be expected to present to children can be overcome.

Autonomy — relative and committed

More and more, in practice as well as in theory, the tasks of the day school (unless it is denominational, in which case several additional considerations come into play) and of the parent religious community are acknowledged as different in respect of RE. The school has an 'appetising' and preliminary role of endeavouring to introduce boys and girls to the wider religious experience of mankind. The end here is that they leave school religiate, though not necessarily religious. In a complementary way, outside the school, in the child's inherited or adopted community of faith, rather more, in explicitly religious terms, will be sought by and for each boy or girl.

The distinction between the educational role of the school and the community of faith is helpful in making the former's task more modest and manageable than it would otherwise be. It would be wrong, however, to polarise the two to the extent that sometimes happens when the term education is used exclusively for the school and nurture for the parent community. For what happens in both contexts may on occasion be both education and nurturing. School and parent community are at one in recognising that a child's religious identity develops over a period of time. The parent community tends to look for a public statement of commitment, ritually expressed, during early adolescence, but the antecedents of this statement go back to birth and include family influence, formal teaching, and either through these or by other means, admit the possibility of divine initiative. The ritual may involve the laying on of hands, the wearing of a sacred vestment, the recitation of some extract from the scriptures, or some other definitive act, but even so the community responsible will scarcely identify this specific stage of the person's development with perfection, or deny that further transformation is expected. In other words, there is implicit in each religious tradition the hope that an individual's development does not finish, but continues beyond youth, even to death and possibly thereafter. Similarly, in the school context, this must be as readily admitted. CSE or GCE exams in RE may for the minority who take them be part of some secular rite of passage to be negotiated before adult society is entered. But any understanding of life and religion that has been achieved in school can be only at the threshold of what is to follow. Thus 'becoming religiate', like becoming numerate and literate, is a provisional condition that opens up a range of experience. Whether a girl or boy chooses to follow any of the ways further, given the help of rudimentary bearings, is beyond the school's educational brief. Nevertheless in school the place of commitment in religion will have been clearly indicated.

On each front, the holding open of personal options is necessary on both educational and theological grounds. The school would beg too many questions if it were to favour one religious or atheistic position over all others. The parent community would be wilfully constricting (increasingly hard in a Western society with its all-pervasive media) if it foreclosed on any expressions of doubt or alternative views. The autonomy to be striven for by all concerned in either context must therefore be related to the insights and affirmations of others, if it is to be other than narcissistic or blind in its dealing with commitment. There is always a danger that an individual, in working out his or her views, may become careless of every other position and closed to any claim on it from beyond.

Reference to 'commitment' being expected of the boy or girl deserves further comment, within the context of the school as well as the faith community. Since William James, it has been a commonplace among psychologists to refer to both once- and twice-born modes of personality development and religious conversion, the one gradual and long term, the other sudden and immediately arrived at. By definition, education is more concerned with the first, though it may directly or indirectly contribute to the second. As a result of RE, some transformation in understanding of both self and the world at large should probably be expected; surface knowledge is less likely to disturb or challenge, whereas genuine appreciation and learning will give rise to deeper resonance and impact. Yet it is only when children become personally engaged – excited, frightened, charmed, provoked, challenged with a story, a festival, an intellectual ideal, a pictorial emblem of faith – that any depth of meaning can be perceived. In this sense, therefore, RE calls for commitment from its participants, teacher and pupils alike, to enter into its distinctive vehicles of expression.

Commitment of this kind is not the same as making a particular confession of faith, although it ought to equip a boy or girl better to understand the implications of such. Rather, it is a willingness to try to enter into the spirit of human adventuring that has moved men and women, past and present to respond to visions and challenges that would re-order their lives and the world around them. What moved the Pilgrim Fathers to leave the confining structures of the old world and strive to realise the new priorities of God's Kingdom in North America? Long marches, Zions – Semitic or Black, the land reform of Vinobe Bhave, the monastery that is Iona, Taizé, or Indian ashram, the believer's daily routine that is seen as shot through with divinity – these cry out to be followed and fathomed.

If this sounds too grand for a classroom, or too dangerous and difficult for children to attempt, we may need quickly to remind ourselves that comparable engagements are taking place anyway. They are found in the following and fervour given to a soccer club, the school team or the first division favourite, and when too much is expected of what after all is a simple game, it cannot bear the weight of life and death, and disorder surges out. Engagement is found in the admiration, quiet or noisy, given to the hero in some television saga, or to the latest pop star. Intellectual explanations by the boys or girls concerned of what it is they are attracted by, may be put into words only with difficulty or very briefly, but there is no doubt that they feel 'grabbed'. And, of course, the media men and advertisers know this; they have done their market research and have developed well-tried techniques for guaranteeing take-up. They are able to devise how to trigger conscious and unconscious associations with loyalties and yearnings, hopes and fears, that are layered deep inside the adult, as well as the child. When we speak of becoming engaged in RE and developing skills for handling commitment, we too are dealing with the nerve centres of individual choice and decision which make us who and what we are.

It follows from this that there is a place in both school and parent community for putting commitments under scrutiny. If they are ignored and left to look after themselves, then any models for living or ranking of interests will be haphazard echoes and not the sources for creative selection which they might otherwise be. Only as a result of opportunity to try and test them can second-hand beliefs and rejections of belief be seen as shapeless and full of holes, or alternatively enhancing the person who decides to live with them.

Conclusion

Any concession to child-centredness in the classroom provides an incentive to make more careful provision for RE in schools. For it is evident that religion is variously part of the 'life world' of children and young people. Any sensitivity to religious traditions provides a range of resources with which to delight and enrich our common humanity irrespective of age. Preferential teaching to establish Christian belief should indeed be avoided – not to encourage doubt, as Plowden feared, but to enable boys and girls to develop a strong sense of commitment with which they may illuminate their lives.

Notes and references

1 Department of Education and Science, *Children and their Primary Schools* (London: HMSO, 1967).

2 Nationwide Initiative in Evangelism, *Prospects for the Eighties* (London: Bible Society, 1980).

3 Contrary to the impression sometimes given, members of newly settled minority groups are not invariably more devout than the host population.

4 As illustration of 'occasional conformity', membership statistics of the Church of England reveal that approximately three-fifths of the total population of this country are baptised and one-fifth confirmed. See *Statistical Supplement to the Church of England Yearbook* (London: Church Information Office, 1981).

5 M. Argyle and B. Beit-Hallahmi, *Social Psychology of Religion* (London: RKP, 1975).

6 Such is the claim advanced by Leslie Francis in several recent research reports. See *Christianity and the Child Today: A Research Perspective on the Situation in England* (Oxford: Farmington Institute for Christian Studies, 1981).

7 See also C. Alves, *Religion and the Secondary School* (London: SCM Press, 1968), chapter 3; J. Greer, *A Questioning Generation* (Church of Ireland Board of Education, 1972).

8 H. Loukes, *New Ground in Christian Education* (London: SCM Press, 1965), chapter 5.

9 M. H. Duke and E. Whitton, *A Kind of Believing* (London: General Synod Board of Education, 1977); detailed examples of the content of young people's responses during interviews are given in the full research report: B. Martin and R. Pluck, *Young People's Beliefs* (Board of Education, 1977), mimeo.

10 B. E. Gates, 'Religion in the child's own core curriculum' in *Learning for Living*, 17:1, 1977, pp. 9–15.

11 See A. Hardy, *The Spiritual Nature of Man* (Oxford: OUP, 1979);
    M. Laski, *Everyday Ecstasy* (London: Thames & Hudson, 1980). For
    related experiences in childhood, see E. A. Robinson, *Original Vision*
    (Oxford: Religious Experience Research Unit, 1977); M. Paffard,
    Inglorious Wordsworths (London: Hodder, 1973).

12 op.cit., vol. 1, pp. 489–92.

13 R. Goldman, *Religious Thinking from Childhood to Adolescence* (London:
    RKP, 1964).

14 Peatling's research study is reported in *Learning for Living*, 16:3, 1977,
    pp. 99–108.

15 Independently, the work of D. Elkind and R. Williams in North
    America, of A. Godin in Belgium, of K. Tamminen in Finland, and of
    G. Westling and S. Pettersson in Sweden has built on the same
    Piagetian base with similar results.

Further Reading

Violet Madge, *Children in Search of Meaning* (London: SCM Press, 1965)
captures the quality of infant and junior interests and puzzlements and
sets RE in this context; Harold Loukes in *Teenage Religion* (London: SCM
Press, 1961) represents the concerns of older pupils in a similar way. The
limiting implications of Piagetian stages of intellectual development for a
child's ability to handle theological concepts are set out in Ronald
Goldman, *Religious Thinking from Childhood to Adolescence* (London:
Routledge, 1965). Direct opposition to this view is expressed by Edward
A. Robinson in *The Original Vision* (Oxford: Religious Experience
Research Unit, 1977) in which he draws extensively on adult recollections
of childhood experience. The sheer power of childhood imagination in
Fynn's *Mr God, this is Anna* (London: Fontana, 1974) is dynamite to any
easy categorisations!

Most of the British literature has been written from within a framework
of Christian belief, but in this respect, *A Kind of Believing* (London: Church
House, 1977) sounds a caveat against assuming that an informed
understanding of Christianity persists among young people; ignorance
too is reported in Brian Gates's 'The politics of RE', in M. Taylor (ed.),
Progress and Problems in Moral Education (Slough: NFER, 1975). Increasingly more attention is being paid to children from other religious
backgrounds. Alan G. James, *Sikh Children in Britain* (London: OUP,
1974) provides a close-up of one minority; J. Taylor in *The Half Way
Generation* (Slough: NFER, 1976) looks at new families more generally in
north-east England.

The classroom implications of children's religious development in the
face of diversity of belief in our society are treated positively in the Schools
Council's *Discovering an Approach* (London: Macmillan, 1977) and

also in Carol Mumford, *Young Children and RE* (Leeds University Press, 1979).

Playground encounters between boys and girls of different religious backgrounds provide the basis of a classroom text in G. Cleverley and B. Phillips, *Northbourne Tales of Belief and Understanding* (London: McGraw Hill, 1975), and Elizabeth Cook, *The Ordinary and the Fabulous* (London: Cambridge University Press, 1969) displays the treasure-trove of stories available for any teacher to dally with.

12
World Religions and Personal Development

Michael Grimmitt

'To be educated is to learn to be a person.'—G. Langford[1]

'First, by what criteria are we to determine that someone is developing as a person in distinction from mathematically, scientifically and so on? Second, how are these more specialised forms of development related to personal development? This is not simply a speculative problem that it might be fun to solve; it is one of considerable practical importance.'—R. S. Peters[2]

In the last fifteen years, religious educators have sought to accommodate at least two different sets of educational concerns and techniques within RE. Both have involved them in reformulating their views of RE and of its contribution to the personal development of pupils, and reformulating their views of religion and of its relationship to education. The first set of concerns arose from insights taken from developmental psychology and child-centred theories of education. These concerns were accommodated in the 1960s by defining religion in terms of a natural theology of experience with strongly Christian affinities and seeing RE as promoting among pupils an activity of theological reflection which would lead them to a Christian interpretation of human experience.[3] The other set of concerns arose from insights gained from the use of conceptual analysis in educational philosophy and from techniques deriving from the history of religions. These concerns were accommodated in the 1970s by defining religion in terms of a form of knowledge relating to a significant aspect of human experience, and seeing RE as promoting among pupils under-standing of that discipline (its structure, central concepts, language, verification procedures, etc.,) and how it is expressed in and through social phenomena.[4] Various names have been given to the two main teaching approaches developed as a result of these accommodations, the most common being *experiential* and *phenomenological*. It is not the intention of this chapter to describe these approaches in detail,[5] but rather to explore their conflicting estimates of what it means for RE to contribute to the personal development of the pupil.

The contribution of an experiential approach to personal development

The experiential approach which dominated the 1960s and inspired other versions of it,[6] was that proposed by Ronald Goldman.[7] Despite the *particular* theological assumptions underlying it which are now seen to be inappropriate, I suggest that the approach is based upon principles which continue to have value and application to RE, namely:

1 that education is concerned with the whole person and with encouraging the personal development of each child;
2 that religious and theological concerns of various kinds contribute to and influence views of education in general and views of RE in particular, especially in defining the meaning and end of personal development;
3 that a coherence should exist between the aims of education and the aims of RE and that attention should be given to identifying the distinctive contribution of RE to education;
4 that for the religious person, religion fulfils an integrating role in the interpretation of all experience and knowledge and that RE should seek to make this explicit;
5 that the needs of the child are of central importance in education and that RE should be directed towards the fulfilment of the child's personal needs, including religious and spiritual ones, as they are felt at the various stages of his development;
6 that RE should be developmental in so far as its purpose, content and methods should (i) relate to the child's needs, experiences and stage of conceptual development, and (ii) assist him towards succeeding stages in his personal development;
7 that the approach to the content of RE should be experience-based and thematic as this allows for a greater possibility of learning being related to the child's needs, interests, experiences, questions and conceptual abilities.

If these principles have largely been neglected in recent years by religious educators it is not because they have been shown to be educationally unsound but because of their close association with a form of Christian education no longer tolerable in the state schools of a pluralist, secular society. In *Readiness for Religion*, Goldman offers a religious view of education, or, more precisely, a Christian theology of education. Consistent with child-centred theorists he sees education as a process directed towards the encouragement of personal growth. His view of religion is similar: it too is concerned with the development of the person. Consequently he sees no educational or theological reason why education and religion cannot be combined into a complementary process directed towards the same goal – the personal development of the individual. But this goal needs to be defined more precisely. *Growth* and *development* in themselves can offer no sense of direction for the process.

Goldman thus chooses to define personal development and personal growth in terms of a Christian view of man because Christianity 'answers the deepest needs of human nature, and without a knowledge of the love of God and a relationship with him men and women will live impoverished lives . . .'[8] Education in general, and RE in particular, is, therefore, to be directed towards the promotion of a Christian outlook among pupils as a desirable and necessary part of their personal development. RE is best able to contribute to this goal when it combines three interrelated concerns:

1 the fulfilment of the child's personal needs as they are felt at various stages of his development;[9]
2 the encouragement of the child's religious development and spiritual growth;[10]
3 the development of religious thinking and an understanding of religion at an intellectual level.[11]

By combining these three concerns within a developmental programme Goldman seeks to devise a form of religious education 'which prepares children for the succeeding stages of their development, as well as answering the spiritual needs of the moment'.[12] RE is not, therefore, to be seen only as an opportunity for pupils to learn about religion but rather as an opportunity for them to engage in a *personal religious quest*. It is for this reason among others that Goldman rejects 'the assumption that religion can be taught as a body of knowledge to be absorbed by pupils, as other facts are learned'.[13]

The contribution of a phenomenological approach to personal development

The contrast in assumptions between those underlying Goldman's experiential approach and those underlying a more recent phenomenological approach are well illustrated by the following observation made by Ninian Smart:

> . . . religious studies should be governed by their inner logic, whatever the parahistorical premises from which people start. They should also, I believe, be governed by the principle of the essential unity of education.[14]

Unlike Goldman, Smart does not make any theological assumptions about religion and education or about the way in which they may be said to relate to each other. The unity of education is determined by the inner logic of its subjects or disciplines, not by its coherence within a religious framework. Religion is like any other discipline in that it too possesses its own inner logic; it is this which governs how it is to be studied, not some claim that it fulfils an integrating role in relation to all experience and knowledge. Accordingly the overriding concern of education is to induct pupils into an understanding of the logic of the disciplines, including religion, for these are seen as the fundamental categories of all truth-seeking activities. The contribution which the study of religion makes to the pupil's development is thus seen in terms of 'creating certain capacities to understand and think about religion'.[15] A capacity to understand religion is, according to this view, dependent upon pupils being able to distance themselves from their own presuppositions and beliefs and re-present the subjective consciousness of the religious believer. The application of this skill is seen as essential if a religion is to be understood as it is felt to be by those who practise it. The reasons for engaging in such a study are given as, 'the interest of religion, the importance of religion and the question of the truth of religion',[16] and elsewhere Smart comments: 'If, then, we are to justify the science of religion, it is centrally upon intellectual grounds, not on the ground of its utility or of its capacity to improve people . . .'[17] These statements are in sharp contrast to those of Goldman in which the value of religion, and the purpose for studying it, is located in the contribution it makes to meeting the child's personal needs. Rather than provide pupils with an opportunity to engage in a personal religious quest, this approach would appear to be advocating that they engage in a *scientific investigation* of religion, the value of which is essentially intellectual.

Religious education: personal religious quest or scientific investigation?

From a practical point of view there can be little doubt that with the adoption of what is sometimes mistakenly and misleadingly called 'an objective approach' to the study of religion,[18] RE has become content-centred. The heavy concentrations of biblical content characteristic of agreed syllabuses in pre-Goldman times have often been replaced by equally heavy concentrations of content drawn from the world's religions. The ways that have been adopted for structuring content vary but in the main they are determined by an appeal to the inner logic of religion. For example, while one syllabus favours studying each major religion in turn, another chooses to organise content by means of themes, such as Founders, Festivals, Sacred Places, Sacred Scriptures, Pilgrimages, and so on. A popular alternative is the type of thematic treatment based on the religious concept of the *rite of passage* where content from a number of religions is grouped under headings such as Birth, Marriage, Death, etc. Lying behind these thematic approaches is a basic principle of phenomenology of religion – that one moves from the description of the phenomena to a comparison and contrast of common features of different religions in order eventually to be able to elucidate the universal essences and structure of religion itself. But the level of understanding of which pupils may be capable means that the study of religion may rarely move beyond the descriptive level and this raises a query about the value of choosing and structuring content solely by reference to such phenomenological principles. To introduce other principles, such as those which I have suggested underlie Goldman's experiential approach, would, however, be seen by those favouring this sort of phenomenological approach to be in conflict with phenomenological method and so impair its educational validity.

But there is more to this conflict than a disagreement over educational aims and methods; theological factors are involved. Fundamental to the type of phenomenological approach that I have described is the belief that religion is a unique phenomenon and that religious experience is distinctive with its own essence and structure. It follows that there is a dichotomy between the sacred and the profane which is incapable of being bridged and that ordinary experience cannot therefore be the starting-point of religious experience or a basis for understanding it. By contrast, fundamental to an experiential approach such as Goldman's is the belief that all experience is essentially religious and that religion is, therefore, a dimension of all human experience. It follows that there is no dichotomy between the sacred and the profane and that ordinary experience can be the starting-point of religious experience and a basis for understanding it for all religious concepts are grounded in such experiences.

What we have here are two conflicting views of religion, each promoting a different understanding of the nature and purpose of RE. Thus, whereas Goldman sees the implications of his view of religion and education to be that any educational rationale for RE needs a theological underpinning and religious aims, Smart's view of religion and education enables him to advocate an educational rationale for RE which is free of theological assumptions with aims consistent with secular education. There can be little doubt that RE has gained from adopting this latter type of educational rationale. For example, it has enabled religious educators to show quite conclusively that RE can no longer be seen as a branch of piety but is a respectable academic discipline deserving a reputable place alongside other subjects in the curriculum. But has this gain only been made by appearing to adapt the subject to a social science and limiting its concern to making pupils knowledgeable about religion? The task of formulating an appropriate educational rationale for RE requires that the relationship between the personal religious quest and the scientific investigation of religion is not ignored but worked out more carefully. In other words, an educational rationale for RE needs to be as acceptable theologically as it is educationally. This would involve considering how a phenomenological approach could be given various theological underpinnings which would enable religious educators to be confident that in using the approach they are not distorting religion or precluding a concern for the pupil's personal religious or spiritual development. The few attempts that have, so far, been made to do this have been grounded in a Christian theological perspective,[19] but the antipathy which members of other faiths, especially Muslims, express towards the current stress on objectivity and openness in RE is a clear indication of the need for this task to also be undertaken from other theological perspectives. What follows is a tentative outline of a possible approach to this task with some indications of work still to be done.

Humanising concerns and the curriculum

A central issue is our view of education. It needs to be broad enough to permit the disciplines to occupy a central place in the process without allowing them to prescribe the only criteria by which development of the individual is to be determined and assessed. One such view might be that education 'is a process by, in and through which pupils may begin to explore what it is, and what it means to be human'.[20] To describe education as a *process* is to stress the on-going nature of the enterprise – that it starts at birth and continues until death and operates through a number of different contexts; the home, the peer group, the local community, through groups to which we belong (including faith communities), the work experience, the marriage experience, the experience of ageing, and so on. Here, though, we are concerned with the relatively short period of formal schooling and its contribution to that on-going process. The value of the school experience is most likely to be found in the way in which it can set children on the paths towards being receptive to the lessons to be learned from life as a whole – by helping them to acquire the skills and attitudes which will enable them to grapple more effectively with changing circumstances and new experiences. Providing children with a large amount of knowledge is unlikely to assist them in this because it can so easily become inert or just forgotten. What we give to pupils must be readily transferred and effectively applied in personal terms. And because education is a continuing process, we must avoid pressing pupils to commit themselves to final answers, especially in the religious and moral spheres.

To accept this view of education involves accepting that *all* subjects in the curriculum should contribute to its overall aim and hold a number of *humanising* educational concerns in common. Naturally each subject will have its own concerns appropriate to its own subject matter and those disciplines which are of central importance to it, but each subject should also assess how, and in what manner, it is able to make a distinctive contribution to these wider educational concerns. Six common concerns might be the following:

1 to provide pupils with an opportunity to become aware of the fundamental questions and dilemmas posed by the human condition, especially those which prompt the formulation of normative views of what it means to be human;

2 to help pupils acquire the knowledge, skills and attitudes necessary to enable them to participate consciously and critically in the processes by which they and their lives are shaped;

3 to explore and reflect on those civilising or humanising beliefs, values and attitudes which provide the basis for a society's sense of cultural continuity and its recognisable identity;

4 to assist pupils in the task of clarifying their own beliefs, values and attitudes as a necessary preliminary to taking responsibility for their own life-styles;

5 to contribute to pupils' self-knowledge and the development of capacities for personal, social, moral and religious decision-making;

6 to enrich pupils' stocks of models of the human, expanding their visions of self, others, the world, life, etc., and extending their repertoires of responses beyond those inculcated by family, peer group, subculture, culture, etc.

We might now ask what distinctive contribution RE can make to furthering each of these six concerns. I suggest that RE could provide the pupil with an opportunity to:

Concern 1 (a) learn about the nature and demands of those inescapable questions which being human poses, and to investigate what it means to make a 'faith response' to such questions;

(b) investigate and evaluate those areas of human thought, experience and action which reflect or prompt a religious interpretation of life and/or the adoption of moral perspectives and principles;

(c) gain insight into a religious interpretation of life as a distinctive way of responding to ultimate questions and interpreting human experiences, beliefs and values.

Concern 2 (a) consider the relationship between what one believes and what one becomes;

(b) understand that the ways in which one responds to life's fundamental questions (by faith) and how one defines one's ultimate concerns (by making a commitment to particular beliefs, values and attitudes) play a significant part in shaping one as a human being;

(c) recognise and be able to describe the different ways in which one has been, and continues to be, shaped as a human being, especially those which involve the transmission of beliefs, values and attitudes.

Concern 3 (a) consider the relationship between human values and religious values;

(b) understand the contribution that religion makes to human culture.

Concerns 4, 5 and 6 (a) discover that in learning *about* religion one can also learn *from* religion about oneself and how one defines one's own concerns and priorities;

(b) evaluate the claims of religion and a religious interpretation of life by engaging in an open and critical exploration of the interplay between what one perceives to be the central teachings

of religions and one's own questions, feelings, experiences and
ideas about life;

(c) discover that learning about other people's beliefs and
commitments can contribute to one's own self-knowledge and
the development of capacities for personal decision-making.

Learning about and learning from religion

Only a moment's reflection on what is commonly taught in RE should
persuade us that much of it is unlikely to promote the sort of learning
which is relevant to these concerns. Thus, instead of content being
determined solely by an appeal to the structure and key concepts of
religion and being studied strictly in accordance with phenomenological
principles, these concerns provide criteria for deciding which aspects of
religion might most profitably be studied in ways which promote personal
growth as well as academic understanding. Consequently, although
phenomenology of religion has some application to RE by providing a
useful methodology for *learning about* religion, RE must venture beyond
the more limited and specialised purpose of this type of phenomenology if
it is to be its concern that pupils also *learn from* religion.[21]

Enabling pupils to *learn from* religion means helping them to transfer
insights gained from their study of religion to their own situations where
they can be used to stimulate and assist them in coming to terms with
questions about their own identities, their own values and life-styles, their
own priorities and commitments, and their own frames of reference for
viewing life and giving it meaning. This process inevitably involves the
evaluation of the truth, significance and personal relevance of what is being
studied – something which this type of phenomenology discourages.

There is a need for us to be clearer about this form of evaluation – what
it involves, how it takes place, what it does for the individual, and so on.
What I am proposing is that RE should encourage the evaluation of one's
understanding of religion in *personal* terms and the evaluation of one's
understanding of self in *religious* terms (i.e. in terms of the religions being
studied). In promoting this type of understanding – that which yields self-
knowledge – I suggest that we are coming as near as it is possible to come
within the school context to encouraging the development of what might
be called the personal religious or spiritual dimension of each pupil's
experience of self. On this view, encouraging development of this
dimension of a pupil's experience of self is the distinctive contribution that
RE can make to his or her personal development within the curriculum.
Other subjects in the curriculum can contribute to the development of
other dimensions of his experience of self – the aesthetic, the linguistic, the
physical, the intellectual, and so on, and clearly all of these can be fostered
in some measure by all subjects, as can be the religious and spiritual
dimension. Development of each of these dimensions combines to further
the pupil's self-knowledge. The following stages in self-knowledge may be

identified; being aware of how one sees oneself to be (the cognised or known self); how one feels about, or values oneself (self-acceptance); how one has come to be the person that one is (self-illumination). Beyond this lies participation in the conscious reconstruction of self in which one explores possibilities of an ideal-self, considers how one might adjust to such an ideal, and, finally, reflects on the new identity which has emerged from this process - a process which will repeat itself again and again throughout life. It is this sort of process which is implied when one speaks of education as 'a process, by, in and through which pupils may begin to explore what it is, and what it means to be human'. It is also implied when one speaks of RE 'stimulating and assisting pupils in their own search for meaning and identity etc.'.

But, it may be argued, this view is open to a number of objections. For example, that it conceives of education as a psychological process and of RE as a form of psychotherapy and that it domesticates religion by making it fulfil an instrumental role in the curriculum. There may be some substance to such objections but equally there may be some substance to the claim that such a view allows for the interpenetration of philosophical, psychological, phenomenological and theological insights in ways which enable them to be related more effectively to the requirements of modern educational theory and the concerns of RE.[22] How this is to be done is a complex matter and here we can only hint at possible ways in which, for example, insights from phenomenology and world religions might be related to the process we have outlined.

The contribution of phenomenology to education

Most religious educators have been introduced to phenomenology by way of the phenomenology of religion. As we have indicated, this has an important part to play within RE in that it provides a useful methodology for the study of religion. But the phenomenology of religion is only one branch of phenomenology - a term which encompasses a wide variety of viewpoints, subject areas and methods. There are, then, other branches of phenomenology which may have relevance to an educational enterprise such as RE, especially, perhaps, the branch linked with existentialism.[23] Phenomenology focuses on the interior experience or *life-world* of the individual - how he both perceives the external world and reacts to his perceptions, particularly before he attempts to fit these personal experiences into any kind of impersonal or public mode of understanding. Its main concerns are, firstly, to expose certain essential structures of *consciousness* and to shed light on how these enable the individual to order his interior experience and create personal meanings. Secondly, phenomenology is interested in indicating how the individual re-orders these personal meanings in such a way as to accommodate them within public modes of expression, such as academic disciplines, including religion.[24]

There are several ways in which phenomenology has a direct

application to education. First, it offers valuable insights, complementary to those which have emerged from developmental psychology, into how pupils learn. In so doing it points to the inadequacy of structuring content only by reference to the inner logic of a subject or discipline. It shows that attention must also be given 'to the ways of thinking, the reflective experience and the modes of operating of those who are to learn, for it is this – the rich and complex mental life they already have – which is to be educated'.[25] Here phenomenology lends some support to the 'new directions' movement in sociology which insists that the definitions and categories of knowledge are treated as problematic and that 'the pupil's own viewpoint, his own construction of reality, needs to be respected, even though it does not fit those viewpoints, those categories "legitimated" by the school'.[26] Second, it reveals the need for the development of a pedagogy which encourages self-consciousness and an intuitive grasping of the situational elements within which each individual forms personal meanings (i.e. why he sees things as he does). Such a pedagogy could take a number of directions. The one suggested in this chapter equates self-consciousness with an awareness of the personal self or identity and suggests that the RE curriculum might be used as a means of encouraging pupils to reflect on the shaping properties which beliefs and values have had, and continue to have on their lives. Such self-consciousness is seen as a necessary prerequisite to their being able to participate consciously in making decisions about the directions in which they are to develop as human beings.[27]

The contribution of world religions to personal development

We can turn to religion itself as it is manifested within the faith of given historic communities – Christian, Hindu, Jewish, Muslim, and so on, to provide a theological underpinning for the view of education and RE offered in this chapter.[28] Here we might concentrate on what each religion understands by the notion of the religious or spiritual quest. We would need to identify the distinctive experiences, practices and teachings which each faith commends to adherents as paths to understanding, ways of discipleship, or modes of salvation. We would need to be clear about each religion's doctrine of man and its place within each religion's eschatological and soteriological framework. Parallel to understanding these formal aspects of each religion we would need to find out from individual Christians, Hindus, Jews, etc., about their own perceptions of what it means to be a Christian, a Hindu, a Jew – how they have appropriated and personalised a religious perspective and how this is influential in the way they respond to everyday situations and experiences. We would expect to encounter responses which were idiosyncratic and unorthodox but these would be important to our purpose in so far as they would illustrate how individuals make meaning at a personal level.

What, I think, we would confirm from these investigations would be that each religion not only prescribes a *model of the human* but also the means by which it can be realised in the life of the individual; in other words, that implicit in each religion's understanding of the religious or spiritual quest is its understanding of the meaning and end of personal development. There will, of course, be considerable differences between the viewpoints of the different religions but as it is not our intention to induce pupils to commit themselves to any one viewpoint nor to posit that one viewpoint is normative for their own personal development, this is not a problem. Indeed it is the existence of a variety of models of the human that constitutes the *educational* value of studying world religions (see Concern 6). We could follow the phenomenologist of religion in seeking to compare the common features of different religions and so lay bare the essence of a religious response to human personality. In my view, a more profitable approach would be to try to determine whether there are stages within the religious or spiritual quest of each religion which are, in some senses, illustrative of those stages in self-knowledge which were identified earlier. If this could be shown to be the case we could then choose content from the world's religions which was most able to fulfil the twin purposes of promoting awareness and understanding of the nature and purpose of the religious or spiritual quest within different religions, and promoting reflection, on the part of the pupil, on the implications that the adoption of a religious view of life would have for his own understanding of self and for his consequent development as a person. This latter type of reflection – which was referred to earlier as 'the evaluation of one's understanding of religion in personal terms and the evaluation of one's understanding of self in religious terms' – would thus permit the possibility of the pupil's discerning a religious or spiritual dimension within his own experience of self. It is in providing him with an opportunity to consider this possibility and its implications for how he defines himself that RE would make a distinctive contribution to his personal development. Such a rationale for RE would be true to both education and religion and, at the same time, enable the subject to contribute to meeting the pupil's religious, spiritual and personal needs without falling into the traps of confessionalism or intellectualism.

Notes and references

This chapter is based on one of five lectures given to the Seventh National Conference of the Australian Association for Religious Education at the University of Brisbane in 1978.

1 G. Langford, *Philosophy and Education* (London: Macmillan, 1968), p. 60.

2 R. S. Peters, 'Education and human development', *Education and Reason*, Part 3, R. F. Dearden, P. H. Hirst and R. S. Peters (eds),

International Library of the Philosophy of Education (London: Routledge & Kegan Paul, 1972), p. 111.

3 See e.g. R. J. Goldman, *Readiness for Religion* (London: Routledge & Kegan Paul, 1965); H. Loukes, *New Ground in Christian Education*, (London: SCM Press, 1965).

4 See e.g. Schools Council RE Committee Bulletin: *A Groundplan for the Study of Religion* (Schools Council, 1977).

5 For a description of these approaches, see e.g. M. H. Grimmitt, *What Can I do in RE?* (Essex: Mayhew-McCrimmon, 1973), chapters 5 and 6.

6 ibid. Also e.g. J. Holm, *Teaching Religion in School* (Oxford: OUP 1975).

7 R. J. Goldman, op. cit.

8 ibid., p. 59.

9 ibid., pp. 66–7.

10 ibid., p. 26, p. 200.

11 ibid., p. 34, p. 204.

12 ibid., p. 38.

13 ibid., p. 6.

14 N. Smart, *Secular Education and the Logic of Religion* (London: Faber, 1968), p. 99.

15 ibid., pp. 96–7.

16 N. Smart, 'The exploration of religion and education', *Oxford Review of Education*, vol. 1, no. 2, (1975), p. 102.

17 N. Smart, *The Science of Religion and the Sociology of Knowledge* (Princeton University Press, 1977), p. 8.

18 J. Holm, op. cit., p. 6, p. 53; City of Birmingham Education Committee, *Agreed Syllabus of Religious Instruction*, 1975, p. 5.

19 See e.g. M. H. Grimmitt, op. cit., chapter 5; K. Surin, 'Can the experiential and the phenomenological approaches be reconciled?', *British Journal of Religious Education*, vol. 2, no. 3, (Spring 1980), pp. 99–103.

20 M. H. Grimmitt and G. T. Read, *Teaching Christianity in RE* (Essex: Kevin Mayhew, 1978), p. 4.

21 For a more detailed analysis of the differences between religious studies and religious education see my article, 'When is "commitment" a problem in RE?', *British Journal of Educational Studies*, vol. 29, no. 1, (February 1981).

22 For an analysis of the way theology mirrors key ideas in humanistic psychology and an examination of the promise it holds for RE, see

D. Webster, 'Creativity within RE: a note towards the significance for RE of a dialogue between Christian theology and Humanistic psychology', *British Journal of Religious Education*, vol. 2, no. 4, (Summer 1980), pp. 129–35.

23 See e.g. the writings of Kierkegaard, Nietzsche, Sartre, Berdyaev, Marcel, Jaspers, Merleau-Ponty, Ricoeur.

24 See e.g. B. Curtis and W. Mays (eds), *Phenomenology and Education* (London: Methuen, 1978).

25 R. Pring, *Knowledge and Schooling* (London: Open Books Publishing Co., 1976), p. 84.

26 ibid., p. 68.

27 The process envisaged here resembles what Paulo Freire calls 'background awareness' of an existential situation actually lived before the codifications (i.e. public modes of thinking, including religion) make new perceptions possible. See P. Freire, *Pedagogy of the Oppressed* (Middlesex: Penguin Books, 1972), chapters 3 and 4.

28 Equally we could turn to natural theology to provide a theological underpinning for the view of education and RE expressed in this chapter. See, for example, Philip Phenix's use of transcendence in the interpretation and evaluation of educational theory and practice, in 'Transcendence and the curriculum', in W. Pinar (ed.), *Curriculum Theorizing* (California: McCutchen, 1975), pp. 323–37.

Further reading

In addition to Ronald Goldman's *Readiness for Religion* (London: Routledge & Kegan Paul, 1965), two recent books on RE have stressed the contribution that religion can make to the child's personal development. These are *Discovering an Approach* (Schools Council, London; Macmillan, 1977) and Raymond Holley's *Religious Education and Religious Understanding* (London: Routledge & Kegan Paul, 1978), although the views expressed by Holley contrast sharply with those expressed in this chapter. It is, however, from literature outside RE that further insights into the concept of personal growth or development may be obtained. For example, Robert Dearden's article, 'Education as a process of growth' in *A Critique of Current Educational Aims*, Part 1 of *Education and the Development of Reason*, edited by R. F. Dearden, P. H. Hirst and R. S. Peters (London: Routledge & Kegan Paul, 1972), points to the pitfalls, from a philosophical point of view, which exist for the educator who seeks to stress notions of 'self-realisation' and 'being oneself'. In the main, though, more attention has been given to the concept of personal development by educators working outside the UK than by British educators. For example, there is an abundance of American literature dealing with the psychological foundations of personal growth. J. Loevinger, *Ego Development* (San Francisco: Jossey-Bass Press, 1976) offers alternative models of personal development, and the collection of papers edited by C. E. Moustakas, *The Self: Explorations in Personal Growth* (New York: Harper & Row, new edition 1975) is of value to those seeking to accommodate such views within RE. The works of Erik H. Erikson are a landmark in this field, especially *Identity: Youth and Crisis* (New York: Norton, 1968) and *Dimensions of a New Identity* (New York: Norton, 1974). Alternative views and uses of phenomenology are typified by the contrasting views of Carl R. Rogers in *On Becoming a Person* (London: Constable & Co. Ltd, 1974) and of Paulo Freire who, in *Education for Critical Consciousness* (London: Sheed & Ward, 1974) presents a view of humanisation to which this chapter is particularly indebted. The concept of humanisation is also explored in an interesting manner in R. R. Leeper (ed.), *Humanizing Education: The Person in the Process* (Washington DC: Association for Supervision and Curriculum Development, 1967). Insights into how individuals make meaning at a personal level are provided by Roger Poole in *Towards Deep Subjectivity* (London: Penguin, 1972) and, in an autobiographical manner, by Harvey Cox in *The Seduction of the Spirit* (London: Wildwood, 1973).

13
Realisation and Religious Education

Simon Weightman

Few people make a conscious distinction between the *actual* and the *real*. Whatever the reasons for this failure to differentiate, present purposes require that a clear distinction is made between the two. To actualise, or to make actual, whatever else the process may entail, always has the effect of rendering *knowable*, and hence can be associated with fact. Realisation, or to make real, disregarding for the moment other aspects of the process, always has the effect of rendering *concrete*, usually in a wider context of meaning and value. Thus when one speaks of realising an aim, or realising a value, there is always implied a transition from the abstract to the concrete, for concreteness is a measure of reality.[1]

The distinction may be further pursued by means of examples. When in conversation with certain Europeans, it is not uncommon to hear the speaker pronounce the English 'very' as 'wery'. In such situations what the speaker *actually* says is 'wery'. This is the actuality, the fact of the matter. But what the speaker is *really* saying is 'very'. This is the reality, the meaning and value of what was uttered in the concrete situation of spoken English. A second example can be the position of a mother who wishes to convey to her child that she does not wish him to go outside, but does not want to appear too severe. She may well say: 'What a pity. It's raining.' This is what she would *actually* say, but what she is *really* saying is: 'I'm sorry, you can't go out.' In this case the actuality resides in the literal meaning, and the reality in the potentiality of the implication. The child hears the actual words and grasps the literal meaning, but more is required. He must also seek the significance of what is said in the context of his situation if he is to realise what his mother is implying. If the child takes the words literally and reaches for his raincoat, the mother has failed. The mother starts by knowing what she intends to imply, but must find a formulation in actual words through which the child is able to realise the implication, and she herself realise her intention.

These two examples permit the introduction of two further related but antithetical notions, *essence* and *existence*. While these two concepts have had a long and controversial history, it is possible to be reasonably precise here as to how these terms are to be understood. Existence, it has been said, is the supreme fact, and we shall associate the term existential with the factual side of things. In the first example above, 'wery' would be the existential aspect of the utterance. Essence we associate broadly with values and purposes and it would be possible, in one sense, to think of 'very' as the essence of the utterance since we can accept as one definition of essence 'the property within any entity of being itself and not other'. In the second example the existential aspect is the actual statement and its literal meaning, while the implication of the statement is its essence. This permits a further definition of essence, 'the intrinsic possibility of being real that resides in every entity'. Existence is poised between the limits of life and death, essence between the limits of reality and unreality.

Elaborating further, it can be seen that both existence and essence are in themselves only half real. Existence compensates for the poverty of value and purpose by the *certainty* of its facticity: essence pays the price for the richness of purpose and value in the *uncertainty* of its realisation. Essence is only the possibility of being real. There is no guarantee at all in our examples that 'wery' will be understood as 'very' or that the child will realise what his mother intends. It is the uncertainty of realisation of essence that brings hazard into our experience, thus making life both interesting and dramatic. Only when existence and essence merge do we meet with the concrete significance of reality. When the child seeks to discover the significance of his mother's statement we can see existence seeking the essential *content* of reality: when the mother seeks for words that will carry her implication we see essence seeking the existential *vehicle* of reality. Both processes are necessary otherwise we are left on the one hand with a catalogue of uninteresting facts and, on the other, with a series of unreal values and intentions. The existential must be rendered meaningful through finding its essential counterpart, and essence must be realised through its embodiment in existential forms. Only then do we confront the real.

Although these concepts and processes have been elaborated from concrete examples, in no field are they more clearly exemplified than in education, and especially in religious education. We can feel a real difference between existential 'bare factual instruction' and essential 'true education'. Every teacher knows that factual recitation is safe but leads nowhere unless the facts are rendered meaningful for the pupils. Equally, however lofty the ideals and aims of 'true education', it is clear that their realisation is hazardous in the extreme. Education, moreover, without an adequate factual grounding is vacuous and unreal well-meaningness, while the dispensation of knowledge without educational aims and values does nothing for the development of the child. Education, it has been said very pertinently, is what remains when you have forgotten all that you learnt at school.

If there is one domain of human life and experience that belongs above all others to the essential side of human nature, it is religion. Religion is concerned both with the realisation of essential values and purposes and also with the 'spiritualisation' of existence – 'Who sweeps a room as for Thy laws makes that and the action fine'. Some appear to look almost exclusively to religious education to awaken and develop the essential side of children's natures and to balance the existential skills and knowledge that form so much of schooling. But obedience, self-discipline, responsibility, obligation to others, questing and achieving, awareness of right and wrong in concrete situations and other similar qualities all develop, or fail to develop, within the overall educational process. If they do develop naturally in the course of school life, albeit in a somewhat unscheduled manner, they form an important part of the growth of a child's essence.

Turning now specifically to religious education itself, it is important to examine the real nature of the opportunity that is offered by the introduction of world religions into the teaching arena. Clearly a, perhaps, the, primary function of religious education is the explication, understanding and appreciation of the religious tradition of the pupils. Since the majority of school children in this country have their essential roots in the Christian tradition, and since it is likely that the religious influences and values to which they are exposed both in and out of school are Christian, there can be little doubt that Christianity should figure large in the teaching of religious education. But the presentation of Christianity can now take place in a totally new perspective: that is, as a world religion, alongside other world religions. Man can now be seen as *homo religiosus*, religion as a universal human concern, and Christianity as one mode of experiencing within the total religious experience of mankind. To be human is to be faced with certain essential questions and dilemmas, and these are not necessarily the same as those that confront the adherents of any particular religion. What the teaching of world religions opens up is not so much the chance to understand our non-Christian neighbours, although that is valuable in its own right, but the opportunity to understand *ourselves*, to face what it means to be a human being, subsisting as an atom of humanity on the skin of life we call the biosphere which covers this insignificant planet, within a vast and incomprehensible universe.

One particularly helpful way of understanding any purposeful activity is to examine it as a four-term system, and this we can do with religious education. The usual representation of such a system is set out below.

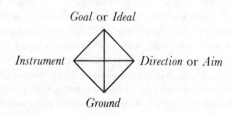

The operational axis is Instrument – Direction, and the motivational axis is Ground – Goal or Ideal. Without further elaboration on the general principles of such a model, we can apply it directly to religious education. The Ground is the raw stuff that we seek to transform by means of the process. Here it is all the haphazard, unorganised raw data available to us encompassed within the term 'world religions'. It is also the uninformed pupils and even the teachers. The Instrument is Teaching with all the methods available to it. Since this principally involves the presentation of facts, that is, the knowable, we associate it with the existential aspects of religions. The Direction or Aim is Understanding which we associate with the essential side of religions since understanding is concerned with why, with purposes and intentions and the values that motivate them. The Goal or Ideal is that which informs and inspires the whole process: it is what we hope for in terms of the personal development of children. This can now be represented on the model.

Goal or *Ideal*

Teaching	*Understanding*, why
Facts, Knowable	Purposes and values
Existential aspect	Essential aspect

Raw data of 'world religions'
Uninformed pupils
Teachers

The six lines connecting the four sources of the process have been designated 'interplays' to indicate that they represent the balance to be maintained between the two sources or a blending of the qualities that derive from each. The interplay between Teaching (Instrument) and Understanding (Direction or Aim) is the directed operation of religious education which can now be considered in the light of the previous discussion. There is a sense in which Teaching can be self-directional: there can be a syllabus and an examination and the facts become meaningful within the context of passing the examination. This, however, is only a proximate aim which might take one perhaps half-way along the connecting line. To understand something is very much more than to know about something, yet equally one cannot understand something one does not know about. As we have seen true understanding can only be attained when existential forms and formulations meet with their own essential content. Only when the existential meets the essential do we encounter *significance*. Facts without understanding the purposes and values that inform them are insignificant, values and purposes without the factual ground in which they are exemplified are unreal. This interplay with its arrows indicates the blending of both which is necessary if we are to create an understanding of the significance of what we seek to teach.

It is possible to trace St Paul across Asia Minor and to read and study the Epistles. But unless we can show why St Paul travelled, his purposes in writing what he did, and the crucial role he played in the realisation of Christianity in the world, there can be no understanding of the life, the writings or the significance of St Paul. Another example is marriage, which is a subject many properly teach, showing the different forms of rites and ceremonies and the different social implications it has in the various world religions. The most immediate and seemingly straightforward religion in which to explore marriage is Christianity. For some children this might be one of the very few occasions that takes them into Church. There is, too, the ideal textbook for this in the marriage service contained in the Prayer Book. The service not only contains directions for the various ceremonial and ritual acts, but provides an explanation of the symbolism of each as well as a clear exposition of the meaning and purpose of marriage in Christianity. Most of this is accessible and understandable. There is, however, at a deeper level of symbolism, the question of marriage representing the mystical Union of Christ and His Church. Although, therefore, one can reach a certain degree of understanding of Christian marriage from the service, its full significance within Christianity can only be understood through a proper appreciation of the totality. One single life cycle rite leads out into unimaginable mysteries.

When a teacher shows a film, for example, of a Hindu wedding, it is equally desirable that he is able to explain the rich symbolism of each element in the rite or the purposes and implications of marriage within Hinduism. One simple example is the fact that in a Hindu wedding the couple are dressed and treated as gods. The underlying reason for this is that in the Hindu life cycle the sacrament of marriage represents the point of maximum purity between the pollution created by birth and the pollution generated at death. This leads out of wedding ceremony to the central place of purity and pollution within Hindu religious belief. This is only a small point which leads out to something much bigger, a part of the total essential content of Hindu marriage that would be necessary to enable the pupils to reach a real understanding of the significance of marriage within Hinduism.

There is no doubt that to try to understand the religions of the world is both a proper and a noble aim, but the realisation of any aim is difficult and uncertain, and the higher the aim, the more hazardous the undertaking. One major danger can be illustrated here from the example of teaching about marriage. To see films of Hindu weddings, Jewish weddings, Muslim weddings and so on, without real understanding, leads to the view that, beneath the rich diversity of ritual and symbolism, there is one institution 'marriage' common to all religions. The assumption then grows that marriage is essentially the same in all religions and only the forms vary. Even more dangerous is the general assumption that can arise that beneath all their diversity, all religions are essentially the same. This is manifestly absurd. If one has real experience and understanding of marriage in different religions it becomes quite clear that the significance and values of marriage within each religion are essentially different. To understand Hindu marriage fully is to enter a completely different religious universe. Each world religion constitutes a unique and essentially distinct religious universe within which each element has its own distinctive configuration and pattern of relationships to every other element within that universe. Understanding is both the means and the reward of entry into these universes. Those who have never entered another religious universe and seen how different everything looks and how differently everything is arranged and interrelated can only pass comment from *without*. They either then assume that inside everything is the same as that which they know, or they make formal equations that lead to confusion. To a Christian, Christianity is quite obviously a monotheistic religion. Seeing that Hinduism has many *devas*, it is designated polytheism. Yet every Indian peasant knows that '*Bhagavan ek hai*', 'God is one'. The *devas* in Hinduism are much nearer to the 'Heavenly Host' of Christianity when seen from *within* Hinduism and the formal equation is misleading. To a Muslim, Christianity is not monotheistic because of the Trinity, yet from *within* Christianity it very clearly is. Teaching world religions can demonstrate that other people from various faiths see things *differently* and can show that there are other entire religious universes that can be opened up and explored. To enter one of these other worlds and to taste what it feels like from within, even for a moment, is an unforgettable and liberating experience. It opens one up. To teach without understanding is to close possibilities, to create misleading assumptions and to produce exactly the opposite result to that intended.

Returning to the model, the interplay between Ground and Teaching can be interpreted as the proper use of resources. The raw data have to be organised and brought into a form in which they can be presented in a way appropriate to the pupils concerned. This interplay then represents teaching skills and the production and utilisation of materials and resources suitable for each age group and each type of class. It is often the case in classes of mixed religions that a teacher will use members of the class as a 'teaching resource' since all that is available can be made use of by the skilful teacher.

The interplay between Ground and Understanding can best be designated *discrimination*. It is the guiding principle that keeps the whole process on the right lines. It requires the teacher to be self-aware, alert to the extent of his own degree of understanding, or lack of it, and to be constantly questioning the material available to him from the world religions, asking why, where do you fit into your religious universe, and to what questions are you the answer. The teacher must also be particularly sensitive to the pupils, assessing what is within the understanding of each age group. Each age has its own capacity and quality of understanding and it is the teacher's discrimination that enables him to provide topics or themes from the world religions that the particular pupils can understand. Without this discrimination, this self-aware questioning sensitivity, which connects the Ground with the Aim, the whole process will break down.

So far we have considered only the instrumental or operational axis and the two interplays of teaching skills and discrimination that connect the Ground to the operation. Now it is necessary to consider the motivational axis that links the Ground with the Goal or Ideal. Beginning first with the Ground, we can say that it is motivated by *need*. First the teachers need to teach because that is their responsibility and law requires that there shall be religious education. Secondly the raw data need to be rendered significant through knowledge and understanding. Finally, and most crucially, the children have needs. Their inner natures, their essences, are open, hungry and beginning to formulate questions about themselves and the world in which they live. This then is the motivation of the Ground.

The Goal or Ideal is motivated by *aspiration*. The Goal or Ideal is *not* the Aim, it is not the development of an understanding of a religion, several religions or even of 'religion' as a generalised concept, but rather what we hope such a development can do to and for children. The Goal or Ideal has to do with the aspirations of education itself, with the personal development of children and, in this case, with the awakening of some form of inner awareness, of essential values and with the implanting of questioning about the meaning and purpose of life. The Goal or Ideal remains hidden, out of sight, undefinable, yet it influences everything and is the source of all our aspirations. Every formulation of the goal or ideal of religious education has proved in some way to be either unsatisfactory or inadequate, and the more so the more specific it is. Yet many agree that religious education is important, indeed, increasingly important in the present era. We could offer a formulation such as 'the preparation of children to become *real* human beings, having an inner and an outer life, with their existential nature in balance with their essence'. Such a formulation is unobjectionable and a very high ideal. Yet if we try to break it down further into details, then we lose it. Perhaps the Goal must remain hidden because it belongs to the hidden part of children, or because it bears fruit in later life. But it is in no way diminished through being undefined; rather it is better that our aspirations should remain unconstrained, free from the limitation of some collective formulation, so that there is scope for spontaneity and creativity in the classroom. There *is* an Ideal, a Goal, which informs the whole, even if it eludes us, and those who do not feel religious education to be inherently worthwhile should not be involved with children in this most sensitive area.

The interplay between Goal and Aim represents the balance between doing the job for its own sake, producing an understanding of aspects of various religions, and doing it to serve a higher purpose, Goal, which has to do with the personal development of children. What is required from this interplay is that the teacher constantly questions whether an understanding of a particular religious element will help a child's own inner life to grow or awaken. We can designate this interplay *enlightenment* since enlightened teaching results when the teacher's aims are informed by a higher ideal. These two interplays, discrimination and enlightenment, which connect with understanding, can be said to produce the 'essential syllabus', that is, understandings and values which, on the one hand, are within the capacity of the pupils concerned, and, on the other hand, will produce experiences for the pupils which will help in some way with their personal inner development.

The interplay between Goal or Ideal and Instrument, Teaching, can be designated *integrity*. This is to indicate that the process should not be divided against itself. This can happen in various ways. It is indisputable that when one is dealing with the essence of children, excessive facts can only blunt the sensitivity. But if the burden and boredom of excessive fact is deadening, cynicism is murderous. If a teacher is cynical and this is reflected in his attitudes and in the tone of his teaching, he can destroy real possibilities for the children, which is unforgivable. At the other end of the scale to the cynic is the narrowly or existentially committed, who is equally dangerous. He has no respect for the child's individuality, no wish that the child should find his or her own reality, but seeks to mould the unformed essence to his own pattern. These are all examples of how possibilities of development can be destroyed for children when the educational process is divided against itself, when it lacks integrity. Another possible designation of this interplay is *faith*. This does not mean a specific faith, but that the teacher should have faith that there is an Ideal and that what he is doing is truly valuable.

The final interplay is that which connects Goal or Ideal with Ground, that is, the motivational axis. Here we have immediate needs rising upwards requiring to be met, meeting and blending with the aspirations that descend from the Ideal. In trying to cope with immediate needs we must never lose our aspirations, but equally we must not in our aspiring neglect the needs of the present. As with all interplays the teacher is required to blend the two motivating influences to attain the right balance.

The findings so far can now be put into the model so that we can see the whole educational process as a structured totality with the central point representing the maximum degree of rightness when all the various sources of initiative are working in balance and harmony.

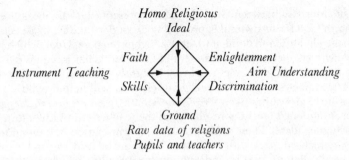

It is now necessary to begin to draw some conclusions from this investigation. If we posit a notional *homo religiosus* at the Goal or Ideal, as has been done above, it is not difficult to imagine that, amongst other things, he lives in the face of certain questions which have come to be called ultimate questions. These questions can be seen as part of that which descends from the Ideal. It would be possible to enumerate some of them, but it seems to me that most can be reached by confronting two specific dilemmas, provided it is done ruthlessly and penetratingly enough, though it is possible that others would see and formulate these 'ultimate questions' quite differently. These two dilemmas which should not be separated can be stated simply as: 'Who am I?' and 'Thy Will be done'. At first sight it appears that the first calls forth an act of affirmation and the second an act of receptivity and submission. Furthermore a relationship is established between an immanent 'I' and a transcendent 'Thou'. But when one really confronts the question 'Who am I?' ruthless self-examination reveals that in each of us there are a multitude of passing states, moods, reactions, personalities which all claim to be 'I' and usurp the place wherein should be our true individuality. It appears we are very far from being real men with a permanent personal individuality which can answer 'I'. This leads out into a whole complex of questions about the nature of man and the need for, and the methods of, *transformation* that play so central a part in all religions. A similar examination of 'Thy Will be done' raises any number of questions about 'Thou', 'Thy Will' and what it is for me at any given moment, what is the purpose of life on earth and even of the Creation itself. These are all questions that are to be found, in one form or another, in all the religions of the world.

The immediate needs of pupils vary enormously, and not only in accordance with age. They may range from a total lack of interest which needs to be transformed into curiosity, to burning questions which can be about almost anything. A good teacher will coax these questions out because each one constitutes a *real* starting point. This means there must be room in the teaching for spontaneity and for private questions to emerge. I can recall having such a question myself which might crudely be put as a bewildered incomprehension as to why people were so beastly to one another. I was fortunate in having a particularly enlightened teacher who simply quoted to me Martin Buber's saying: 'We judge others by their actions and ourselves by our intentions.' When I coupled this with the knowledge that we very rarely indeed realise our intentions in our actions, I was given an insight into the human condition that has been invaluable to me ever since, especially in understanding how marriages break down.

This process of bringing out the immediate questions, awarenesses and experiences of the pupils on the one hand, and the implanting and awakening of ultimate questions, a sense of the miracle and wonder of life and the dimensions of transcendence and holiness on the other, takes place within the framework and context of presenting material from the various world religions and wrestling to understand and assent to its essential values. There is scarcely any element that is likely to be introduced that cannot be used in this way, provided that it is fully understood and freedom is allowed for a spontaneous response from the pupils upon which the teacher can build. The Evil Eye is often disregarded as a superstition even though it is one of the most widespread beliefs in the world. Yet, when one examines it, it embodies the principle that if one creates a situation which evokes envy in another, the consequences may be dire. This principle, in its own way and at a practical level, is probably more effective than any commandment 'Thou shalt not envy'. The Sermon on the Mount, if it is truly faced, makes demands that are quite *impossible* for nearly all of us in our present condition. This is the reality of the situation and it raises fundamental questions about ourselves and Christianity which can bring a class alive with interest and enquiry. Yet these awesome requirements are almost never faced. They are glossed over, neutralised and rendered safe until they become almost comfortable, and many real possibilities are thus destroyed. Total honesty with oneself and with one's pupils is surely the absolute and prime requisite for teaching religion.

This is not the place to elaborate further on all that could be introduced in class, since we are concerned here not with the 'what', but with the 'how' and 'why'. I have written elsewhere of how material from Hinduism could be used in the way suggested here.[2] What really matters is that what is presented as religion should be *real*: real in its own right, not valueless facts or unreal values: real for the children, so that they can relate it to themselves and their world: and real in that it is an authentic part of man's religious experience on this planet.

The word realisation has been used in the title to convey not only the necessity of making religion real for the children, but also the fact that, by doing so, something is realised in their essential natures. In the final analysis religion is primarily concerned with realisation: whether it is the Creator realising His divine purpose, a saint or a seeker struggling to realise the divine within himself, or a community striving to realise essential values in its conduct, its worship or its art. Examples of realisation should figure large in teaching from whatever source they are taken. The lives and writings of saints are too often neglected, yet they offer wonderful material. Gandhi realising the essential religious value of non-violence in the improbable arena of India's political struggle for independence is, of course, often used. Examples abound at every level and on every scale.

But what is it that we hope can be realised by all this? Before each lesson my prayer would be: 'Let nothing I do or say destroy a possibility for a child, may what emerges be real "essence food" for the children, but, above all else, may each child, at some time in its schooldays, have at least one *real* moment.' This is what I would wish, for *real* moments are very rare – most people have only very few in their entire lives – but their significance cannot be measured by frequency for they stand out as sunlit mountain peaks and their influence on our lives is of a quite different order from even our most moving or most exquisite experiences. After such a moment one can never remain content to exist as an automaton passing from birth to death, because one *knows* that true living is to struggle against unreality towards the realisation of one's own personal individuality which alone is capable of such moments. Our hope must be that, in our fumbling but sincere efforts to teach world religions, something will happen in each child which at some stage will set them in search of their own reality, on the path towards the realisation of their own essential natures. As teachers we can aspire no higher than this. Some teachers, when they speak of other religions, do so in hushed and pious tones, but this is surely misplaced. The religions of the world will survive whatever assaults we make on them. It is the inner natures of the children that are vulnerable and that, however intractable and unpromising their exteriors may appear, truly deserve our reverence and respect.

References

1 Many of these concepts and the model of a four term system are taken from J. G. Bennett, *The Dramatic Universe* (London: Hodder & Stoughton, 1966).

2 Robert Jackson (ed.), *Perspectives on World Religions* (London: School of Oriental and African Studies, 1978), chapter 2.

Part
Moral and Political Education

Introduction

A number of curriculum areas have been developed in recent years that can both contribute to religious education, and benefit themselves from the insights of religious education. This section is devoted to three such areas – moral education, political education and world studies – and considers the contribution that a study of world religions can make to each of them. In turn, important insights are also to be gained by religious educators from these other curriculum developments.

In chapter 14 Allan Hawke gives some of the reasons why the organisers of moral education projects, which are themselves different in rationale, have agreed in assuming the independence of religion and morality and in recommending the development of skills for autonomy as a key goal of moral education. In drawing attention to the work, particularly in philosophy and psychology, that has influenced these projects, Hawke notes the controversial nature of such assumptions and recommendations. At classroom level he acknowledges that religious education – through the study of what Ninian Smart has called the moral dimension of religion – can make a valuable contribution to pupils' moral education. At the same time moral education can draw upon the study of religions, in that a serious consideration of morality raises fundamental human questions about which the various religions have much to say. Taking the examples of Islam and Hinduism, Hawke discusses some of the ways in which RE and ME may interact in the classroom. In particular he notes how RE can make a distinctive contribution to ME in developing an awareness in pupils of how a person's moral views may be affected by his or her religious beliefs.

In recent years there has been a growing interest in political education in this country, but so far its relationship with religious education has remained unexplored. Richard Tames (Chapter 15), using the example of Islam, considers the contribution that the study of world religions can make to pupils' understanding of political concepts. Tames argues that political ideas can be more readily grasped by pupils when they encounter them within political and social structures that are different from their own. In studying Islam, pupils can be encouraged both to scrutinise Islamic prescriptions and practices from a Western stance and to examine Western institutions and attitudes from the Muslim point of view. Such an approach should lead to an increase in political and religious understanding. Note that religious responses to political questions (in this case Christian responses) are included by Owen Cole in his suggested programme for Christian studies in schools (Chapter 7, p. 83).

Closely related to both moral and political education is the group of subjects with such names as 'development studies', 'third world studies', 'modern studies' and 'education for international understanding'. The twentieth-century revolution in technology has afforded unprecedented opportunities for international understanding and co-operation, yet at the same time it has dramatically increased the threat of war on a vast scale. It is with the aim of promoting the former and preventing the latter that such bodies as Unesco have encouraged school courses with an international perspective. That the study of world religions can contribute significantly to such courses may appear obvious, but there has been as yet little discussion of the relationship between the study of world religions and the 'world studies' family of courses. Robin Richardson, in Chapter 16, explores the relationship between the two by presenting a critique of the teaching of world religions from the stance of world studies followed by a reply from the point of view of religious education. Like Richard Tames, Richardson points to the tendency in teachers of RE to avoid such issues as political conflict, power and justice. In particular he is concerned – in common with several other contributors to this book – with the lack of opportunity offered by many RE teachers for pupils to evaluate religion. He goes on to criticise the simplistic understanding of 'Christian responsibility' to be found in many RE syllabuses, and further suggests that RE teachers might derive from world studies more vital theories of teaching and learning than those underlying much religious education. In formulating a reply to these criticisms on behalf of teachers of world religions, Richardson identifies some distinctive contributions to world studies that can be made by religious education. Religious education can encourage in pupils an awareness of the humanity of the victims of injustice and, therefore, an awareness of their own humanity; in addition, a knowledge of world religions helps pupils to understand the issues that arise in a world society; but most important of all, says Richardson, the teacher of world religions can remind other teachers of the importance of metaphysical and existential questions.

R.J.

14

Moral Education in a Multi-religious Society

R. Allan Hawke

At one time it used to be assumed that the chief vehicle for moral education was the school assembly and the daily or weekly dose of 'scripture' or 'religious instruction'. For many today the assumption still holds. Some committed Christians may be heard to bemoan the decline in moral standards, which they attribute to the decline in commitment to religious belief and practice. Even those with no strong Christian commitment may share a similar assumption: ask student-teachers doing general curriculum studies in religious education to prepare a scheme of work for use in school, and often they will come up with 'Caring and sharing' or 'The family', and will be very surprised when the tutor suggests that the scheme they have prepared is moral rather than religious education. The old problem of 'Bible boredom' – pupils being bored by successive treatment of the parables of Jesus or favourite stories from the Old Testament from infant school through to secondary school – is now sometimes replaced by 'ethical *ennui*'. This may result from too many encounters with drugs, sex, violence and so on, introduced as topics for study by well-meaning RE teachers who assume that morality is the special concern of their subject, oblivious of the fact that the English or the integrated studies departments also regard these topics as their province.

This assumption of a link between RE and ME, so that the two virtually become synonymous, would look strange in some other countries. In the United States for example, it is well known that religious instruction is not permitted in public (i.e. state) schools, yet there is a great concern for moral or social education. In the Soviet Union there is a heavy moral emphasis on children's duties to work hard, respect their teachers, grow to be useful soviet citizens and so on, and frequent condemnation of the moral decadence of the West; and all this from an ideological standpoint of 'scientific atheism'. Both these countries, in their different ways, stand as examples of the feasibility in practice of divorcing moral education from religious ideology or religious education. (It is beside the point to argue about the results of this divorce. Assessments of the moral health of nations, of moral progress or moral decline, are notoriously difficult to make, even with reference to one's own society. Furthermore, the results of the British tradition of linking moral with religious education are not obviously better than their American or Russian counterparts.)

A further practical reason for separating moral and religious education is sometimes heard from humanists. They say that there is a danger that, if morality and religion are presented as a package, morality may be rejected along with religion when children come to adolescence. An extension of this point may be made with reference to a multi-cultural, and more specifically a multi-religious, society. The linking of ME and RE meant in practice the linking of moral education with *Christian* ethics. Difficulties will obviously arise if this stance is maintained when dealing with Jewish, Muslim, Hindu or Sikh pupils.

To these practical difficulties and dangers must be added an important theoretical point concerning the nature of morality and religion. P. H. Hirst has argued that the *logic* of morality is distinct from that of religion: they are two separate 'forms of knowledge' or modes of human experience, each with its own structure of distinctive concepts and its own mode of verification.[1] Whether or not one agrees with Hirst's analysis of human knowledge into a handful of fundamental logical forms, the particular argument concerning religion and morality has been expressed by other philosophers, from Plato onwards, in other ways. Plato (in the *Euthyphro*) asked: 'Do the gods love piety because it is pious, or is it pious because they love it?' In more modern guise the point is made under the heading of the 'naturalistic fallacy', which can be extended into what might be called the 'supernaturalistic fallacy'. The point is that values cannot logically be derived from facts, 'ought' from 'is', ethics from nature or even supernature. It does not logically follow from the statement, 'God wills X' (fact), that 'X is right' (value), unless one presumes that 'God always wills the right'.[2] To this logical objection to linking religion and morality there may be philosophical replies,[3] but the point is put forcefully by M. Downey and A. V. Kelly in this way:

> A religious morality must essentially be an authoritarian morality. Our reason for accepting those moral principles that have their basis in religion and for adopting as a consequence certain kinds of behaviour must be that they are recommended, if not demanded, by the godhead. This is true of any religious code of ethics no matter what religion it emanates from.[4]

Needless to say, Downey and Kelly see this inherent authoritarianism of religious morality as grounds for objecting to the religious – moral link.

It is interesting to note in this context a link with psychological research into children's moral development. Both Piaget and Kohlberg[5] have postulated stages of moral development which children go through, and both postulate stages of heteronomous or authority-based morality, which they identify with moral immaturity. This, if accepted, has some rather startling implications for those religious moralities of the world which do emphasise authority. Two issues arise. One is whether such developmental schemes are guilty of smuggling ethical evaluation into their empirical research ('mature' is, after all, as much a term of commendation as description). The other is whether a closer examination of the concept 'authority' in relation to morality might not remove some of the pejorative associations of 'authoritarian'. Note, for example, that 'authoritative' is another adjective derived from 'authority', and one with less pejorative overtones: this might remove some of the sting of Downey and Kelly's criticism, mentioned above.

As well as philosophers and psychologists, sociologists too provide grounds for separating moral and religious education. It has become a commonplace to refer to Western industrial society as 'secular'. Although this might be challenged in respect of countries like Britain, and other terms preferred such as 'post-Christian', 'Christianised', 'multi-religious', it serves to show that there is no agreed basis of religious consensus on which moral judgements or conduct can be based. In the world as we know it now, religious moralities join in the maelstrom of conflict with one another and with secular moral views over issues such as birth control, abortion, sexual freedom, women's liberation, revolutionary politics and so on.

It is such arguments from philosophy, psychology and sociology which form the background to practical curriculum suggestions for moral education in schools. The best-known moral education projects in Britain are the work of the Farmington Trust, begun by John Wilson and his team in 1965,[6] and the Schools Council projects *Lifeline*[7] (for secondary schools) and *Startline*[8] (for the middle years), directed by Peter McPhail. Although these projects are very different in rationale and content, they agree in putting forward ideas for moral education which make it independent of religious education. Both aim to develop in pupils the skills necessary for making their own moral judgements: skills of knowledge, imagination, sensitivity, insight, reasoning and so on, which the autonomous moral agent (and 'autonomy' is a key concept for moral educators) requires for the difficult process of decision-making. Both projects lay emphasis on moral *education* rather than moral instruction or moral training (and if the difference is not immediately obvious consider the implications of 'sex education', 'sex instruction' and 'sex training').

Given that this 'skills/autonomy' view is the received opinion among moral educators, what is one to say of the traditional British link between moral and religious education and of the new situation in which religious education tries to orientate itself to a multi-religious world? Firstly, it may help for clarity's sake, even at the risk of over-simplification, to see the RE – ME connection as a one-way relationship. That is to say, religious education, involving the study of religions, cannot but include the study of the moral dimension of religions. Ninian Smart's analysis of the six dimensions of religion[9] is too well known to need outlining here, but it will be remembered that the ethical dimension is one of the six which he finds characteristic of the religious experience of mankind. To this extent religious education is bound to contribute to pupils' moral education: at the very least it is giving information about the ethical systems or moral values and practices of the world's religions; one hopes that by developing qualities of empathic understanding it is doing more than merely transmitting information. The RE – ME relationship is one-way because in practice one simply could not study religion without studying morality as part of religion. But the converse does not apply: one could in practice (and in the curriculum projects mentioned one *does*) engage in moral education without reference to religion.

However, the situation is more complex than this. It could be argued that a deep study of morality gives rise to general questions about human nature, meaning and purpose in life, the possibility of life beyond death, the nature of moral justification and so on, about which religions have much to say. In this case there would be a link from ME to RE. It may be that a full study of morality must include an examination of such questions, but there are two caveats. One is that a practical programme of guidance in moral decision-making may not be able to wait for the settlement of such broad questions, and that for many pupils whose level of abstract conceptual thinking is limited, it would not be appropriate anyway. The other is that the raising of such questions does not necessarily imply the acceptance of religious answers. Thus moral education, for some, may lead on to religious education, but it does not necessarily lead on to religious commitment.

What aspects of the major world religions are likely to be studied in school RE today? What contribution can such religious studies make towards a pupil's moral education? I propose to take two examples, Islam and Hinduism, in order to examine some of the possibilities and problems that may arise. In both cases I have two considerations in mind. One is what a 'neutral', 'secular', 'post-Christian' pupil might learn about human morality from these religions. The other is what the effect of the 'autonomous moral education' movement might be on practising adherents of these faiths.

Islam

With Islam we are up against a conflict between the general tone of authority and instruction which the religion carries and the emphasis on autonomy which the moral educators favour. *Islam* means submission, and morality is set firmly in a context of divinely revealed laws which it is man's duty to obey. The sources of Islamic Law (*shari'a*) are fourfold: the *Qur'an*, held to be absolute and eternal; the traditions (*hadith*) concerning the customs (*sunna*) of Muhammad, the moral ideal; the application of human reason in working out analogy (*qiyas*) from scripture (for example extending the Qur'anic prohibition on wine to all alcohol); the consensus (*ijma*) of the community, traditionally exercised by expert scholars (*'ulama*). *Shi'a* Muslims (for example in Iran and some from India and Pakistan) replace *ijma* by reliance on *imams*, blood descendants of Muhammad, for authoritative guidance. (For *Sunni* Muslims, the majority, the *imam* is merely a prayer leader in the mosque.)

This emphasis on authoritative tradition presents both a problem and an opportunity for the non-Muslim pupil in learning about Islam. The problem is that in moral education the very notion of authority is likely to be unpopular, not only amongst the pupils, but also among the moral education 'experts', as we saw above. Furthermore, acceptance of the specific moral authority in Islam depends on accepting the religious authority of Muhammad, the *Qur'an*, the *hadith* and so on. The opportunity for advancing one's moral education that can come from a study of the ethical dimension of Islam lies precisely in the recognition that for millions of the world's population (not only Muslims, but Jews and some Christians also) authority is a key concept in moral discourse. Difficult as it may be to deal with at school level, there *is* an issue between autonomy and authority.

For the Muslim pupil taking part in moral education in many British schools (through RE, English or social studies) there must be many tensions. The whole ethos of discussion among laymen of moral problems is foreign to Islamic tradition, where moral education is seen as moral instruction. Depending on the strength of parental allegiance to traditional Islam, the Muslim pupil may feel that such discussion is for him or her beside the point. (Many Muslim parents would, of course, for moral and religious reasons, prefer to have their children educated in exclusively Muslim schools.) However, it is perhaps more likely in the multi-faith school that the Muslim pupil may feel obliged to defend in argument the traditional moral stance of his faith or culture on certain issues, for example the status of women or arranged marriages. This in itself can be a betrayal of Islamic principles, for morality is not to be justified by human reason. 'Man is not meant to argue for democracy on the grounds of inalienable rights.'[10] But one must not give the impression that Islam is totally conservative, traditional and static. By sheer force of world economics, there are increasing encounters between traditional Islamic cultures and new situations in the 'global market-place' to which there are varying responses within Islam. The present writer has heard very different arguments on the role of women in society from Muslim men and Muslim women in the University of Kabul, Afghanistan. There are indications of similar differences between Muslim parents and their teenage children in Britain.

It is such issues as these, rather than theoretical discussions of authority, that are likely to form the main context of moral education discussion, or drama improvisation and role-play, in schools today. 'Education for personal relationships' is the sort of title given to an aspect of moral education designed to put 'sex education' into a broader framework. It cannot be denied that here is a conflict between the traditional Muslim and the contemporary Western viewpoints. One must try to distinguish between what is authentically Muslim, in the sense of being in the *Qur'an* or derived from the *sunna/hadith*, and what is part of custom and culture, for example on the issue of how women should dress, but this is not always easy to do. At all costs the teacher must get his facts right about what is Muslim law or custom, and where there is a difference of viewpoint, either between Islam and the West or within Islam, try to see the various sides of the argument, and encourage pupils to do so. For example, the prevailing Muslim custom is still to see marriage as a contract from which a relationship can grow, whereas the contemporary Western view (and it *is* contemporary, not having always been the case in the Christianised West) is to see the contract as the fulfilment of a relationship. There is something to be said for both points of view. This is not to argue for moral neutrality, but for every effort to be made to stand in the other person's shoes in the process of forming one's own views.

The issue of the status of women in Islam is notoriously controversial and space precludes a full examination of it here. There are other issues which are just as controversial, with which pupils are likely to become familiar via the media, for example the penalties for consuming alcohol, for theft or for adultery in some Muslim countries. Again, these are difficult and sensitive issues on which not all Muslims agree, and on which Muslim pupils themselves may not be fully informed. One is driven back to the *Qur'an* for precise guidance, and then the problem of interpretation arises, as well as that of authority. The *Qur'an* certainly takes a robust attitude to the punishment of offenders, in both this life and the hereafter, but it is also much concerned with the mercy of God towards man and justice and kindness in human relations:

> The righteous man is he who believes in Allah and the Last Day, in the angels and the Scriptures and the prophets; who for the love of Allah gives his wealth to his kinsfolk, to the orphans, to the needy, to the wayfarers and to the beggars, and for the redemption of captives; who attends to his prayers and pays the alms-tax; who is true to his promises and steadfast in trial and adversity and in times of war. Such are the true believers; such are the God-fearing.[11]

A final comment on Islam and moral education takes us back to the question of the relationship between religious and moral education. It should be obvious that for Islam the two are indissoluble. There is no division between sacred and secular, God and Caesar or God and mammon. The sacred book at the heart of Islam gives guidance for all life, often in precise detail. Of its 6,000 or so verses, it has been estimated that 2,000 are strictly legislative. Furthermore, on that question of the broader considerations concerning human nature which, it was said, might lead from moral to religious education, Islam takes the view that, properly educated about the will of God, man can in fact attain it. There is no original sin to hold man back from the practical realisation of the will of God on earth. Islam is 'a total way of life, known and learned from Divine disclosure and attainable in political, social, and economic existence by men on earth'.[12]

Hinduism

As with so many aspects of Hinduism the ethical dimension is complex, wide-ranging and diverse. Instead of the clear-cut sources and directions of Islam, based ultimately on a single revelatory origin, Hinduism presents a range of traditions and a complexity of ideas which are difficult to deal with at an advanced level of study, let alone at school.[13]

At the heart of Hindu ethics is the concept of *dharma*. This, it has been said, is impossible to translate by any single English word, although 'duty' is often used as a rough approximation. *Dharma* is the law defining the essential nature of a thing, so that to fulfil one's *dharma* is, to adapt a phrase of St Augustine's, to become what one is. There is a general *dharma* which applies to all men, involving such general principles as the avoidance of violence, theft, sexual licence and so on, and particular *dharmas* which apply to one's class or caste. For example, the traditional virtues of the brahmin or priestly class are self-control, austerity, purity, forbearance and wisdom; and those of the kshatriya or warrior class are heroism, vigour, generosity and leadership.[14] Or again, it is the duty of a brahmin to study the most ancient and hallowed Hindu scriptures, the *Vedas*, but this is forbidden to the lowest class, the shudras. On the other hand a person of the lowest class may drink liquor, which is forbidden to brahmins. This idea of duties appropriate to one's station in life is not without parallel in the Christian tradition, but it is not likely to be easily understood in a secular, egalitarian climate. This will be referred to again.

There are other concepts fundamental to Hinduism to which *dharma* is related, notably *samsara*, the round of rebirth (reincarnation); *karma*, the law of moral cause and effect which links actions and their consequences; and *moksha*, spiritual liberation or release. This again brings up the question of the connection between morality and religion. One of the distinctive contributions of religious education to moral education is the awareness of how one's sense of moral direction, one's perspective on the whole purpose of morality, may be affected by the religious beliefs one holds. S. C. Thakur argues that religious ethics are inherently teleological, morality is seen as purposive: 'What shall I do to inherit eternal life?' is a question that makes sense in Christianity and in Hinduism, where *dharma* is ultimately for the sake of *moksha*.[15]

There is much in Hinduism's ethical dimension which can be paralleled with Christianity. Indeed, Thakur's argument is that there is an overall similarity both of particular moral injunctions and of theoretical ethical underpinning. This seems to me to ignore certain important differences, particularly concerned with the soteriological aspect of Christian doctrine, but it is instructive to compare, for example, the Ten Commandments with the Laws of Manu[16] and to realise that the injunction against murder has its counterpart in the principle of *ahimsa*, non-violence, that against false witness in the principle of *satya*, veracity, and so on. It is well known that Mahatma Gandhi drew on both the Sermon on the Mount and the *Bhagavad Gita* for moral inspiration, and the Gita's central principle of 'detached action' (a 'Kantian ethic in a religious setting', as Thakur calls it)[17] certainly has its parallel in Christianity, even if it is mainly confined to the mystical tradition.

Nevertheless, however much head teachers and those who arrange multi-faith assemblies like to stress the common ground of religions, in their ethical if not their other dimensions, one has to face the fact that there are differences which are going to emerge once pupils start discussing moral issues in the classroom. One such difference has already been referred to and will be taken up briefly again now, that of class or caste in Hinduism. 'The idea that all men are fundamentally equal,' says A. L. Basham, 'is to be found in Buddhism' (and, one would add, in Islam and Christianity), 'but it is quite foreign to classical Hinduism.'[18] He goes on to outline the four classes (*varnas*) into which Aryan society was divided and the thousands of castes (*jatis*) which exist today in every region of India. It should be noted that the Indian Constitution of 26 January 1950 is against caste discrimination and declares the equality of all citizens before the law. The modern Indian government strives to overcome caste divisions by means of official propaganda in cinema and poster advertisements and the like, but it seems to be generally agreed that caste is still pervasive throughout Indian society. 'Caste continues to determine the function, the status, the job opportunities, as well as the social handicaps of a very large majority of the population.'[19] As with the subject of the status of women in Islam (and a similar question arises with regard to women in Hinduism) one needs to investigate carefully the facts concerning caste and the different ethical evaluations of those facts. It is possible to argue that the principle of caste, if not always the reality, far from being a social evil, is a form of 'harmony unifying diversity',[20] or social integration, linked with the religious notion of progress towards *moksha* through the progressive fulfilment of appropriate *dharma*.

A further notion in Hinduism suggests a possible exercise which could have interesting results in a multi-cultural class. From time to time there have been surveys of pupils' ambitions and expectations of life, designed to bring out what in fact adolescents do value. 'My life in 20 years' time' is the sort of topic an English teacher might set for an essay, which could link well with moral education. At the time of writing a survey has just been completed amongst polytechnic students, showing that they value happiness, freedom and honesty above everything else, that they have a low opinion of the importance of politeness, cleanliness and obedience, and that only business studies students rate 'a comfortable life' very highly in their preferences, others consigning it to the bottom half of their list.[21] It might be interesting to carry out such an exercise with school-age pupils and compare the results with the 'Three Aims' referred to in the Hindu lawbooks, ranked in order of priority as the pursuit of religious merit, wealth and pleasure.[22] This scheme, together with the notion of four ideal stages of life – the pupil, the householder, the hermit and the wandering holy man – sets a framework for the Hindu moral quest which again brings us back to the all-important notion of *dharma*, that pattern of conduct which is appropriate not only to one's general humanity and particular status in life, but also to one's stage along the way.

Finally, there are two points to be added on the contribution that a study of Hinduism might make to moral education. The first is a negative one. It is often claimed that the basic orientation of Hinduism is life-renouncing rather than life-affirming, that Hindu ethics are seen as relative and in a sense illusory (*maya*), that ultimate reality is beyond good and evil, and that consequently there has been a lack of concern with active social reform such as one finds in the history of Christianity. These are fascinating questions; there are theoretical and empirical points to be made for and against; but they are at a level of abstraction which makes them unlikely to be dealt with in school except perhaps at sixth form level. There is much groundwork ethics of a positive nature with which it would be more appropriate to deal. The second point follows on from this and may serve as a conclusion to this whole discussion of world religions and moral education. I have perhaps tended to emphasise the moral *teachings* of religions and the business of discussion and debate of controversial viewpoints. This is perhaps an over-intellectual perspective. I would not want to neglect another important contribution which religious educa-tion can make to moral education: that of the imaginative realisation of moral ideals in stories of saints and heroes, seen as 'moral models'. Children perhaps gain their moral notions more from Robin Hood or Batman and Robin, than from lists of commandments. For Christians Jesus is the living exemplar of Christian ethics, for Muslims Muhammad is the embodiment of the Qur'anic ideal, for Hindus the mythological figures of Krishna, or Rama and Sita, serve this purpose. Nor should one always look *backwards* to the past for models. Contemporary history and television news can provide examples also, whether it be Mahatma Gandhi or Mother Teresa.

Notes and references

1 P. H. Hirst, 'Liberal education and the nature of knowledge', in R. D. Archambault (ed.), *Philosophical Analysis and Education* (London: Routledge & Kegan Paul, 1965). See also P. H. Hirst and R. S. Peters, *The Logic of Education* (London: Routledge & Kegan Paul, 1970), chapter 4.

2 For a brief but pointed statement of this argument see P. H. Nowell-Smith, *Ethics* (Penguin, 1954), pp. 192f. For a fuller and very clear

exposition, see R. F. Dearden, *The Philosophy of Primary Education* (London: Routledge & Kegan Paul, 1968), chapter 8.

3 For example W. W. Bartley III, *Morality and Religion* (London: Macmillan, 1971).

4 M. Downey and A. V. Kelly, *Moral Education* (London: Harper & Row, 1978), p. 6.

5 Downey and Kelly, op. cit., give useful summaries of the work of Piaget and Kohlberg in chapter 3.

6 See J. Wilson, N. Williams and B. Sugarman, *Introduction to Moral Education* (Penguin, 1967), and subsequent works of Wilson.

7 Schools Council Project in Moral Education: *Lifeline* (London: Longman, 1972).

8 Schools Council Moral Education 8–13 Project: *Startline* (London: Longman, 1978).

9 N. Smart, *The Religious Experience of Mankind* (London: Fontana, 1976 edition), chapter 1.

10 K. Cragg, *The Call of the Minaret* (NY/OUP, 1956), p. 143.

11 *The Koran*, tr. N. J. Dawood (Penguin, 1956), pp. 341f.

12 K. Cragg, op. cit., pp. 142f.

13 For a thorough theoretical study of Hindu ethics see S. C. Thakur, *Christian and Hindu Ethics* (London: George Allen & Unwin, 1969).

14 ibid., p. 145.

15 ibid., chapter 1.

16 ibid., chapter 5.

17 ibid., p. 68.

18 A. L. Basham, 'Hinduism', in R. C. Zaehner (ed.), *The Concise Encyclopedia of Living Faiths* (London: Hutchinson, 1959), p. 244.

19 R. Lannoy, *The Speaking Tree* (OUP, 1971), p. 248. Lannoy is a most useful source for information on and analysis of Indian social and cultural life.

20 ibid., p. 138.

21 *The Times Higher Education Supplement*, 11 April 1980.

22 A. L. Basham, op. cit., p. 242.

Further reading

Moral Education: Theory and Practice, M. Downey and A. V. Kelly (Macmillan, 1978), gives a wide-ranging summary of philosophical and psychological perspectives on moral education, including the work of key figures such as Lawrence Kohlberg, and also summarises the practical implications for the curriculum and organisation of schools. Paul Hirst is a noted writer on philosophy of education and his *Moral Education in a Secular Society* (University of London Press/National Children's Home, 1974), is well worth reading. Those interested in the logical relationship of morality to religion will find several useful articles in *Christian Ethics and Contemporary Philosophy*, edited by Ian Ramsey (SCM Press, 1966). Bishop Kenneth Cragg is well known for his sympathetic insight into Muslim belief and practice, as evidenced in *The Call of the Minaret* (OUP, 1956). An insider's view of Islam, expressed in the form of letters written from prison to his son, is given by Mohammad Fadhel Jamali in *Letters on Islam* (OUP, 1965). A detailed comparison of *Christian and Hindu Ethics* is provided in the book of that title by S. C. Thakur, an Indian who became professor of philosophy at an English university (Allen & Unwin, 1969). A more phenomenological viewpoint is to be found in R. Lannoy's *The Speaking Tree* (OUP, 1971), a fascinating study of Indian social and cultural life. Finally, the two best-known curriculum projects on moral education, although they do not take a particularly multi-cultural perspective, are the Schools Council projects *Lifeline* and *Startline* on the one hand (Longman, 1972 and 1978), and the project led by John Wilson on the other. Wilson has written several works, for example *Teacher's Guide to Moral Education* (Collier-Macmillan, 1973) and *Practical Methods of Moral Education* (Heinemann, 1972).

15
Islam and Political Education

Richard Tames

I would like to go [to Saudi Arabia] . . . with a large armed force, blow up the wogs and take over the oilfields and bring the economic situation under control so's to have more money to spend on arms to attack the Soviet Union. This would then possibly result in world peace and prosperity, thus enabling the rich western powers to help the smaller underdeveloped nations. I would also put the smelly arabs onto a world slave market.—Fourth-year pupil in a south Essex comprehensive school

This quotation may lack sophistication; it does not lack vigour. It was written a few months before the outbreak of the Iranian revolution, in response to the following assignment: 'Why I would or would not like to visit Saudi Arabia.' The respondents were drawn literally (but not in the strictly statistical sense) at random from a number of secondary schools in the Home Counties. Their views are noteworthy on two counts: (a) roughly twice as many were opposed to visiting Saudi Arabia as were in favour of going; (b) roughly half based their views, for or against, on some moral/social value as opposed to a purely aesthetic/pedagogic concern (such as to see the desert/eat the food).

'I would like to attend the public trials and whippings of people who have crimed.' (*sic*)
'As the country is a Muslim one the people have lives dominated by religion, which I do not agree with.'
'They are very strict and put you in prison for drinking whisky.'
'. . . they have no freedom there.'
'We do not force Christianity onto Muslims that enter Britain, so why should they be able to push their religion on us.'

It should not be necessary to labour the point that secondary age pupils of average ability habitually and spontaneously think in 'political' terms, that is they make judgements according to scales of value which necessarily involve questions of authority and social relationships.

More than half a century has passed since the idea that 'every teacher is a teacher of English' was advanced as a radical and challenging proposition. Perhaps it will take a little less time for it to be recognised as a truism that every teacher is also a teacher of politics. This is simply an inevitable consequence of the teacher's relationship with his/her pupils, an acknowledgment of the fact that he/she stands for certain values. RE teachers, having a special and conscious commitment to the problematic area of 'values education' obviously have a central role to play. It may well be that that role is both more urgent and more demanding than the role currently being assumed by the teacher now consciously confronting the challenge of 'political education', a challenge too often conceived to lie entirely within a framework of concepts and issues derived from the Western tradition of political thought. As the above quotations imply, our pupils often ask very broad, basic questions which range beyond the very parameters within which our arguments are habitually conducted. It may well be that the RE teacher with a 'world religions' background is more adequately equipped to cope with this situation than the politics teacher whose training has been limited to a rigorous study of Western political theory and institutions. This is not to say that the task is one to be undertaken lightly; it is fraught with difficulties and some very real dangers.

The idea of 'political education' has gained general currency in Britain over the course of the last decade, thanks very largely to the efforts of Professor Bernard Crick of Birkbeck College, London, the Politics Association, the Hansard Society for Parliamentary Government and the Nuffield Foundation.[1] Only one Local Education Authority, Sheffield, has gone so far as to appoint a specialist adviser in political education,[2] although other authorities have allocated responsibility for this area to other advisers, for example in history or social studies, but Her Majesty's Inspectorate has given enthusiastic backing to the cause.[3] It is curious and noteworthy, however, that virtually no effort has been made, either intellectually or institutionally, to explore and develop the large areas of common concern which are shared by teachers of politics and teachers of RE. It is also worth mentioning, in passing, that the GCE A level examinations in religious studies do contain explicitly political questions such as the following: 'Describe the attempts of one Muslim country to harmonize Muslim religious faith and practice with modern social and political life' (London 1977); 'Consider the suggestion that Islam is a religion which perpetuates the inferior status of women' (JMB 1976).

Crick has emphasised consistently that 'political literacy' is to be achieved not through the memorisation of the minutiae of the so-called 'British Constitution' which once provided the staple fodder of 'civics' courses, but through the mastery of key concepts such as justice, representation, order.[4] I wish to argue that these concepts may more readily be grasped in their entirety when we come at them indirectly, by considering political and social structures in which they have either no part to play at all or at least a very different one. Islam offers particularly clear advantages in this regard.

The Schools Council publication *Humanities for the Young School Leaver: An Approach through Religious Education* declares:

> Religion is not an optional extra in the interpretation of human life . . . It is,
> rather, a dimension of all experience. It is the full understanding of the whole of
> life – life viewed *sub specie aeternitatis*. It follows that any problem, if pushed far
> enough, becomes a religious problem.[5]

In Islam one does not have to push very far.

This Schools Council publication goes on to argue that 'our young
people' are inextricably involved in human situations which they can well
appreciate lead them necessarily to confront the problems of (a) living in
groups, (b) being affected by rules, (c) satisfying needs and wants, (d)
understanding beliefs, and (e) coping with change. Islam has, of course,
distinctive perspectives to offer on each of these matters.

Islam is, as its followers so constantly assert, more than a religion in the
narrow, Western sense; it is an entire way of life. Islam offers, therefore, a
direct challenge to conventional modes of thinking with regard to social
and political affairs. It acknowledges no distinction between the realms of
Caesar and of God, the secular and the sacred, the public and the private.
In the candid words of the Pakistani ideologist, Abul A'la Mawdudi, the
sphere of activity of an Islamic state 'is co-extensive with the whole of
human life . . . In such a state no one can regard any field of his affairs as
personal and private. Considered from this aspect the Islamic state bears
a kind of resemblance to the Fascist and Communist states.'[6]

In the ideal Islamic state, therefore, the scope of state power is
determined not by popular sovereignty, the axiomatic and usually
unexamined basis of Western-style democracy, but by divine revelation
('They ask, "Have we also got some authority?" Say "All authority
belongs to God alone".' *Qur'an* 3:154).

This necessarily gives rise to some interesting issues which are bound to
lead to energetic debate in the classroom. As Professor N. J. Coulson
notes, the traditional criminal law in Islamic states 'was largely confined
to the exposition of specific offences – illicit sexual relations, slanderous
allegations of unchastity, theft, wine-drinking, armed robbery and
apostasy – in which the notion of man's obligations towards God
predominated.'[7] A recently published textbook for West African Muslim
students takes a broadly similar line:

> God hates these [i.e. sexual] offences and they are harmful to us. They are
> social crimes in the same way as stealing or murder are social crimes. If they are
> allowed to happen, without any legal check, their bad effects will gradually
> spread through the community.[8]

Islam not only determines the scope of public authority, extending it to
cover what are regarded in the West as personal matters of morality and
lifestyle, it also affects such fundamental political issues as the process of
public decision-making, the nature and obligations of citizenship and the
limits of dissent and opposition. In Islam the emphasis shifts from 'rights'
to 'right' and, indeed, to righteousness. As W. C. Smith put it:

In the message that God communicated is to be found, in the Muslim view, not what is true so much, though, of course, they do hold to this, but what is *right* . . . it is a revelation *from* God, more than *of* God. The apostle or prophet is one who conveys to men the message that God wants them to know; namely, how they should live.

The result is that 'any attempt to impose a purely human yoke on man's neck is an infringement not only of human dignity, but of cosmic order, and to submit to it would be sin'.[9]

This is not, of course, to say that the ideal Islamic state is readily to be found. Islam, in this sense, like democracy, is an ideal, an aspiration, which each generation must struggle to realise, whether this means maintaining the values and institutions that it has inherited or establishing them *de novo* after a period of societal degeneration. It is essential, therefore, that the comparisons which will inevitably be made, whether crude or subtle, should match like with like, judging Muslim ideals against non-Muslim ideals, Muslim practice against non-Muslim practice.

A re-evaluation of the historical experience of Muslim peoples is, therefore, overdue. This need not imply an uncritical assessment of the achievements of Muslim statehood. Michael Hudson warns that the norm was 'despotism punctuated by rebellion and chronic succession crises' but emphasises that 'rulers and the ruled shared basic values, most rulers did not impose alien norms on their subjects and so tyranny in the sense of wrong rule was the exception'.[10]

Islam is, in other words, different. It envisages a role for the state, for law, for public officials, quite distinct from these conventionally assumed within the Western tradition. This alone might make it worthy of attention and interest. But the perspective of comparison can be reversed. We can not only examine Islamic practices and prescriptions from a Western point of view; we can also look at Western institutions and attitudes from the Islamic point of view.

One of the most outspoken Muslim critics of the Western political tradition has been Colonel Muammar Gadaffi of Libya, proponent of the 'Third International Theory' and author of *The Green Book*. According to Colonel Gadaffi, 'A parliament is a misrepresentation of the people and parliamentary governments are a misleading solution to the problem of democracy.' A one-party state is justified on the grounds that 'the existence of many parties escalates the struggle for power and this results in the destruction of any achievements of the people and of any socially beneficial plans'. In Gadaffi's view 'there is no difference between party struggles and tribal or sectarian struggles for power'. The party is, moreover, 'a dictatorial instrument of governing that enables those with one outlook and a common interest to rule the people as a whole'.[11] These criticisms would seem to ignore some basic distinctions between parties, tribes and sects, in respect of the manner in which members are recruited and the nature of the commitments that their membership involves. If careful consideration of Gadaffi's strictures of Western parliamentarism makes these distinctions clear the effort will surely have been worthwhile.

There is, of course, a prudential as well as a purely pedagogic argument to be made. The plain fact is that Islam – whatever that may mean – is 'news', and that states whose political style and outlook are largely conditioned by Islamic tradition have acquired immense political 'clout'.

Iran and Saudi Arabia, Nigeria and Indonesia, Kuwait and the United Arab Emirates *matter* in a way and to an extent that would have been virtually inconceivable a decade ago. Libya, a state with a population smaller than that of Wales, has played a significant role in the recent political history of countries as diverse and distant as Uganda, Ulster, Chad, Palestine, Malta and the Philippines.

The fifty or so states in which Muslims form a majority of the population are all, moreover, developing countries. They include states with substantial industrial sectors, such as Turkey and Algeria, and states which are among the poorest in the world, such as Mauritania and Bangladesh. And their Islamic traditions are directly relevant to any consideration of their status and prospects as developing countries, for Islam is intimately bound up with many of the most fundamental aspects of the daily life of the mass of ordinary people – the content of education, the role of women and the inheritance of property to name but three of the most crucial. Religious personnel, deriving their prestige from tradition and esoteric knowledge, can wield immense influence. Bill and Leiden stress that

> the practising Muslim will turn to the cleric for protection and support against secular forces considered corrupt and oppressive. He finds it difficult to believe that individuals who have consistently exploited should suddenly become the standard-bearers of reform. Thus when the mullah seeks to resist modernizing programmes, he will do so more effectively because of the strong bonds of trust that he has often developed with the people themselves. This is one reason why some scholars strongly argue that reform must develop through traditional channels if it is to be at all effective.[12]

The twentieth century affords numerous examples of political leaders in Muslim countries struggling to reconcile the force of Islamic tradition with the imperatives of modern statehood. The rejectionist stance of Mustafa Kemal Atatürk is well known. Suppressing the Sufi orders in 1925 he asserted that 'to seek help from the dead (i.e. through the intercession of the spiritual hierarchy of past Sufi divines) is a disgrace to a civilised community . . . The straightest, truest way is the way of civilisation (i.e. the West). To be a man, it is enough to do what civilisation requires.'[13] What is less often acknowledged is that although Atatürk may have secularised the policy-making elite and reduced religion to a matter of private preference in their lives, he did little to change the basic orientation of the masses for whom Islam continues to define the basis of the social order.

The ideal of an authentically Islamic form of state provided the *raison d'être* for the establishment of Pakistan in 1947. It is likewise supposed to have provided the inspiration for the Libyan 'Jamahiriyyah' which through its students' and workers' committees is claimed to optimise mass participation and 'People's Power'. Contemporary Iran provides an even more dramatic case study in Islamic state-building. Leonard Binder, the distinguished American political scientist, has sketched out the lineaments of an Islamic state:

> Such a state will declare the sovereignty of God as the foundation of the legitimacy of its government . . . The law of the state will be based upon the Qur'an and the traditions . . . The Head of the state will have power of interpreting the sacred law in applying it to new situations . . . The Head of state and assembly will be elected, but there will be only one party or perhaps none at all . . . The composition of the assembly may reflect economic interests but probably not geographical areas. The law will be a respecter of persons in regard to religious differences. Only Muslims will be able to hold policy-making positions, but non-Muslims will be permitted to live in accordance with their personal status law. Private property will be safe-guarded but exceptionally large accumulations of wealth will be prohibited. Women will be excluded from public life and secluded in the home wherever possible. The major domestic duty of the government will be to foster the good and repress evil in encouraging the growth of a truly Muslim society.[14]

Matching Binder's ideal type against current realities could prove to be a thought-provoking exercise.

Supporters of 'development education' as much as of political education cannot, therefore, afford to underestimate the significance of Islam, not least because the notion of an *umma*, the universal brotherhood of believers, challenges the very notion of the nation-state, which has conventionally provided the social and territorial framework, established the priorities and mobilised the resources for the development process itself.

The President of OPEC, Mana Said Al-Oteiba, has stated bluntly that 'if there is another world war, it will be over petroleum'.[15] There is nothing intrinsically Islamic about the problematic issues that this raises for the West, but the Islamic dimension cannot be ignored. And the West is at last waking up to the fact. As Henry Fairlie noted with customary acerbity, 'all of Washington is speed-reading the Qur'an'. A *Sunday Times* editorial made much the same point though in rather a different vein: 'We will get nowhere as agents of stability in the Middle East if we begin by despising the people who live there.'[16]

So we are, perhaps, becoming more disposed to learn a little. But the task is not easy. As the media coverage of the Iranian revolution has revealed, Western journalists have little conception of how to analyse the events they are compelled to report. Ayatollah Khomeini's words are apposite:

'All this about "reactionary mullahs, reactionary mullahs". Those who write these words either have no understanding or their pens are on loan to the enemies of Islam.'[17] Perhaps the former explanation will suffice.

Notes and references

1 See especially *Political Education and Political Literacy*, edited by Bernard Crick and Alex Porter (Longman, 1978), which contains Crick's fundamental theoretical contribution to the elaboration of the concept of 'political literacy' as well as numerous schemes of work and case studies of actual practice.

2 See *The Times Educational Supplement*, 22 February 1980.

3 See 'Political Competence', the curriculum 11–16. Discussion Papers, DES November 1978.

4 Crick and Porter, op. cit., especially sections 2.2 and 2.3.

5 *Humanities for the Young School Leaver: An Approach through Religious Education*, Schools Council (Evans/Methuen Educational, 1969).

6 Abul A'la Mawdudi, 'Islamic Law and Constitution', quoted in Kurshid Ahmad (ed.), *Islam: Its Meaning and Message* (Islamic Council of Europe, 1975), p. 166. See also Seyyed Hossein Nasr, *Ideals and Realities of Islam* (Allen & Unwin, second edition 1975).

7 N. J. Coulson, *A History of Islamic Law* (Edinburgh University Press, 1964), p. 124.

8 B. Aisha Lemu, *A Student's Introduction to Islam* (Macmillan, 1971), p. 35.

9 W. C. Smith, *The Faith of Other Men* (CBC Toronto, 1962), pp. 32 and 34. There are, of course, numerous Qur'anic references in support of this view, for example Surat Al-Ma'idah (5 – The Food) 15: 'Indeed there has come to you from Allah a light and a clear book whereby Allah guides such as follow His pleasure into the ways of peace and brings them out of darkness into light by His will, and guides them to the right path.'

10 M. C. Hudson, *Arab Politics: The Search for Legitimacy* (Yale University Press, 1977), pp. 91 and 99.

11 Quotations from *Arab Dawn Report.No. 2 (Revised) – The Green Book* – the text of two public discussions in London, (Press Department, Embassy of the Socialist Peoples' Libyan Arab Jamahiriyya, 1977). Copies of *The Green Book* can be obtained free of charge from The Information Department, The Libyan People's Bureau of the Socialist Libyan Arab Jamahiriyya, 5 St James's Square, London SW1.

12 James A. Bill and Carl Leiden, *The Middle East: Politics and Power* (Boston: Allyn & Bacon, 1974), p. 38.

13 Quoted in B. Lewis, *The Emergence of Modern Turkey* (OUP, second edition 1968), pp. 410–11.

14 Quoted in R. Tames, *The World of Islam: A Teachers' Handbook* (School of Oriental and African Studies, 1977), p. 130.

15 Public statement at Vienna, 3 October 1979.

16 *The Sunday Times*, 6 January 1980.

17 Quoted in *The Guardian*, 17 September 1979. See also Edward Said, *Covering Islam* (Routledge & Kegan Paul, 1981) for an analysis of Western reporting on Iran.

Further reading

What Western thought would categorise as the political aspects of 'classical' (i.e. pre-modern) Islam are dealt with in chapter 9, 'Law and the State', of J. E. Schacht and C. E. Bosworth, *The Legacy of Islam* (OUP second edition, 1974), and at greater length in R. Levy, *The Social Structure of Islam* (CUP, 1957); P. M. Holt, A. K. S. Lambton and B. Lewis (eds), *The Cambridge History of Islam*, Vol. 2 (CUP, 1970) Part 8, chapters 3 and 4; and in W. M. Watt's *Islam and the Integration of Society* (Routledge & Kegan Paul, 1961). Bernard Lewis, *Islam: From the Prophet Muhammad to the Fall of Constantinople* (Harper & Row, 1974) presents a selection of documentary materials.

The standard orientalist accounts of Islamic modernism are H. A. R. Gibb, *Modern Trends in Islam* (Librairie du Liban, 1975), and Kenneth Cragg, *Counsels in Contemporary Islam* (Edinburgh University Press, 1965). For Muslim views see parts 2 and 3 of *The Challenge of Islam* (Islamic Council of Europe, 1978) edited by Altaf Gauhar, and Charis Waddy's rather eclectic anthology *The Muslim Mind* (Longman, 1976).

G. H. Jansen's *Militant Islam* (Panther, 1979) is a more thoughtful and carefully researched study that its lurid cover would suggest, whereas John Laffin's *The Dagger of Islam* (Sphere, 1979) does bear out the promise of its title. Two sociological accounts are Morroe Berger's descriptive and slightly dated *Islam in Egypt Today* (CUP, 1970) and the more theoretical work by M. Jamil Hanifi, *Islam and the Transformation of Culture* (Asia Publishing House, 1974) which focuses on Turkey. South Asia is dealt with in chapters 15, 16 and 17 of R. Jackson (ed.), *Perspectives on World Religions* (School of Oriental and African Studies, University of London, 1978 – available from SOAS, Malet St. London WCIE 7HP). K. H. Karpat's *Political and Social Thought in the Contemporary Middle East* (Praeger, 1968) presents a range of twentieth-century viewpoints. Highly critical accounts of contemporary Europe from the fundamentalist viewpoint can be found in F. J. Goulding's translation of Sayid Mijtaba Rukru Musawi Lari's *Western Civilization Through Muslim Eyes* (Worthing: Optimus Books, 1977) and in *Jihad: A Groundplan* (Diwan Press, 1978) by 'Abd al-Qadir as-Sufi, an English Muslim.

16
World Studies and World Religions

Robin Richardson

'Quite a curiosity, isn't he? Now tell me doctor – you've been all over the world – don't you think that's a bit of a Hindoo we've got hold of here?'

The speaker, a character in a short story by Joseph Conrad, is a farmer in a tiny village on the south coast of England.[1] It is the 1870s. The curiosity of which the farmer speaks is the sole survivor of a shipwreck in the Channel. At the moment he is extremely weak, drenched, barely alive. But soon he recovers from the ordeal of the shipwreck. Conrad describes how he stays on in the village, learns English, and eventually – after a fashion – settles down. However, the villagers never really get used to him. His foreignness, says Conrad, 'had a peculiar and indelible stamp'.

> . . . his rapid, skimming walk; his swarthy complexion; his hat cocked on the left ear; his habit, on warm evenings, of wearing his coat over one shoulder, like a hussar's dolman; his manner of leaping over the stiles, not as a feat of agility, but in the ordinary course of progression – all these peculiarities were, as one may say, so many causes of scorn and offence to the inhabitants of the village. *They* wouldn't in their dinner hour lie flat on their backs on the grass to stare at the sky. Neither did they go about the fields screaming dismal tunes . . .

Conrad's story is a beautiful and prophetic (and, incidentally, tragic) exploration of what nowadays we call inter-cultural communication. It was in the 1870s that the rate of social and economic change in Europe really began to speed up, so that only three or four generations later there would be a whole new family of words and phrases to evoke the basic social and political environment of all human beings: world society, spaceship earth, global village, one world, small planet. And within this overall world society most individual societies are now multi-cultural, and multi-ethnic. Compared with Conrad's villagers in the 1870s we are all of us today much more used to foreigners. We do not, it is true, much appreciate the 'peculiar and indelible stamp' of their foreignness. But we cannot avoid it. Every newspaper we read and every television news bulletin we see reminds us, indirectly or in as many words, that most major human problems have to be seen in a world context, not a local or national context, if they are to be adequately analysed and managed; and that therefore the perceptions and preferences of foreigners have to be taken into account. We no longer live, as Conrad's villagers did, in separate communities scattered over the face of the world, with only the occasional explosive accident to stop foreign ships passing in the night. The passengers and goods from foreign ships – and also their 'bads', their sanctions and brute coercion – are in the very weft and warp of our lives.

There has been a variety of responses amongst teachers and other educators to the increasing interdependence of the modern world, and to the increasingly multi-cultural and multi-ethnic nature of most individual societies. The responses are evoked by terms such as development education, peace education, global education, multi-cultural education, world studies, education for international understanding.[2] Amongst the people who use these terms there are certain differences of emphasis and priority, and there are consequent tensions. For the purposes of this chapter it can usefully be suggested that the tensions are between 'world studies' on the one hand and 'world religions' on the other.

The distinction and tension between world studies and world religions is part of a wider tension – between those who emphasise teaching about world politics and those who emphasise teaching about world cultures. The latter are concerned not only with world religions but also with the history of other parts of the world, everyday customs and lifestyles, arts, architecture, folklore, literature, and so on. In practice they devote their attention mainly to Asia, Africa and the Caribbean. The proponents of world studies, however, are concerned with world society as a whole rather than with distinct bits and pieces of it, and are severely critical of any attempt to teach about culture, for example about religion, without including what they consider to be the more important notions of interaction, conflict, dominance, power and justice.

In addition to tensions and disagreements there are also, of course, several points of contact and meeting. The choice is not really between the one approach or the other – *either* politics *or* cultures. It is possible and desirable, on the contrary, for each of these two main approaches to challenge and to enrich the other. In this chapter, accordingly, the concern is with synthesis as well as with antithesis. First, a critique will be made from a world studies perspective of the priorities and concerns of much teaching about world religions. Second, there will be a kind of reply. The tone of the reply will be one of 'Yes, but . . .'. That is, it will not attempt to counter or refute the earlier criticisms, but will draw attention to certain important things which the world studies approach can learn from the concern for world religions. Some of these things can also be learnt, it will be recalled, from imaginative literature – for example, from Conrad's short story about the foreigner in a Sussex village.

Three main criticisms of much teaching about world religions are to be recalled. First, there is the omission of issues to do with conflict and justice; second (partly as a consequence), there is a naïve understanding of, as many school syllabuses call it, 'Christian responsibility'; third, there is a rather impoverished theory of learning and teaching.

With regard to issues of conflict and justice, the most immediately striking aspect of much teaching about world religions is the lack of reference to colonialism and racism, and to inter-ethnic relationships in the inner cities of modern Europe. We teach about the 5 K's of Sikhism or about Guru Nanak more readily than about the massacre at Amritsar; about the gods and festivals of Hinduism more readily than about the destruction of the Indian cotton industry by British capitalism or Kipling's infamous proposal that non-Europeans are 'half-devil and half-child'; about the prayers and mosques of Islam more readily than about petro-dollars or the second-class status of Muslim children in many European schools; about the synagogue, sabbath and bar mitzvah more readily than about Shylock and Fagin, or the holocaust.

This kind of omission is serious for three separate reasons. First, it ignores a very major part of the reality which is supposedly being studied. For 'the power of religion depends, in the last resort, upon the credibility of the banners which it puts into the hands of men as they stand before death, or more accurately, as they walk, inevitably, toward it',[3] and death comes not only naturally but also at the hands of other human beings. To understand a religion as a human phenomenon you have to understand also, amongst other things, the metaphysical chaos which is conceived to be its alternative. And to understand any particular religious community you have to understand the threats to its integrity and to its very existence which it has had to withstand from other human beings. In the case of religions other than Christianity, some (though certainly not all) of the main threats to their integrity and existence during the last 500 years have been made by Christianity in particular or Western culture in general. This fundamental point about religions and religious communities cannot be ignored if we really do want to understand them – as distinct from convert them, or 'cover' or 'do' them in a school syllabus.

A second reason for deploring the omission of conflict and justice from teaching about world religions is that all too often such teaching contains in consequence no value judgements. Instead, there is a woolly relativism: the various dimensions of a religion (doctrinal, ethical, ritual, and so on) are described in painstaking detail, and there is explanation also of their significance for believers, but at no point are pupils expected to form judgements about the actual rights and wrongs of religious belief.[4] Certainly it is better to judge slowly than to judge swiftly, and better not to judge at all than to judge selfishly and ethnocentrically. But nevertheless the aims of a course on world faiths must surely include the capacity to make judgements – not least judgements about the appalling role which many religions have played over the centuries, and continue to play, in blessing and reinforcing inequality between social classes, and between men and women.

A third reason for regretting these omissions is more practical: that is to say, it is nearer to the everyday concerns and strategies of the classroom teacher. It is that to focus attention in one's teaching on issues of conflict and justice is to make one's lessons more immediately interesting – all the world loves a scrap, or at least observing one and arguing about it. There is also the point that most of one's pupils probably have hostile feelings against all kinds of foreignness and strangeness, and that these are daily reinforced and confirmed by the mass media. (Also in their conversations and chat with each other – 'Irish' jokes for instance.) It is elementary common-sense for a teacher to acknowledge the pupils' prejudices, and to work cheerfully with them as acceptable starting-places, rather than to pretend that they are not there at all.

Many RE syllabuses nowadays contain reference not only to world religions but also to 'Christian responsibility', and in this latter connection they typically refer to the Third World, and to the work of agencies such as Christian Aid. Explicitly or implicitly they often recall the parable of the Good Samaritan. 'Who is my neighbour?' asks the parable. 'My neighbour', replies the syllabus, 'is every starving and naked person in the Third World. I should bring them succour and comfort for the same reason that the Samaritan was right to pause on his journey in the parable – they are *there*.' Now this may or may not be good Christian humanitarianism, but it is certainly bad politics. For from a political point of view, the real villains in the original parable are not the people who passed by on the other side but the thieves amongst whom the man fell in the first place. The political obligation on the thieves not to beat people up, or at least to make reparation once they have done so, is surely greater than the obligation on third parties to succour and comfort their victims. But anyway, supposing the Samaritan himself was a receiver of stolen goods? Perhaps the money he gave to the innkeeper had previously been slipped to him by the very thieves whose victim he was now helping? Surely he is no longer then a model for us to admire and to imitate?

Questions such as these have to be asked about aid to the Third World and also – even more importantly – about aid to so-called immigrants in European cities. To translate the metaphor, the point is that no serious consideration of 'Christian responsibility' dare ignore the challenge of, for example, a report of the 1970s written by a West Indian for a working party at the British Council of Churches:[5]

Everyone seems to forget that the West Indian as we know him today is a creation of Western capitalist countries, Spain, France, Britain, and of the Gospel that accompanied their exploits . . . The race debate in this country is carried out as if the presence of black people here bears no relevance to the responsibilities of Britain and the rest of the capitalist world in the social and economic affairs of their countries of origin . . . It is supremely ironical that, having appropriated to itself an unfair share of the world's resources, having denuded the 'under-developed' world of its natural resources, and its opportunities for growth and self-sufficiency, Britain could turn to those same territories and say: Come and be employed as cheap-labour in England rather than be unemployed cheap-labour in Asia and the West Indies. Now that you lack the capacity to produce riches for me on your own soil, come to the metropolis and enable me to maintain and improve the standard of living here that your toil there had enabled me to achieve . . . Even if the Church, encapsulated as it is within the oppressive culture so that it cannot stand with the poor and oppressed, refuses to proclaim the Gospel of deliverance that Christ preached (Luke 4:18), and accept the mission that the Gospel enjoins, a mission which poses the Church as a contradiction to the status quo, we as black people could do no other than identify with the struggles for liberation of the oppressed peoples of the world.

With regard to teaching and learning, the world studies perspective has a single main point to put to teachers of world religions (and, indeed, to teachers of many other subjects). It is that the typical classroom situation is itself characterised by inequality, between teacher and pupils, and that a major part of the teacher's responsibility is to diminish, and to equip and empower the pupils to diminish, the imbalance of power in which they find themselves. This is partly a matter of practical techniques and methods. 'One of the saddest things to me about "phenomenological" approaches to RE,' a teacher complains ruefully and accurately, 'is the incredible dullness of style. Teachers who would never dream of using chalk-and-talk all the time in Biblical lessons seem to see nothing wrong with reading from a textbook or dictating notes in the area of World Faiths.' She goes on to recall 'that we all learn from the *how* as well as the *what*', and says, 'So teach Islam in a Muslim way. Teach Judaism in the Jewish way. There's no actual Hebrew word for "religion". Use songs, blessings, discussion, ritual actions, stories, food and lots of humour, because these are how *Jews* communicate. Be Jewish about your Judaism course.'[6]

Such suggestions are stimulating and important. It is also vital, if one is concerned with issues of justice both in the wider world and in the immediate teaching/learning situation itself, to work with the kind of general pedagogy famously outlined by Paulo Freire.[7] One account of this, written with European classrooms in mind rather than non-formal education in Third World villages, proposes that a course of study should have three distinct phases: climate, enquiry, synthesis.[8] The tasks of the first phase include establishing and valuing the knowledge and experience which pupils already have, and accepting their knowledge and experience as a valid starting point; giving them a chance to find out more about each other's opinions and attitudes, and to trust and respect one another; helping them to develop self-confidence through the successful completion of simple tasks; providing opportunities for them to recognise on their own initiative that there are gaps in their knowledge and inconsistencies in their values; and requiring them to take a measure of responsibility for designing and managing the rest of the course. The second phase of the course, enquiry, includes direct or simulated experience of the subject being studied. The third phase, synthesis, involves drawing up not only general principles and guidelines but also specific plans for action, and ends in action itself.

Faced with the criticisms and proposals which have been outlined so far in this chapter, the teacher of world religions can make two main kinds of reply. The one involves saying 'No!' – no, these criticisms are based on inadequate understanding of what we actually do in our classrooms, and of the syllabuses with which we are working. The criticisms are therefore unfair. In any case the criticisms seem to take for granted a left-wing ideology which is neither reasonable nor desirable in the urgent and giddy business of everyday classroom teaching, and in the lobbying and pressure for more money and time to be spent on RE by the school. An alternative approach to the criticisms is to say 'Yes, but . . .'. This latter approach is more concerned to qualify the criticisms than to argue flatly against them, and to point to possible weaknesses and omissions in the perspective of those who make them. It is this second approach which is to be adopted here – even though the first does have, certainly, its attractions.

The first point that teachers of world religions should put to teachers of world studies is that commitment to justice must go hand in hand with (and is indeed mere dead rhetoric without) a keen and vivid sense of the humanity of the victims of injustice and – therefore – a keen and vivid sense of one's own humanity. This point can be illustrated and emphasised by a passage in Thomas Hardy's novel *Tess of the d'Urbervilles*. The main character, Angel Clare, is a middle-class intellectual who goes to live and work amongst farm labourers. Before this experience he has a stereotype image of farm labourers. He thinks of all of them as 'Hodge' – a bunch of country bumpkins, yokels, peasants, clodhoppers. But much to his surprise, writes Hardy, Clare takes 'a real delight in their companionship'.

> The conventional farm-folk of his imagination – personified by the pitiable dummy known as Hodge – were obliterated after a few days residence. At close quarters no Hodge was to be seen . . . His host and his host's household, his men and his maids, as they became intimately known to Clare, began to differentiate themselves as in a chemical process . . . The typical and unvarying Hodge ceased to exist. He had been disintegrated into a number of varied fellow-creatures – beings of many minds, beings infinite in difference; some happy, many serene, a few depressed, one here and there bright even to genius, some stupid, others wanton, others austere; some mutely Miltonic, some potentially Cromwellian; into men who had private views of each other, as he had of his friends; who could applaud or condemn each other, amuse or sadden themselves by the contemplation of each other's foibles or vices; men every one of whom walked in his own individual way the road to dusty death.[9]

The understanding of a 'foreign' culture which Hardy so beautifully describes here can also be achieved through a study of world religions. It is crucially relevant to questions of justice and conflict in world society. To be committed to justice in world society is to hold the view that in conflicts of material interest the perceptions and needs of foreigners are to count in principle as equal to one's own. This is a moral commitment not just a matter of Realpolitik: it is morally irrelevant (even though politically, of course, of huge importance) whether a foreigner has bads or clout with which to threaten us, or goods (raw materials, manufactures, markets, capital, expertise) with which to woo us. Such moral commitment needs to be informed and inspired by the kind of experience and understanding which Hardy describes in Angel Clare. Otherwise it remains cold, brittle, fragile.

Clare's experience has four main aspects. The same four aspects are present also in successful teaching and learning about world religions. First, there is personal pleasure and enjoyment – 'he took a real delight in their companionship'. Second, Clare sees the farm people as being different from each other. He can no longer generalise about *all* people who live on the land. Similarly, no one who has had a similar kind of experience can generalise about all Muslims, all Jews, all Christians. Third, Clare sees people as being centres of consciousness – subjects not objects. They have anxieties and hopes, and intentions and will-power. They can and do shape their own lives. They are not cogs in a machine, or corks on a wave, at the mercy of impersonal forces. Certainly they cannot be manipulated by Clare himself. Fourth, Clare learns from them – he is changed by interaction with them. The main thing which he learns is something about his own identity and destiny as a mortal being.

Hardy's points can be translated from his own poetic metaphors and allusions into the more abstract framework of an academic psychologist. The Swedish psychologist Stig Lindholm, for example, has proposed that there is a continuum, in our knowledge and understanding of a foreign country or culture, between 'external' and 'internal' relationships.[10] At the one end of the continuum, which in Hardy's term might be called the Hodge end:

> . . . one regards the other person as an object, which in turn implies that the person is regarded as a pawn, or one whose behaviour is guided or determined by external causes, rather than his or her own desires and objectives . . . one views the other more as the occupant of a given role than as an individual . . . the external relationship implies a dehumanisation, a depersonification, of the other person.

At the other end of the continuum, however:

> . . . the other person is conceived of as an individual, a living person with goals and intentions; the person is not static, like the occupant of a role, but rather he is in the process of developing, or possesses an innate potential to develop.

An alternative way of picturing much the same continuum draws a distinction between 'instrumental' and 'communicative' action.[11] In the one instance it is a matter of 'manipulation and domination'. In the other, '. . . we encounter . . . speaking and acting subjects. In principle, they can be understood through symbols . . . we are interested in comprehension and communication without the desire of domination.'

Concepts and distinctions such as these emphasise the first and most important point that teachers of world religions can make to teachers of world studies. To study religion can be to develop internal relationships with people who have world views different from one's own, and to develop skills of communicative action. To summarise the point very briefly: respect for the political rights of a Muslim (or whoever) has to be rooted in gratitude for a Muslim's insights.

A second point is almost too obvious to be worth making. It is that one is in a better position to understand issues in world society, in other words better able to do world studies, if one has knowledge and understanding of how those issues are seen by people in countries and cultures other than one's own – in other words if one has studied (amongst other things) world religions. This is a particularly important point when one recalls and emphasises that most religious loyalties in the modern world cut across national boundaries. One consequence of this is that the history of the Middle East during the next fifteen years or so (and therefore the history of the whole world) is going to be affected by Jewish people in the United States as well as in Israel, and by Muslim people in Europe, Africa, the Soviet Union and Indonesia as well as in the Middle East itself. Conversely, inter-ethnic tensions in British inner cities are continually going to be affected by events in the Middle East. (Some teachers already suggest that every time OPEC puts the price of oil up, or every time an Arab country expels a Western diplomat, there is a measurable increase in the number of 'Asian' girls at their school who decline to accept the school's conventions for dress, meals and games, and in the number of parents who press for Urdu to feature on the school timetable.)

Finally, and no doubt most importantly of all, the teacher of world religions has something to say to all other teachers about metaphysical and existential questions. The basic point has been vividly emphasised by Peter Berger:

> Modern society has not only sealed up old metaphysical questions in practice, but . . . has generated philosophical positions that deny the meaningfulness of these questions: 'What is the purpose of my life?' 'Why must I die?' 'Where do I come from and where will I go?' 'Who am I?' – all such questions are not only suppressed in practice but are theoretically liquidated by relegating them to meaninglessness . . . The reality of a middle-aged businessman drowsily digesting his lunch is elevated to the status of final philosophical authority. All questions that do not correspond to this reality are ruled to be inadmissible. The denial of metaphysics may here be identified with the triumph of triviality.[12]

Now certainly teachers of world studies would pride themselves on being very distant and different from a middle-aged businessman drowsily digesting his lunch. But distant also from a teenager at a disco, a student in a demo, a tennis player in a match, a soldier in a battle, a parent with a young child? These people too cannot engage in reflective thought as long as they remain in their situation: they cannot stop to wonder (in both senses) at any length about 'Where do I come from and where will I go?' Similarly teachers of world studies are in a giddy rush for a great deal of their time, because of the stresses of teaching and the giddy, ever-changing world society it is their job to study. From world religions they can receive the command to be still. They can receive it also from that short story of Joseph Conrad's, about the foreigner shipwrecked on the south coast of England. The man is, says Conrad, 'cast out mysteriously by the sea to perish in the supreme disaster of loneliness and despair'. The man dies with two separate words on his lips: 'Why?' and 'Merciful!' Conrad does not explain the latter. But he does describe the tone of the former: 'He cried in the penetrating and indignant voice of a man calling to a responsible Maker.' And Conrad adds: 'A gust of wind and a swish of rain answered'.

Final despair or final mercy? Teachers of world religions challenge teachers of world studies to ask this question, continually and with divine unrest. Students of world society and intercultural communication are called in their turn to maintain, with Conrad, that the answer is at the present time not clear.

References

1 Joseph Conrad, *Amy Foster* (first published in *Typhoon and Other Stories*, 1903).

2 For a discussion of these terms, and of tensions and differences amongst them, see D. Heater, *World Studies: Education for International Understanding in Britain* (London: Harrap, 1980).

3 P. Berger, *The Social Reality of Religion* (London: Faber. 1969), p. 52.

4 Judgements about religion are explicitly encouraged in *A Groundplan for the Study of Religion* (London: Schools Council, 1977).

5 G. John, 'The Black experience of Britain', in *The New Black Presence in Britain: a Christian Scrutiny* (London: British Council of Churches, 1976).

6 A. Wood, 'Judaism in the home, synagogue and classroom', in W. O. Cole (ed.), *Shap Mailing: 1979* (London: Commission for Racial Equality, 1979).

7 A useful discussion of Freire's ideas in relation to teaching about Christianity and religion is to be found in B. Wren, *Education for Justice* (London: SCM Press, 1977). The best introduction by Freire himself is probably *Education as the Practice of Freedom* (London: Writers and Readers Publishing Co-operative, 1977).

8 R. Richardson (ed.), *Learning for Change in World Society* (London: One World Trust), pp. 122–3 of the 1979 edition.

9 Chapter 18 of *Tess of the d'Urbervilles* (first published 1891).

10 S. Lindholm, *Seeing for Oneself* (Stockholm: Swedish International Development Agency, 1975), pp. 10–11.

11 P. Connerton (ed.), *Critical Sociology* (London: Penguin, 1977), p. 30.

12 P. Berger, *A Rumour of Angels* (London: Allen Lane, The Penguin Press, 1970), p. 95.

Further reading

For the development of world studies in Britain in the period 1960–80 the most influential single person, as author, advocate and campaigner, was James Henderson. His books *World Questions: A Study Guide* (Methuen, 1963), and *Education for World Understanding* (Pergamon, 1968), summarised the concerns of the 1960s, and set the stage for the 1970s. Publications of the 1970s which reflected Henderson's influence, intellectual or personal or both, included the three handbooks produced by the World Studies Project of the One World Trust, *Learning for Change in World Society* (1976). *Debate and Decision* (1979), and *Ideas into Action* (1980); numerous articles in journals, particularly *The New Era* and latterly the *World Studies Journal*; textbooks and other materials for use in classrooms, for example the Nelson *World Studies* series by Robin Richardson (1978); the Routledge *World Studies* series for scholars; and Derek Heater's *World Studies: Education for International Understanding in Britain* (Harrap, 1980).

In the United States the single most important book of the 1970s was Lee Anderson's *Schooling and Citizenship in a Global Age* (Indiana University, 1979).

In the related fields of development education and multicultural education important books included those of Chris Searle, for example, *This New Season* (Calder & Boyars, 1973) and *The World in a Classroom* (Writers and Readers Publishing Co-operative, 1976), Brian Wren's *Education for Justice* (SCM Press, 1977), Rob Jeffcoate's *Positive Image* (Chameleon Books, 1979), and David Hicks's *Minorities* (Heinemann, 1981).

The two principal organisations providing information and resources for teachers are the Centre for World Development Education, 128 Buckingham Palace Road, London, SW1 and the Council for Education in World Citizenship, 26 Blackfriars Lane, London EC4V 6EB.

Index